# MAKING
# VICTORIAN
# COSTUMES
## FOR MEN

# MAKING
# VICTORIAN
# COSTUMES
## FOR MEN

Sil Devilly

THE CROWOOD PRESS

First published in 2019 by
The Crowood Press Ltd
Ramsbury, Marlborough
Wiltshire SN8 2HR

**www.crowood.com**

British Library Cataloguing-in-Publication Data
A catalogue record for this book is available from the British Library.

**ISBN 978 1 78500 575 6**

Typeset by Sharon Dainton Design.
Printed and bound in India by Replika Press Pvt Ltd.

# Contents

# Introduction

*Making Victorian Costume for Men is designed to guide the reader through the process of creating period gentlemen's clothing, using a mixture of traditional and modern tailoring techniques along with costume-making methods.*

There are many reasons for making Victorian costume, from wanting to create tailored menswear based on Victorian fashions for theatrical productions or re-enactment to using elements of Victorian costume and adapting them to use as a basis for steampunk, live action role-playing (LARP) or cosplay costume. Each individual costume has its own rationale with endless options and possibilities.

Some of the techniques used are based on traditional methods, although it is impossible to recreate true Victorian tailoring without using both original methods and materials. The idea of this book is to produce garments that may appear to be very much like Victorian men's clothing while using techniques that are appropriate for the materials available to the modern maker, the assumption being that you are going to make a version of costume rather than replica garments.

Although the skills and techniques outlined in this book have been streamlined wherever possible, they are not easy, coming as they do from established tailoring methods. With patience and persistence, allowing yourself to both practise and develop an understanding of the construction systems, you will enhance your coordination and start expanding your sympathy for fabrics and gain a greater 'feel' for the construction process.

Queen Victoria's reign lasted sixty-three years, during which there were constant, often subtle, changes to men's clothing within the large and growing population, all of whom had different occupations, incomes and interests. The outfits chosen as construction examples represent portions of this time period when they were popular. Each outfit starts with the coat or jacket and includes the other garments needed to build a complete costume, in order to tell the history of men's clothing through this timespan. The garments and patterns in this book cover a broad spectrum of time and styles; each of the outfits, although based in a specific decade, represents items that were made during a longer period of time and would have been worn by men from many walks of life.

I am a costume maker with over twenty years of experience in costume design interpretation and costume construction. Initially self-taught, I started making costume as a hobby in my free time. I returned to education to learn how to make costume 'properly'

and completed the Theatre Wardrobe course in Liverpool. I have worked on a huge variety of costumes, both in theatre workrooms and as a freelance maker ever since.

Every costume-making project is different and provides new opportunities to learn. I have been extremely fortunate to work with a wonderful group of people, colleagues whose generosity has been boundless in sharing with me their hints, tips and techniques picked up during their careers.

Some of my accumulated skills and experience I am able to pass on in my role as a costume construction teacher and lecturer. I hope to use this book as an opportunity to share more of this useful knowledge.

The recent completion of an MA in Creative Pattern Cutting gave me the confidence to take on the writing of this book, which provided my biggest challenge to date – condensing Victorian menswear and the techniques needed to make it into just one book!

It is my intention that this book will be useful to people who are able to sew and who already have an underst-anding of garment construction and patterns, but who would like to broaden their range of technical abilities. My sincerest wish is to help you enjoy the process of creating Victorian costume for men.

Left: Fig. 0.1 Footmen sharing snuff, captioned 'A Friendly Pinch'. From *A Practical Guide for the Tailor's Cutting Room, XIX Footman's Dresses* (National Museums Liverpool). The two footmen are wearing quite different styles of uniform: on the right the livery resembles military uniform; the man on the left is wearing an outfit more closely based on the fashionable dress of the 1840s – a cutaway tailcoat with epaulettes, horizontally striped waistcoat and narrow trousers.

# Chapter 1
# Exploring Victorian Costume

*Each period of history has its own distinctive clothing styles influenced by the main themes of the time, including the arts, science, technology and important events. Most fashions progress from existing ideas; there are developments and adaptations of previous styles which can go on to mass popularity if they are taken up by influential people or catch the public mood. Fashions rarely start without a traceable history, demonstrating the evolution of the various influences that subsequently bring about what appeared to be an original innovation.*

The Victorian era is one of the longest periods of rule for a monarch. Victoria reigned for sixty-three years from 1837 to 1901. Such a lengthy reign covered many changes in fashion and taste.

The men's clothing covered by this period seems practical and restrained as compared to the flamboyance of women's clothing with its fluctuating skirt, bodice and sleeve shapes; there are resemblances and echoes of the changes in men's dress but with different results. The social conventions of the time applied strict rules to masculine dress, with different occasions demanding stringent dress codes to be adhered to. The upper-class man was expected to change his clothing sometimes several times a day to the appropriate outfit for the occasion.

The growing population produced a new, larger and wealthier middle class, members of which had the disposable income to spend on clothing and used the upper class as a style guide. New cities and larger towns contained more people who were involved in the types of social scenes which required the following of changing clothing trends.

## The Development of Men's Costume through Queen Victoria's Reign

### The Coat

Victorian men's coats changed according to the fashionable shape of the time: waistlines rose and fell; coat skirt lengths varied or became wider or narrower; the coat could be double- or single-breasted; the sleeve fit, shape and cuff changed; and of course the collar and lapels followed the varying fashionable lines. The major coat styles of the period were the frock coat, the tailcoat, the cutaway coat and the short jacket – each style had a variety of names help to distinguish between the different cuts, eras and fashions.

### The Waistcoat

Waistcoats through the period fluctuated more modestly with fashion. A smooth, close fit was a constant requirement, with various waist alteration methods on the back to draw in the body of the waistcoat. The length, which had been rising towards the waist since the beginning of the nineteenth century, continued to stay around that level for the whole period, continuing to this day where waistcoats are still worn at a similar length. Between the 1830s and 1870s the shawl collar was the dominant collar style, with variations in width or length of opening, and this could appear in double- or single-breasted versions. Welt pockets were popular.

Padding was added to both coats and waistcoats at various times, adding to the natural shape and giving a more fashionable look.

### Trousers

Trousers had begun to be worn at the beginning of the century in preference to breeches. Initially they were very tight with a fall front waist opening; the fly came into use in around the 1840s. Up to the end of the 1840s trousers often had a stirrup or strap under the foot to keep the trouser leg taut. The Victorian man was keen on having the trouser fit in exactly the right way over the foot, consequently many trouser drafts have shaping around the ankle to give the desired shape. Throughout the century trouser shaping changed from very tight to gathered at the waist with varying widths of leg; by the end of the century trousers had become fairly straight-legged.

### Shirts, Collars and Neckwear

The new shirt shaping began to evolve at the start of Victoria's reign, becoming the shirt we recognize today. Throughout the period very little of it would be seen, especially during the day when most of it would be covered by the coat and neckwear; for evening wear it was generally acceptable to have more shirt front on show, with the appropriate fashionable modifications. Collars, cuffs and bib fronts were stiffened and became detachable, a popular development, essential to maintain the respectable look of a gentleman. Neckwear, ties, cravats and bow ties in all their fashionable varieties completed the look.

### Hats

When out of doors, all respectable Victorian men would have worn a hat. There were, of course, many different

Left: Fig. 1.1 Illustration from a story in *The Strand Magazine* from 1894 showing two very different styles of men's dress. Drawings accompanying stories outline the silhouette of clothing worn by the characters but do not show every detail of the garments.

styles that could be expected to be worn with particular outfits. Top hats changed shape according to fashion, moving from daywear to becoming only formal wear by the end of the century, when bowler hats came into use as less formal daywear, and soft fabric or straw hats were adopted for leisure and sport.

## Fabric and Colours

Wool remained a popular fibre for men's clothes; there were many different pure wool fabrics, also cloth made from wool mixed with other fibres. The availability of cotton increased, taking over from linen for shirts and underwear. The fashionable man started the period with rather restrained colours, probably a plain dark coat and light-coloured legwear, white shirt and neckwear. Darker-coloured striped trousers commenced the sombre palette of the Victorian man, with colour being introduced into the outfit through waistcoats, either with the fabric itself or with decoration. Throughout the years a huge range of coloured and patterned fabrics were available; part or all of the huge outfit could be expected to be made from the same fabric at different times.

## Second-hand Clothing

The trade in second-hand clothes provided employment, redistributing clothing and textiles and helping to keep the poor clothed when they could not afford new garments.

### Paving the Way for the Victorians

Making interesting and essential contributions to both the development of clothing and the general social history of the time were the inventions of new manufacturing processes and their evolution. Significant industrial developments (like many of history's momentous events) do not fit neatly into any historical period; I have therefore included events and inventions which, although set in

motion before Victoria came to the throne, became essential parts of both Victorian historical narrative and the evolution of clothing at the time and, in some prominent examples, into the future.

The agricultural revolution of the seventeenth century allowed farmers to produce more food than was needed for the mere survival of their families. The subsequent food surpluses freed some people to take up work away from the land, giving rise to the growth of urban populations and factory systems which had a profound effect on the Victorian era.

The British industrial revolution is generally considered as lasting from the 1760s to the 1840s. Its advances made the Victorians memorable and significantly changed the landscape of daily life, manufacturing, business and textile and garment production.

The population of England doubled between 1800 and 1850 to 18 million, partly as an effect of increased food production, which led to better general health, and there was a similar increase in the populations of western Europe and North America. Although there was dreadful poverty and suffering for much of the working population, there was also more wealth generated, allowing the middle class to grow.

The cotton industry began growing quickly in the 1770s. In 1733 John Kay invented the flying shuttle, speeding up weaving to four times faster than previously. Spinning needed to become faster to keep up and was mechanized in 1764, when James Hargreaves invented the spinning jenny. This was quickly followed by Richard Arkwright's spinning frame, and Samuel Crompton's combination of elements of the two systems created the spinning mule in the late 1770s. Cotton production moved to mills close to sources of power, initially water.

As cotton production grew it became cheaper, its quality improved and it was more widely available, encouraging innovations in printing and dyeing and necessitating the use of the patents system to control copying and the theft of ideas.

Steam power and metal production led to faster, more reliable transport, increasing the trade in textiles, with the export of wool and the import of unprocessed cotton and textiles from around the world. New manufacturing methods led to the availability of goods to a wider portion of the population (Osborne, 2013).

## Wool Production and Tailoring Business Advancements

Britain's wool trade was renowned around the world both for the quality of the fleece and the finished fabric. Until the late eighteenth century the wool trade had been a cottage industry broken down into many separate processes which were often divided throughout the community. In contrast, the industrial revolution promoted increased mechanization and the move to factory systems, often urban.

Precise fit in tailored garments only became a requirement in the early 1800s. Carefully constructed layers of padding were an essential part of tailored clothing. Victorian tailors had an impressive reputation as craftsmen with wool, manipulating the fabric with pressing, shrinking and stretching, adding structure with canvas and padding to mould and sculpt the garment to the body in order to make the customer the appropriate fashionable shape. It was important that the outer fabric lay smoothly over the canvas and padded structure in an effortless manner, the garment appearing as if there were little or no under layers.

During the nineteenth century the systems of production in the tailoring trade, as in other manufacturing businesses, were transformed. The small shop was also supplanted by factory methods for garment making.

## The Position of Women in the Sewing Workforce

Victorian tailors or cutters were always male, although women did have roles in tailoring as seamstresses. Before the advent of the sewing machine the latter would have worked as outworkers, taking the simpler tasks home with them. Once factories were established they formed part of the machinist workforce. Women had always sewn, as sewing for the family was an essential part of the domestic routine. Outworking meant that women could earn money, augmenting the family income, by dressmaking, making clothing for children or making up shirts and men's linens.

## Victorian Inventions

With the turn of the eighteenth to the nineteenth century, there were more significant discoveries and developments that had an enduring impact on costume.

### The Sewing Machine

The sewing machine had a tremendous effect on tailoring and dressmaking, despite its convoluted history. The first sewing machine was patented in 1790 for sewing leather. Barthélemy Thimonnier invented a chain-stitch machine in 1830. In 1834 Walter Hunt invented, but did not patent, a lockstitch machine. Elias Howe

introduced his lockstitch machine, patented in 1846. Developments to the sewing machine continued, including changes to the bobbin and needles. In 1851 Merritt Singer patented a lockstitch machine; his effective marketing and distribution of the machines has ensured they are often still known by his name today (Leoni, 1988).

As can be seen in the picture here, early sewing machine manufacturers created diverse decoration and style details, with the basic practical design for lockstitch machines enduring.

### The Pin

From 1840 the domestic pin began to be made with head and shank all in one, as compared with its former construction method where the head was attached around the end of the shank in a separate process (Willett and Cunnington, 1992).

### Tape Measures and Pattern Drafts

Tailors had been using their own versions of the tape measure since the seventeenth century, utilizing a strip of

fabric, ribbon or paper marked up with the client's dimensions straight from the body. The marks made on the strip would be used with draft instructions to create the pattern.

The standard inch tape measure as we know it today was invented in the early nineteenth century and became popular from around the 1830s. The tape measure was revolutionary in allowing tailors to develop and ultimately print their own pattern drafting systems from accurate measurements of the body. Early systems were extremely difficult to follow but did provide inspiration, encouraging tailors to formulate, refine and produce their own methods (Waugh, 1964).

### Aniline Dyes

William Henry Perkin discovered the first purple dye accidentally while attempting to synthesize quinine for the treatment of malaria in 1856; he called his first aniline dye 'mauveine'. He started the patenting procedure later in the year in order to commercialize the process. Other people started developing aniline dyes and were responsible for further Victorian

Fig. 1.2 Sewing machines from the Museums Sheffield collection. L to R: Jones hand sewing machine, c. 1900; Jones 'D' sewing machine, possibly early 1880s; Weir sewing machine, c. 1860s; S. Davis & Co. 'Beaumont' sewing machine, c. 1900.

favourites; for example, fuchsine – a strong red with a leaning towards fuchsia – and safranine – a deep red with a hint of orange.

## Elastic

India rubber began to be incorporated with thread and into textiles, thus forming elastic products from 1820. Initially they were difficult and fiddly to produce and adversely affected by heat, cold and sweat. The vulcanization process patented in1844 by Thomas Hancock made rubber more practical, transforming its use and causing an upsurge in clothing designs that included elastic (Levitt, 1986).

## Patents

The patent system had been around for hundreds of years, but it had been used increasingly throughout the industrial revolution to register designs protecting inventors' ideas from being copied. Patents also allowed inventors and businessmen sell their rights to inventions. A huge number of patents were taken out for clothing throughout the Victorian period (Levitt, 1986).

## Photography

The first publicly available photographic process, invented by Louis Jacques Daguerre, was introduced in 1839, and the daguerreotype was popular for twenty years. The image was delicate and kept behind glass for protection but by 1860 it was superseded by cheaper processes with easy-to-see images.

Introduced in the 1850s, an ambrotype is a negative photograph on glass which, when placed over a black background, appears to be a positive image. Like the daguerreotype, it was delicate and had to be protected from any kind of rubbing by a glass sheet.

Tintypes were most popular during the 1860s and 1870s, using a thin sheet of metal coated with a dark lacquer or enamel to which the photographic emulsion was applied to make a direct positive. The photograph shown here

was taken in Huddersfield or the surrounding area. Two of the four men are wearing jackets, the other men are in shirts and waistcoats as if they had just stopped working. All the men are wearing hats.

These advancements inspired an explosion in interest and inventions for the photography process, including work with colour. Portable cameras became available to the public and film motion picture cameras were developed.

## Fashion Magazines

The Victorians had access to an increasing range of printed materials to guide sartorial choice. Fashion magazines, or articles about fashion for women, started to become regular features from around the beginning of the 1800s, with articles on men's fashion starting in the middle of the century. These articles, fashion plates, journals, photography and printed material became increasingly popular and had an impact on readers, especially those of the middle classes,

Fig. 1.3 Tintype photograph probably taken at the height of tintype photography, c. late 1860s; the piece of metal measures 9 x 5cm (3 x 2in).

all over the country who could see and be prompted to adopt something of the styles they were seeing and reading about (Willett and Cunnington, 1992). These same materials provide ideal reference for costume historians and costume makers alike.

## Overview

The Victorian period was inundated by wide-ranging changes to many aspects of society and by inventions that worked for or against local textile industry and craftwork and its manufacture. At the same time new methods of transport developed, trains and (later) bicycles had a direct impact on clothing and leisure activities. Artistic movements, literature and the Great Exhibition of 1951 also influenced dress.

Voting reform in 1867 increased the number of voters from the working classes, reducing the separation between them and the middle classes and the wealthy, raising the collective consciousness to conditions for the working and non-working poor. The considerably enlarged number of voters gave working-class men a voice, leading to factory acts and state provision for the poor, beginning the alleviation of extreme poverty, the further development of the trades union movement and pointing towards the eventual emancipation of women.

There were also major changes in education and sanitation and even shopping, all of which helped to transform society over six decades.

# Chapter 2
# Tools and Equipment

*The equipment outlined in this chapter is a subjective list of my preferences, a combination of tools I use all the time and also some items that were useful during the construction of the garments in this book. The modern costume maker has access to a vast range of equipment, from specific tailoring tools to tools used for various textile trades or crafts.*

Traditional tailors of this historical period had a fairly small selection of tools, with which they had to be as efficient as the techniques they employed. The kit I use is somewhat different to that of a traditional tailor although fundamentally it is quite simple and can be inexpensive and portable.

There is some explanation with most of the items in this chapter. Certain tools have been repeated where they feature in more than one section.

## Essential Tools

These items comprise the basic equipment that I consider to be most important and would not like to be without.

**Shears:** ideally you should select scissors that can tackle a variety of fabrics with ease. Choose a pair that are most suited to the work you will be doing and are comfortable to use. Traditionally a pair of shears lasted for a tailor's whole career; now they can be relatively inexpensive and are easy to replace.

**Paper scissors:** have these to hand for paper, card and anything that you do not want to cut with fabric shears.

**Small scissors:** use these for smaller jobs, for everything that the shears are too big for, such as snipping thread or trimming, or cutting pockets open.

They must be sharp all the way to the tip, with strong blades that do not flex when cutting through fabric.

**Tape measures:** tailor's soft tape measure with a metal end, in inches and centimetres, and another tape measure without the metal end.

**PatternMaster®:** this is a clear plastic template with both curved and straight calibrated edges. It is invaluable for many small tasks, such as marking lines, finding and marking 45-degree angles, locating the middle of almost anything, marking button and buttonhole positions, and scaling patterns up and down.

**Calculator:** handy for pattern drafting and small calculations such as working out the distance between buttons.

**Pencils:** 'H' or a mechanical pencil for paper and softer 'B' for fabrics (always note that pencil marks cannot always be erased from the right side of a fabric). Keep a selection of coloured pencils, plus a pencil sharpener and eraser.

**Pins:** 34mm hardened steel dressmaker's pins.

**Needles:** tailors had a range of short needles each of which would be used for a particular hand sewing job. A short needle spends less time passing through the fabric, ultimately saving fractions of a second with every stitch. If you are making a traditionally tailored garment with thousands of hand-sewn stitches all those little bits of time saved will add up. For general sewing use the needle you find most comfortable for the task.

**Thimble:** tailor's thimbles do not have a top for two reasons; firstly, the end of the needle is pushed with the side of the thimble; secondly, the absence of a top allows air to circulate, necessary as they could be worn for hours. Thimbles

Fig.2.2 Tailor's thimble; the needle is pushed with the side of the middle finger wearing the thimble.

take a bit of getting used to, but it's worth doing to stop damage to the skin of the fingers when doing a lot of hand sewing.

There are now so many types of thimble you can try out a few to see which one suits you best. To begin with they may feel a bit alien and keep falling off, but perseverance and perhaps some adhesive tape to hold it on will help you to get used to it.

**Tailor's awl, bradawl, bodkin or stiletto:** a variety of names for a tool that makes a hole in fabric by forcing the threads apart.

**Tracing wheel and carbon paper:** the needle point tracing wheel transfers a neat precise line from the pattern through the carbon paper onto the fabric. Prym have a tracing wheel with an ergonomic handle which works very well and is not quite as damaging to table tops.

Dressmaker's carbon paper or tailors' or dressmakers' tracing paper comes in

Left: Fig. 2.1 My essential tool kit. From top L clockwise round the page: thread, chalk, calculator, small scissors, PatternMaster®, tracing wheel, shears, paper scissors, sewing machine bobbins and needles, pencil, coloured pencil eraser and pencil sharpener, thimble, tailor's awl, pins, needles and a soft tape measure.

a variety of colours; it is used to mark the construction lines on the backing fabrics or the wrong side of the garment panels.

**Tailor's chalk:** square or triangular in shape, this comes in white and a selection of colours (usually yellow, red, blue and black). White chalk comes off fabric fairly easily and is useful for making marks on the right side of the fabric when necessary. Some coloured chalks contain oil which creates a good clear line but should be used cautiously where marks could be seen – these might be difficult to remove. The chalk line should be fine and clear so the chalk must be sharp; use paper scissors to scrape away the chalk to make a sharp edge.

**Pattern paper:** choose between white or brown plain or papers marked with dot and cross or a grid. Papers come in assorted weight according to gsm (grams per square metre), right up to manila card.

**Sewing machine:** a simple domestic machine can be extremely versatile and portable. If space allows, an industrial lockstitch machine is well worth considering, and then perhaps an overlocker if needed. Sewing machines were only invented towards the beginning of 'our' period and would not have been commonly used for some years: consider if visible machine sewing is appropriate for the costume.

**Machine needles:** keep a selection in a range of sizes. You may find that you need ball point or stretch needles, possibly leather needles.

## Pressing

Pressing is a fundamental part of fabric preparation and the construction process. The completed garment is given a professional finish with careful and appropriate use of ironing equipment.

Pressing is the process for which traditional tailors had the most equipment. Alongside a very heavy flat iron, they would have several different ironing boards of varying sizes and specific uses, also steaming and pressing cloths in cotton and linen, a

clapper, sponge and brushes.

As with the general equipment for costume making the stock of essential pressing equipment is actually quite small, easy to acquire and can be inexpensive.

**Iron:** also known traditionally as a flat iron or smoothing iron, this has always been an absolutely essential piece of kit. You can use either a very basic iron with a cotton or linen pressing cloth or the heaviest steam iron you can find, again with a pressing cloth. Industrial

steam irons are ideal but can be expensive and require maintenance; they usually benefit from constant use. Whatever your choice, you will also need an ironing board, a sleeve board, pressing cloths made from cotton and/or linen, plus a clothes brush.

**Pressing ham and pressing roll:** also known as a tailor's or dressmaker's ham and seam pressing roll respectively. These are tightly packed cushions used to press particular shaped areas of a

Fig. 2.3 *A pressing area*. On the left, above the steam iron and ironing board you can see a sleeve board, clapper and point presser, pressing roll and ham, clothes brush (just seen behind the pressing roll), linen and cotton pressing cloths, velvet pressing mat and a small ironing board.

garment.

**Clapper:** a piece of hard wood used to draw heat and/or steam from ironed fabric. After ironing place the clapper on the area and press down to draw out the heat and steam. This flattens and smoothes seams and edges.

**Velvet board:** a metal velvet needle board or mat, although expensive, has long fine needles giving really good results. Nylon velvet needle mats are very much cheaper and are comprised of fine nylon needles on a woven backing, the slight disadvantage being that the needles are not as long or fine as a metal velvet mat. Alternatively, you can press the reverse of the fabric using a spare piece of velvet turned nap or pile upwards on the ironing board.

## Additional Tools

These are oddments that you may only need occasionally.

**Masking tape:** a temporary sticky tape for paper and toile fabric.

**Bias tape maker:** this is a small device that helps you to make bias binding with consistent folds. Various widths are available. Cut fabric strips on the bias. Test the width of bias-cut fabric in the maker; thin fabrics often need to be cut slightly wider.

**Cigarette lighter or matches:** use naked flames with great care. Burning can be used to test fabrics to give an indication of fibre content. You can also stop fraying on synthetic ribbon by melting the edge of the cut ends.

**Stitch unpicker or seam ripper:** the point is particularly useful for taking out individual stitches but use it carefully when ripping seams to avoid damaging the fabric or pile.

**Hole punch, eyelets and eyelet attaching tool:** depending on the context, holes may be made and eyelets inserted with a tool that relies just on hand compression; alternatively you may wish to consider using a hammer closing tool.

**Buttonhole cutter:** this tool enables quick, neat and consistent cutting.

**Buttonhole attachment:** this may be available for your sewing machine. Some machines have keyhole buttonhole program setting.

**Pinking shears:** pink seam allowances to reduce fraying. Heavier fabrics that do not fray can sometimes benefit from being trimmed with pinking shears, as pinking softens the edge, thus slightly reducing the chance of the seam showing through to the right side.

**Glue:** there are several different brands of fray-stopping glue.

**Beeswax:** apply wax to cotton or silk thread for hand sewing; the wax will be absorbed by natural fibres with the addition of heat stiffening the thread and reducing the likelihood of knotting. Pull the thread over the wax block two or three times then draw the thread over the tip of the iron to melt the wax into the thread.

Fig. 2.4 Extra equipment used for constructing the Victorian men's costume in this book. Clockwise from top L: masking tape, tailor's awl, bias tape makers, cigarette lighter, buttonhole cutter and buttonhole attachment, pinking shears, stitch unpicker (seam ripper), eyelets and attaching tools.

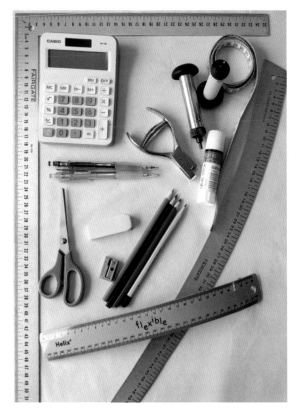

Fig. 2.5 *Pattern-cutting equipment.* Clockwise from top L: tailor's square, calculator, pattern notcher, paper drill, soft tape measure, glue stick, tailor's curved stick, flexible ruler, pencils, coloured pencils, pencil sharpener, eraser, paper scissors and coloured mechanical pencils.

## Pattern Cutting

Pattern making needs only a very few pieces of equipment. The extra items make the process slightly easier and make the finished pattern a pleasing object. Mentioned below is a selection of items not covered elsewhere in this chapter.

**Tailor's square:** L-shaped ruler printed with scales for using with draft instruction or making half-scale patterns.

**Rulers:** short 12 inch or 30cm lengths and a longer length of around a yard or metre, a flexible ruler can be handy for measuring shapes.

**Glue stick:** useful for altering and adding sections to paper patterns.

**Tailor's curved ruler or curved stick:** usually made from aluminium, this is ideal for drawing shapes onto patterns, such as sleeve seams, the inside leg curvature between the knee and crotch, the outside leg from waist round the hip and then the opposite curve below the hip to the knee.

**Paper drill, pattern notcher:** these make holes and notches respectively in paper patterns to indicate darts and balance marks.

**Marking tools for fabric and paper:** tailors only use a minimum amount of marking tools, mainly chalk, thread marks (tailor tacks); garments are cut with consistent seam allowance and inlays in specific places. By comparison, fabric marking for costume making includes a large range of options to be used as appropriate. It is essential to test the marking method chosen to ensure it can be removed or will disappear from the fabric, and to thread mark any marks that could disappear or be removed accidentally.

## Trimmings

'Trimmings' is a tailoring term for all the accessories and supplies needed to complete a garment. The photograph shows some of the trimmings used in the construction of the garments in this book.

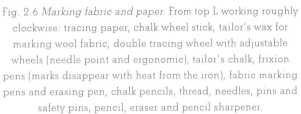

Fig. 2.6 *Marking fabric and paper*. From top L working roughly clockwise: tracing paper, chalk wheel stick, tailor's wax for marking wool fabric, double tracing wheel with adjustable wheels (needle point and ergonomic), tailor's chalk, frixion pens (marks disappear with heat from the iron), fabric marking pens and erasing pen, chalk pencils, thread, needles, pins and safety pins, pencil, eraser and pencil sharpener.

Fig. 2.7 *Trimmings*. Top, L to R: sew-in hair canvas, black synthetic knit fusible interfacing, fusible hair canvas, threads, linen buttons, heavier hair canvas. Centre, L to R: fusible domette, sew-in non-woven interfacing, sew-in chest felt, braces buttons, black and white cotton woven fusible interfacing. Bottom, L to R: fusible hemming tape, sew-in hair canvas, shirt and linen buttons, trouser waist hooks and bars, sew-on and no-sew, collar canvas and edge tape. Calico for toiles, backings and samples has been used for the background.

## Research

At the beginning of the making process it is essential to do some research. Make it as wide-ranging as possible look at the clothing, art and architecture of the time. Even if you are not intending to create exact replicas of men's Victorian costumes it is important to become familiar with them and to develop an understanding of similar garments; this is also necessary when working with designs or references that do not show the whole garment and all its details.

There is an excellent supply of Victorian menswear primary source material, including original Victorian garments, photographs, paintings, art and architecture. Some museums have costume archives that can be visited with an appointment; many museums have online costume archives with photos and additional information, allowing easy access to museum collections all over the world.

Books are the cornerstone of my own research. At the back of this book is a list of the books most directly useful to research and produce the garments in this volume. The list covers both the books that I refer to in the text and some suggestions for further reading.

# Chapter 3
# Preparing to Make Your Costume

## Planning and Beginning, Measuring and Pattern Cutting

Prepare to start making the costume with an overview of areas of consideration. Make an outline of the measurements needed to make the garments and how they can be used. Study the sizes the patterns are and how the patterns can be transcribed, tested and made into a toile. Consider what to look for when fitting the toile of your costume. Think ahead to your choice of fabrics and interfacings and how you will need to work with them.

Making costume is all about precision and practice; practise everything from measuring to making. There are no definitive methods for costume making because the requirements change with each project, so there are many 'right' ways, undo and re-sew until the result is satisfactory. Keep practising and learning.

Why are you making the costume? On the surface this is a simple question easily answered: it may be for your own pleasure, to learn the techniques or a commission.

Who (and what) are you making the costume for? There are many different reasons for wearing a costume, from established performance areas of theatre, film, re-enactment (living history) or as fancy dress for a party or event.

What character or person is the costume representing? Who are they, where do they live, what is their profession? Build up a picture of character in the costume.

A costume design or reference images are essential; refer to them at every stage.

## Costume Requirements

- How long is the costume going to be worn? A few hours or for an hour every day for weeks?
- What is the performer going to be doing in the costume? How much movement is involved? Standing, sitting, dancing, fighting?
- Environmental factors. Is it to be worn indoors? Will there be heating or air-conditioning? Or is it going to be worn outside with all the possible weather and terrain implications that could have?
- Quick change. Will the performer have to get into or out of the costume quickly, thus needing different 'quicker' fastenings?
- Laundry or cleaning. How will it be cleaned and what implications does that have for the maker?

## Meeting the Requirements

Answer the questions above as far as possible and then list the possible consequences for the costume, adding the time frame, fittings and when it has to be delivered. Budget can have a major impact on the costume, especially on choices of fabric, lining, canvas and backing. It can be useful to consider possible breaking-down processes before starting.

Along with costume requirements this is the point at which to choose the construction processes that seem most appropriate.

## Measuring

Measurements alone are not enough to make a well-fitting garment. However carefully they are taken, even with a precisely drawn pattern, it is pretty much essential to have a fitting.

Only a very basic set of measurements are required for the garments in this book. The patterns will need drawing up to full scale and altering to the wearer's basic measurements, then a toile of the pattern needs to be made and fitted.

Horizontal measurements (around the widest or narrowest part): chest, waist, seat, neck.

Vertical measurements: height, nape to back waist, waist to floor (outside leg), inside leg.

When a tailor drafts a pattern, a more complete set of measurements are required, defined by the draft instructions, many of which include a table of comparative measurements, relative to average sizes; these are useful when not all measurements are available.

## Pattern Sizes

Two male stands or mannequins have been used to make the example garments in this book: the 1840s frock coat outfit was made to fit a shop dummy; all the other garments were made to fit a half-scale tailor's dummy. (The advantage of using a half-scale dummy is that it uses about quarter the amount of fabric of a full-scale garment and the processes are exactly the same.)

The 1840s frock coat with waistcoat, the trousers from Chapter 5, and the early Victorian shirt and the 1870s drawers in Chapter 4 made to fit: chest 96cm (38in), waist 79cm (31in), seat 96cm (38in), neck 39cm (15in). Approximate height 183cm (6ft), nape to back waist 46cm (18in), waist to floor 117cm (46in), inside leg

Left: Fig. 3.1 Pad stitching lapel, sewing parallel to break line with work rolled over fingers of other hand.

21

## VICTORIAN TAILORING VERSUS COSTUME MAKING

These are distinctly separate disciplines with contrasting preparation, materials and tools. It is not possible to achieve a truly authentic-looking costume without using traditional tailoring methods; for example, steaming, shrinking and stretching are all processes that work extremely well with skilled hands on traditional wool fabrics but are inappropriate for modern fabrics which do not have the same mobility as wool or could be damaged by heat or steam.

The tailoring profession has developed over hundreds of years, constructing an understandable and desirable mystique. Old reference books show intricate patterns that look complicated but which in skilled hands were the basis for individually tailored garments. As in the past, a modern tailor still spends years learning, practising and refining his or her art; skills are methodically repetitive to develop speed and dexterity and truly make the most of the fabrics, all with the aim of achieving beautifully fitted and finished made-to-measure garments.

The costume tailor can have much more flexibility in his/her approach to construction. A wide variety of sources can be drawn upon: period or modern tailoring, techniques derived from hundreds of years of clothing construction, modern fashion, and techniques developed for theatrical costume making, plus a huge body of knowledge about how best to use new or unusual materials and make them work within the constraints of design, fabric, budget and time to produce appropriately fitting and finished couture garments.

86cm (34in).

The morning dress outfit from Chapter 6, the evening wear from Chapter 7, the 1890s suit from Chapter 8, the working man's waistcoat and breeches from Chapter 9, the square-cut shirt, the late Victorian shirt and the 1890s drawers in Chapter 4 made to fit the half-scale stand of a man who measures: chest 108cm (42in), waist 92cm (36in), seat 111cm (43in), neck 41cm (16in).

Approximate height 178cm (5ft 10in), nape to back waist 44.5cm (17$^1$/$_2$in), outside leg 109cm (43in), inside leg 80cm (31in).

### Pattern Pages: Scale and Abbreviations

The grids on all the patterns indicate one square = 2.5cm (1in).
CF = centre front
CB = centre back
Check the picture here to make sure that you understand the symbols used.

Fig. 3.2 Pattern draft from a tailors' guide of the mid-1850s (National Museums Liverpool).

### Seam Allowances
The patterns have no seam allowances included. The notable exceptions are the square-cut shirt, with a 1.3cm (½in) seam allowance included, and the welt pockets and welt pocket bags, which have a 6mm (¼in) seam allowance included.

## Drawing Up the Pattern

Measure and cut precisely: care and precision are essential at all stages of pattern making.

Isolate each pattern piece on the diagram by drawing a box around it. On a separate piece of paper (either plain or with a 2.5cm/1in marked grid), draw a box to the full-scale measurements of the isolated box on the diagram.

## Counting Squares

The pattern information can be transferred by counting the squares and marking onto your paper where the pattern lines cross the grid. When all the crossing points are marked the lines can be joined. Compare the shape with the original diagram.

It helps to make a mini tape measure; mark the diagram grid divisions as numbered increments along the side of a piece of paper. A numbered mini tape measure reduces the need to count the squares repeatedly.

## Calculation Method

This method works well on plain paper and is fairly straightforward when the measurements are taken in millimetres (and centimetres). Use a calculator and PatternMaster®.

The diagram scale is one square to represent 2.5cm (1in).
10 squares x 25mm (2.5cm) = 250mm (or 25cm).

Calculate the exact size of the squares on the printed diagram, these may vary from page to page. Measure 10 squares of the diagram (example: 10 squares measure 32mm). Divide the measurement by 10; the resulting number is the exact size of a diagram square (example: 32mm ÷ 10 = 3.2mm).

This number (example: 3.2) can now be divided by measurements taken from the diagram and multiplied by 25mm to produce full-scale measurements (example: 32mm ÷ 3.2 = 10 x 25 = 250mm).

The pattern information can be transferred, increasing the measurement to full scale and marking on your paper where the pattern lines cross the grid. When the crossing points are marked the lines can be joined. Compare the shape with the original diagram.

## Pattern Checklist

Look for the following in your pattern. Are the measurements of the construction lines that join pattern pieces together the same? Where panels join, is there a smooth line? (Waistlines are usually straight; armholes and necklines should be smoothly curved without lumps or dips.)

Check that collars fit neatly into necklines with matching collar fold and break lines.

Measure around the armhole and sleeve head; a coat sleeve is about 5cm (2in) bigger than the armhole, whereas the measurements for the same areas on a shirt are nearly the same.

Mark the grain line.

Add balance marks to the seams of panels that join; this is particularly helpful to marry up seams of different shapes.

## Adapting the Patterns

Draw up the pattern and compare the measurements to those of your wearer. In a different colour, mark on the alterations; check that the pattern pieces still resemble the shapes from the diagram.

Modern fashion grading rules can be used to fit different sizes. They do not transfer directly to Victorian garments but can provide a valuable starting place.

The patterns can be modified to your design at two main stages, either by changing the initial pattern (which can be checked at fitting) or by making adaptations at the fitting stage.

## Using Commercial Patterns

Commercially produced patterns will save the time of making your own patterns. They are cut to fit modern figures and often graded to fit a range of sizes. They provide an opportunity to develop an understanding of two-dimensional patterns and build confidence in their use. Always make and fit a toile to check the fit and shape.

Take the included seam allowance off the pattern to easily see and check the shapes. Add your chosen seam allowances to the toile and fitted garment pattern.

## The Toile

When you have drawn up the pattern, make up the toile. Ideally the toile fabric should be roughly similar to the final fabric of the garment: calico is a frequently used and inexpensive

### COSTUME OR TOILE FITTING

#### FITTING CHECKLIST

The most important item at the fitting is the design or reference being used for the costume: keep referring to it.

At the fitting, where possible the right underwear, shoes and accessories should be used.

Make yourself a fitting kit: include in it all tools or fabrics that may be needed, a checklist of the areas to be fitted and considered, plus any questions you might have about how the costume will be used. A notebook is essential and a camera is very useful.

#### AFTER THE FITTING

First, make notes from the fitting. Check the costume and mark on it any alterations. Mark the sleeve position. The alterations can either be transferred back to the pattern or the toile made into a new pattern.

choice. Cut the toile pieces with large seam allowances of about 2.5cm (1in) and a very generous hem allowance for alteration.

Machine tack the pieces together; sleeves can be hand tacked in place for easy removal or be attached during the fitting. Try it on the wearer and alter it to ensure the right fit, shape and proportions.

Fitting a toile allows the flexibility that is essential to make the costume work. It can be cut into as needed or extra fabric can be added in. The toile fabric can be marked with notes, such as where to position pockets or a new waistline, etc.

## Choice of Fabrics and Other Materials

Selecting fabrics is a rare luxury for a costume maker; generally the designer or client chooses the fabric, occasionally asking for guidance or opinion. It is the costume maker's job to make the chosen fabric work for the costume.

When choosing fabric natural fibres are often easier to work with and tend to last better; synthetics do not wear in the same way. Making a tailored costume will take many hours so buy the best quality fabric possible.

### Fabric Quantities

The fitted pattern can be used to work out the exact amount of fabric needed. Lining fabric, cotton sateen or silesia are similar to those used in original garments and easy to work with.

If using patterned, checked or striped fabrics, more is usually required to allow for a less economical layout and cut. Consider how the garment pieces work with the pattern. Is it necessary to match patterns at the centre front or across seams? How do the sleeves and pockets fit in?

### Canvas and Interfacing

Choose a weight of canvas or interfacing complementary to that of the fabric. The costumes in this book have all had the canvas cut without front edge seam allowance; this is not usual. If there is any uncertainty about working with canvas, cut it with a seam allowance and trim it down later in the construction process.

### Fusible Interfacing

The future of the garment has to be considered; fusible interfacing applied in domestic conditions is not always successful in long-term use or there can be problems with the compatibility of the fabric and fusible interfacing. Fusing may even start to separate during construction, presenting a problem for wear or future cleaning. When using fusible interfacing, always test how it works with your fabric; if it is not suitable use a sew-in version or fuse it onto a backing fabric to flat tack to the main fabric.

For backing fabrics, test various options for the appropriate effect. If using calico, consider washing it to shrink it before you start construction.

## Preparing to Sew

### Pressing the Fabric

Iron a piece of fabric to get a feel for it. Not all fabrics are creased but giving your fabric a 'run over' with the iron gives you an opportunity to examine your fabric, to check it over for flaws and to become familiar with its handle. While constructing the garment every seam will need pressing.

Chalk mark the wrong side of the fabric and the pile or nap direction; this will save time examining fabrics with similar right and wrong sides or subtle nap direction.

### Seam Allowances

Decide what seam and hem allowances to use and where extra might be added if the garment might be altered in future. There are not many places to easily alter coats; it can be particularly difficult to let them out, and even the sleeves are not easy to lengthen. Trousers can be let out and taken in at the centre back waist and the length can be changed.

When cutting the seam allowances, be precise and consistent; if the seams have been cut carefully it helps when constructing the garment. Exactly cut seam allowances help when making up parts with offset seams. Although linings must have seam allowance added, I usually suggest not to add any hem allowance.

A consistent seam allowance reduces the amount of construction lines that need to be marked on the garment pieces. It is, of course, important to cut and sew all the seams accurately.

## Marking Up and Preparation

After all the pattern pieces are cut out in fabric, mark on the wrong side all the construction lines and balance marks, along with any information from the pattern that is considered to be important. This is particularly significant for theatrical garments that may have large seam allowances for future alterations. Fabric-marking options are shown in Chapter 2. Any marking method can be used as long as it will last through the making process and will not show through on the outside of the fabric.

Although time-consuming, tacking or flat tacking the chalked or traced seam lines and pattern information is effective and completely removable.

## Garment Construction

Always read the construction instructions carefully.

Throughout the book different methods are used to produce the same thing; for example, the collars are constructed and attached slightly differently. When navigating your way through the book choose the method that suits your particular project best.

Each coat back hook (see Glossary) is formed differently; the frock coat hook in Chapter 5 is the closest to historically accurate with a separate lining for the upper back and skirt supporting and covering the hook on the inside. The other two versions are more 'cheap and cheerful', perhaps not as sturdy but the overall look is acceptable and the back lining can be cut in one piece.

The under collars can be machine or hand pad stitched; construction and fitting is again slightly different on each one, with the closest to a properly tailored collar being the short jacket.

Lapel hand pad stitching is the one process used on all the coats; it does not take long and really is the most effective method to achieve a pleasing shape to the collar.

The front canvas ranges from simple to versions that are more thoroughly constructed with padding and shoulder support.

In this book all the trousers have a button fly and pockets into the side seam. The frock coat trousers have a separate waistband. The breeches have a fall front opening which could be used on trousers. To create different effects for trousers you can vary the leg width, straighten the legs for simplicity or use a shaped hem.

Always make a test sample of any new technique, to see how it works and if you understand the instructions. If possible, make the sample in the real fabric.

## Working with the Instructions

I have tried to make the garment construction as logical and practical as possible. Each coat is constructed using methods varied either to suit the era of the coat or the fabric or to present an alternative solution. With some patience it should be possible to pick through the instructions and choose the ones most appropriate for your project.

Costume construction generally has changing requirements; you need to judge which are the most appropriate combinations of methods and techniques to use. The instructions are guidance: feel free to reinterpret them as is suitable for fabric or performance requirements. Ideally try out the methods in order to make a considered decision about changes.

Read through the garment construction instructions, practise any new techniques and make a sample or two (for example, the pockets) to familiarize yourself with the method. It can seem like a waste of time making something that will not be used, but it is actually an important stage, giving the opportunity to make mistakes or find a better solution.

## Terms and Methods

Before you start, it is really important to work through the Glossary and its 'General Points' section.

# Chapter 4
# Underclothes: Shirts and Drawers

## Beneath the Surface

The shirt is an important part of the look and structure of Victorian men's clothing and should be an early consideration when building a costume, even though often little is seen of it.

Fabrics worn next to the skin are usually washable, with the dual purpose of keeping the dirt of the body from soiling difficult-to-clean outer garments and also to protect the body from rough, heavy or dirty outer clothes. The same innovations that meant cotton was becoming available to the wider population allowed the Victorians to wash their bodies and clothes more frequently than people in previous centuries. Metal utensils for washing clothes and other laundry equipment became cheaper and thus more widely accessible, along with the invention and promotion of laundry additives.

The shirt evolved in cut and shape comparatively quickly over the Victorian period, from the square-cut shirt constructed from squares and rectangles of fabric which had undergone only small changes over nearly two centuries to the garment we would recognize today.

From around 1840 the shirt progressed from the square-cut to a more fitted design. The underarm gusset was superseded by the closer fitting armhole and sleeves and the shoulder was less dropped. The shirt became tailored to the body shape, allowing natural movement.

The visible features of the shirt – the collar, cuffs and bib front – changed according to whim and fashion. The collar developed from a deep rectangle to a narrow shaped band cut with a separate fall. The pleated bib front with an area of gather or tucks below the bib also became an accepted feature of the shirt.

## Early Victorian Shirt

In the 1840s linen was usually used to make the whole shirt. As cotton became more affordable and accessible, shirts were commonly made from two different fabrics: a white linen or fine

Figs 4.2 and 4.3 Early Victorian shirt, front and back views.

Left: Fig. 4.1 Top: Early Victorian shirt (1840s) and drawers (1870s).
Bottom: Late Victorian shirt (1880s) and drawers (1890s).

# Early Victorian shirt

1 Square: 2.5cm (1") No seam allowance included

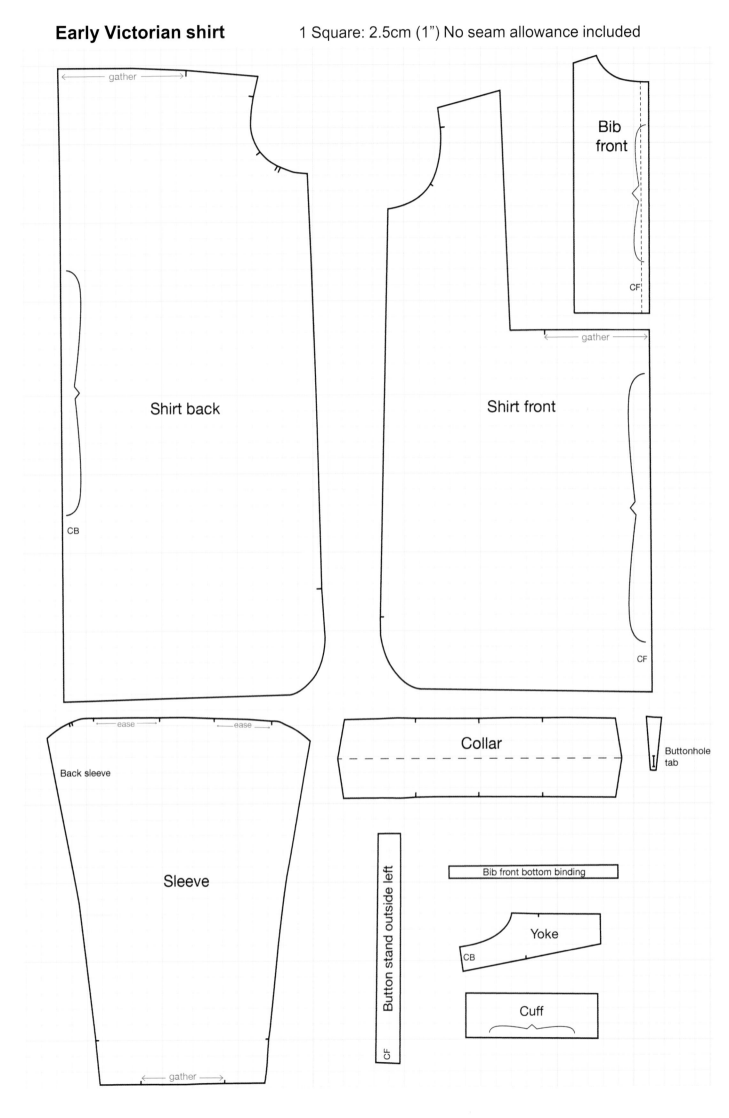

gather

Bib front

CF

Shirt back

CB

gather

Shirt front

CF

ease

ease

Back sleeve

Collar

Buttonhole tab

Sleeve

gather

Button stand outside left

CF

Bib front bottom binding

Yoke

CB

Cuff

**Main fabric:**

Cut one front and one back on the fold; cut two sleeves and four yoke pieces.

**Plain fabric:**

Cut two bib fronts. Cut two cuffs and one collar on the fold. On the straight grain cut one button stand, one band to bind the bottom of the bib front and three buttonhole tab pieces (the third piece acts as an interfacing to strengthen the tab).

**To finish:**

Buttons.

Fig. 4.4 Shirt hem, double rolled and sewn with roll reducing towards side balance mark; hem is shown from both sides (unfinished and finished).

cotton for the areas that would be seen (the collar, bib front and cuffs); the rest was cut from a different fabric, usually a robust but modest material, often a striped or patterned fabric. (Shep and Cariou, 1999).

This early Victorian shirt has features that are recognizable in modern shirts: it is slightly shorter and less voluminous than shirts of the eighteenth century; the tails are rounded; the sleeve head and armhole are shaped; and the creation of the shoulder yoke has enabled a smooth fit around the neckline and shoulder.

This sample shirt is based on an 1845 pattern from *Journal des Desmoiselles*, as examined in *Shirts and Men's Haberdashery 1840s to 1920s* (Shep and Cariou, 1999). In order to simplify the construction, not all the parts of the original shirt pattern have been used.

The shirt is made from a mauve self-striped cotton for the main body of the shirt and sleeves, with the bib, collar and cuffs made from a vintage cotton drill.

This shirt has been cut with 1.3cm (½in) seam allowance except for the sides of the bib front, where it is 2.5cm (1in), and the back and front armholes

and the armhole area of the yoke pieces, where it is 6mm (¼in).

In this example the shirt collar and cuffs are constructed without interfacing. Consider using an interfacing in the collar and cuffs if the fabric being used would benefit from extra structure. If so, it is advisable to use a sew-in interfacing as fusible interfacings may not bond successfully without a fusing press and do not always stand up well to repeated laundering.

## Marking Up and Preparation

Indicate all the balance marks. Ensure the back of the sleeve is marked because the back and front of the sleeve are the same cut, the only difference being that there is less ease at the front. The sleeve head is supposed to be very smooth and flat.

## Construction Instructions
### Gather stitches

Sew lines of gather stitches between balance marks: at the top of the back panel, at the top of the centre front, on either side of the sleeve head and at the bottom of the sleeve.

## Hem and sleeve cuff opening

The shirt has a rolled hem. Starting at a side seam balance mark, sew from the balance mark at the edge of the seam allowance with a very small roll, widening after a few stitches to the desired hem size, usually about 6mm (¼in) doubled over from 1.2cm (½in), and continuing to the balance mark at the other side of the shirt, where the roll is narrowed and the stitching run off the edge of the fabric into the side seam.

The same technique used on the hem is used for finishing off the cuff openings. At the balance mark indicating the length of opening, form a very small rolled hem, widening the roll as you go towards the bottom of the sleeve and then running the stitching off into the seam allowance.

## Bib front preparation

Press under the seam allowance on both sides of the button stand. Fold the bib front panels in half (indicated by the dashed line on the pattern).

Place the button stand on the outside of the wearer's left front, just covering the bib front fold, and attach it to the front by topstitching along both sides of the stand.

With the left bib front over the right and matching the centre fronts (indicated on the pattern by dotted lines), tack the bottom of the opening closed.

On the shirt front, sew reinforcing triangles from the seam allowance to the intersection of the construction lines at the side and bottom of the bib front.

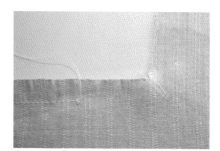

Fig. 4.5 Bib area of shirt front with reinforcing triangle sewn towards construction line pivot point; gather thread for centre front is visible.

## Buttonhole tab

This will be attached to a button on the trousers to keep the bib taught and flat. Sew the three tab pieces together leaving the top open, trim the seam allowances, turn through, press down and topstitch around the edge of the tab. Make a buttonhole at the end of the tab.

## Joining the bib to the shirt front

With wrong sides together match the bib to the shirt front, snip to the end of the reinforced triangle, and match up the construction lines; there is a 2.5cm (1in) seam allowance on the seams along the sides of the bibs and 1.3cm (½in) on the shirt. Pull up the gather stitch threads to fit the area between the balance marks on the bib.

Sew the shirt front to the bib front, starting from the shoulder. Match the point of the 'V' to the corner of the construction line on the bib. Sew to the point of the triangle. With the needle down through the point, pivot the shirt to match to the bottom of the bib, then continue sewing to the other shoulder.

Trim off half the seam allowance next to the main fabric on the underside of the bib front; the remaining seam allowance will be folded back to make a flat-fell seam to finish off the sides of the bib.

Place the buttonhole tab on the centre front of the shirt over the gathers.

## Binding strip to finish off the bottom of the bib front

Press under a seam allowance on one side of the strip. Place the right side of the binding strip to the right side of the shirt. Using the creased line, sew on top of the existing sewing line (ensuring the buttonhole tab is included) and continuing to the unfinished edges. Trim away some of the seam allowance to reduce bulk.

Press the binding strip towards the bib front. Wrap the side seams of the bib front and binding around the shirt and bib front seam allowance, then press.

Sew along the folded seam allowances around the bib front (Fig. 4.7).

## Shoulder yoke

Sew a right and a left yoke piece together along the centre back seam, repeating to create two identical yokes.

Press the seams open.

Place a yoke to the right side of the upper back of the shirt. Pull up the gather stitch to fit the yoke, and sew the yoke to the back. Sew the remaining yoke piece with its right side to the wrong side of the shirt, sandwiching the shirt between the two yoke pieces, and sew them together over the top of the first sewing line. Press both the yoke panels away from the shirt back.

With right sides together, sew the shoulders of the shirt and outside yoke together.

Starting at the armhole, manipulate the yoke so that the right side of the remaining yoke shoulder matches to the wrong side of the shirt front, then pin along the shoulder seam moving towards the neckline. (Look at the picture of the late Victorian shirt yoke later in this chapter.) Some of the shirt will be drawn into the yoke. Sew along the first yoke to shirt sewing line,

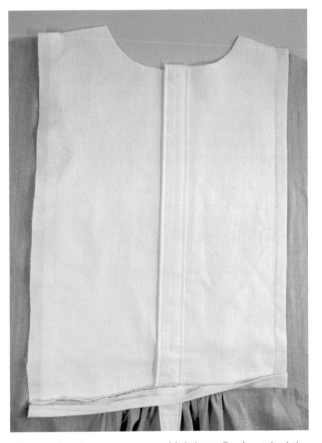

Fig. 4.6 *Shirt front sewn to contrasting bib:* Bib seam allowance next to shirt is trimmed back (seen here partially trimmed); gathered area at centre front of shirt front can be seen at bottom.

Fig. 4.7 *Finishing seams around bib front.* On the right, bib seam allowance has been trimmed and wrapped around shirt; binding strip is joined onto bottom and seam allowances are pressed under.

trapping all three layers together. Turn the yoke to the outside and press. Topstitch along the front shoulder and back of the yoke.

### Shoulder seams and sleeve seams

With wrong sides together, match the front to the back of the shirt, extending the seam allowance of the back panel from under the front to be visible by about 1.3cm (½in).

Prepare the sleeve seams in the same way.

Sew the side seams with a 6mm (¼in) seam allowance, starting from the rolled hem on the shirt tails and from the rolled cuff opening. Press the longer back seam over the front, wrap the larger seam allowance around the smaller one. Topstitch close to the fold. Sew a bar tack across the seam at the join of the shirt tails and cuff opening.

### Collar and cuffs

Press the collar and cuff pieces in half and press one long seam allowance to the inside on each piece. Sew the side seams of the collar and cuffs, sewing over the pressed line. Turn through to the right side and press.

Place the unpressed seam allowance, right side of the collar to the wrong side of the neckline and sew the collar along the neckline.

Place the right side of the unpressed cuff seam allowance to the wrong side

of the bottom of the sleeves, drawing up the gather on the sleeves to fit the cuff. Sew together.

Pin the pressed-under seam allowance of the collar and cuffs, covering the first sewing line with the seam allowance inside, and machine along the fold, closing the collar and cuffs.

### Attaching the sleeves to the body

With right sides together, put the sleeves into the armholes. Extend the sleeve seam allowance by 1.3cm (½in) to be visible under the edge of the shirt armhole seam, and match up seams and balance marks. Pull up the ease stitches to fit the sleeve into the armhole.

Sew the armhole 6mm (¼in) from the cut edge of the shirt armhole; the sewing line will be about 2cm (¾in) inside the cut edge on the sleeve. Press

the seam allowance towards the shirt and wrap the larger seam allowance around the smaller one. Machine close to the fold on the seam to make a flat-fell seam visible on the inside of the shirt with a line of sewing showing on the outside of the shirt.

### Buttonholes and buttons

The placement of the buttons on the collar and bib front were not specified on the original instructions. For this shirt the collar fastens with a button and buttonhole at the base of the collar band and there are two buttons and buttonholes on the button stand of the bib. The pattern instructions did have two cuff buttons and buttonholes towards the top and bottom of the side of the cuff; this example just has one set of fastenings close to where the cuff joins to the shirt.

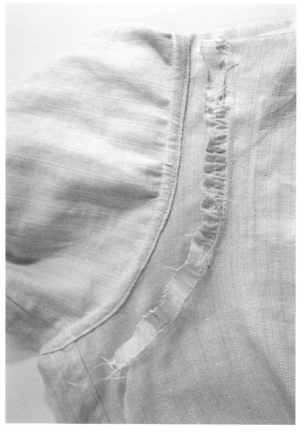

Fig. 4.8 Side seams and underarm seams being made into welt-type seams.

Fig. 4.9 Fitting sleeve into armhole, with sleeve seam extending beyond body to be wrapped around body seam allowance and made into a flat felled seam.

## Late Victorian Shirt

By the 1880s shirt bib fronts had changed from square to rounded and stiffened. The ideal look of the shirt front was flat and smooth without wrinkles. This was achieved by combining several elements: fastening the tab at the bottom of the bib front to a button on the trousers; increasing the stiffness of the bib with lines of sewing, pleats and tucks (even occasionally cording); and application of starch during laundering.

Front openings continued below the bib, either for a short distance or (from the 1880s) all the way down the front. If a shirt had a longer opening or opened completely it did not need the volume of fabric required to pull it on over the head and could therefore be a much closer fit (Willett and Cunnington, 1992). Some shirts opened down the back, which would have had the advantage of keeping the front flat and neat (Levitt, 1986).

For evening wear and later in the period, separate stiffened collars, cuffs and bib fronts were attached to the shirt with studs and cufflinks: such fastenings are easier to use than buttons with seriously stiffened fabrics.

The sample shirt pattern is based on instructions from the *West-End Gazette* of 1884, as explored in *Shirts and Men's Haberdashery 1840s to 1920s* (Shep and Cariou, 1999).

The variety of shirt details were numerous and changed with fashion and can be changed by modern makers as needed; for example, the cuffs could be replaced by rectangular-shaped cuffs or double cuffs.

When making modern versions of the bib front, stiff interfacing can be used. Spray starch can be used after construction.

The area directly below the bib front could be gathered or pleated to fit the excess fabric into the available area. The seam between the back and the back of the yoke can also be gathered or pleated and would vary in width depending on the length of the shirt opening.

This shirt has been cut from two fabrics: a stripe for the body of the shirt and a plain cotton for the bib front, collar and cuffs.

The cuffs could be interfaced with a sew-in interfacing or you could cut an extra cuff depth on the cuff to form a self-interfacing similar to the waistband of the 1870s drawers.

For this example, a 1.3cm (½in) seam allowance has been generally used except on the collar, the post for the cuff opening and the buttonhole tab, where 6mm (¼in) is used. The curved sides of the bib have 2.5cm (1in) seam allowance.

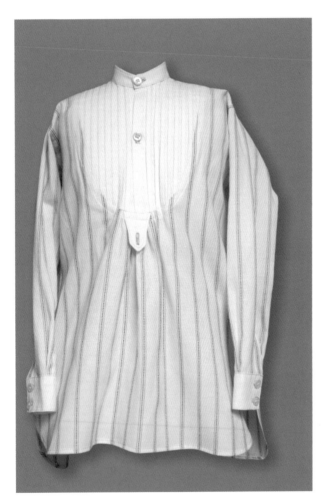 

Figs 4.10 and 4.11 Late Victorian shirt, front and back views.

# Late Victorian shirt

1 Square: 2.5cm (1") No seam allowance included

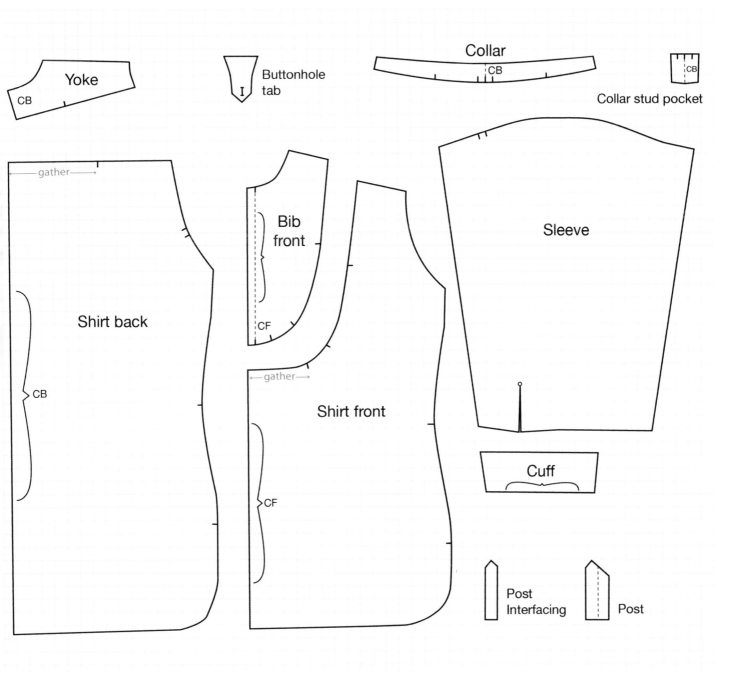

Yoke

CB

Buttonhole
tab

Collar

CB

Collar stud pocket

CB

gather

Shirt back

CB

Bib
front

CF

Sleeve

gather

Shirt front

CF

Cuff

Post
Interfacing

Post

## PIECES NEEDED

**Main fabric:**

Cut one back and one front panel on the fold; cut two sleeves and four yoke pieces.

**Plain fabric:**

Cut two bib fronts; cut one small square to make a back neck collar stud pocket, three buttonhole tab pieces (the third piece acts as an interfacing to strengthen the tab) and two posts for the sleeve opening. Cut two cuffs on the fold. From the leftover fabric cut strips 2.5cm (1in) wide long enough for sixteen generous pleats down the bib front (eight each side).

**Woven fusible interfacing:**

Cut one collar shape and the post shape without seam allowance. Fusible interfacing is not normally recommended for shirts: this exception is because the areas of the narrow stand collar and the cuff post are quite small, so any deterioration during laundry should not be obvious.

**To finish:**

Buttons.

## Marking Up and Preparation

The suggested seam allowances work well. If you are able to cut them precisely there is no need to mark the sewing lines and very little trimming of excess seam allowances is needed. Indicate all the balance marks.

## Construction Instructions
### Gather stitches
Sew lines of gather stitches between the balance marks at the top of the shirt back and the top of the centre front.

### Shirt hem
Construct the hem as suggested for the early Victorian shirt under the side

heading 'Hem and sleeve cuff opening'.

### Bib front with decorative pleating
Each 2.5cm (1in) strip of fabric is folded in half and the two cut edges are machined together with the zigzag stitch straddling the raw edges. Press the strips flat.

Fold the bib fronts in half (along the front fold line) and press. Open out flat. Working with the illustration as a guide, mark the pleat positions on each front, leaving space for the front fastening on both sides.

From the centre front pin the strips with the zigzag edge towards the front fold of the bib. Pin carefully, then, using a straight stitch, sew the strips to the bib front sewing close to the zigzag. Continue until the front is full, checking for even spacing as you go. Press the pleats towards the centre fold covering the zigzag and sewing lines with the pleats. Trim the excess pleat ends.

Re-fold along the front fold line. Mark the construction lines and balance marks on the outside edges of the bib fronts. Flat tack the two layers of the bib fronts together along the construction lines.

Overlap the wearer's left bib front over the right bib front so that the centre front lines (indicated by the dotted lines on the pattern) match.

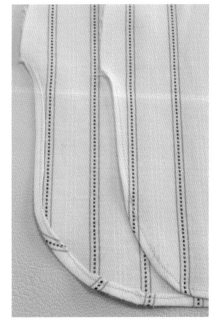

Fig. 4.12 Shirt hem, starting with very small roll at side seam balance mark, increasing to larger roll.

Machine tack the two together at the bottom so that the bib front can be treated as one until buttons and buttonholes are sewn.

### Buttonhole tab
Follow the buttonhole tab instructions for the early Victorian shirt. Pin the buttonhole tab on the centre front of the bib.

### Joining the bib to the shirt front
With right sides together match the

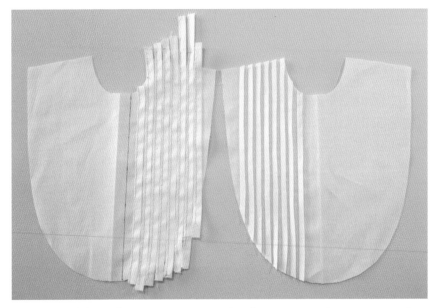

Fig. 4.13 Bib front pleat preparation; on right, pleats are pressed over sewing and trimmed.

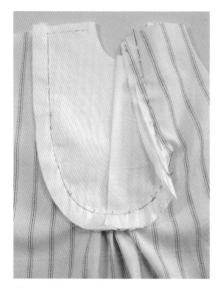

Fig. 4.14 Inside of bib pinned and partly sewn to shirt.

Fig. 4.15 Front shoulder seams of inside and outside yoke sewn, with shirt front shoulder sandwiched between the two; some of the shirt is drawn into the yoke. After sewing the shirt is pulled out of the yoke, turning the seam allowances inside the yoke panels.

construction line of the shirt front bib area to the construction line on the bib front. On this shirt the seam allowance on the bib is larger than that of the front. Pull up the gather stitches to fit the front of the shirt into the available space on the bib. Pin from the shirt to the bib, ensuring the construction lines match.

Machine the front of the shirt to the bib.

Trim the seam allowance of the shirt and the pleated side of the bib evenly to about 6mm ($^1$/4in), leaving the seam allowance on the inside of the bib long. Press the seam allowances towards the shirt. The long seam allowance of the inside of the bib is wrapped round the trimmed seam allowances of the shirt and gathering. Machine along the fold of the seam to the shirt front around the edge of the bib creating a flat-fell seam and sewing over the buttonhole tab so it is pointing towards the bottom of the shirt.

### Shoulder yoke
Construct and fit the yoke pieces as suggested for the early Victorian shirt under the side heading 'Shoulder yoke'.

### Collar
Fuse the collar interfacing to the outer collar.

Join the collar stud pocket to the outer collar. This is done by sewing from the balance mark edge of the seam allowance towards the interfacing or construction line, turning at a right angle to sew along the side of the interfacing, continuing over the centre back to the other balance mark and

turning at a right angle to finish at the edge of the seam allowance balance mark, thus making a three-sided rectangle. Trim and snip close to the stitch at the angles, turn through and topstitch around the shape. At the centre back, make a buttonhole for the collar stud though the collar and facing. Fold the facing over so the seam allowance is in line with the bottom of

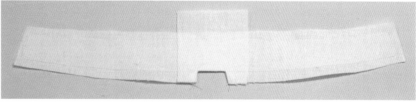

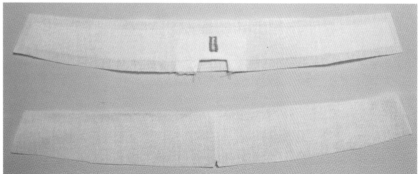

Fig. 4.16 *Collar with stud pocket construction:* Stud pocket facing is bagged out along centre lower collar seam allowance; buttonhole is made; extended facing is folded down in line with collar seam allowance.

the collar.

Press under the neck seam allowance along the edge of the collar interfacing.

Sew the two collars together, offsetting the inside collar piece slightly so it finishes slightly smaller than the interfaced outer collar, then turn through to the right side and press.

### Attaching the collar to the shirt

Place the inside of the collar with its extended seam allowance to the inside of the shirt. Sew the collar to the shirt, matching the construction lines.

Turn the seam allowances into the collar. Sew along the pressed fold just covering the first sewing line, sew across the stud pocket facing, and continue the topstitching around the collar.

### Cuffs

Press the cuffs in half, right sides together, and press under a cuff seam allowance.

Sew the side seams, offsetting the unfolded side of the cuff so that it is slightly smaller and trapping the pressed-under seam allowance. Turn through and press.

### Cuff posts

Fuse the interfacing to the post with the points in line. Press the fabric seam allowance over the edge of the interfacing and continue the fold from the post top along the top of the side extension.

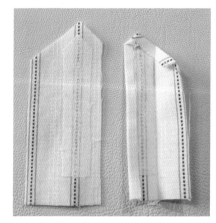

Fig. 4.17 Cuff posts with fused interfacing and seam allowance pressed back along edge of interfacing, continuing pressed-back seam allowance from side of point along extension.

### Making the cuff opening

With the wrong side of the sleeve facing up, sew a small rolled hem on the side of the opening closest to the sleeve side seam. At the top of the opening make the roll run off to almost nothing. Continue sewing at a right angle along the top of the opening. Sew on the post extension, placing the right side of the post to the wrong side of the shirt sleeve and then stitch down the other side of the opening to the cuff.

Press the seam allowance towards the post and bring the rest of the post to the outside of the shirt.

Topstitch the post to the sleeve. Starting at the cuff edge of the sleeve

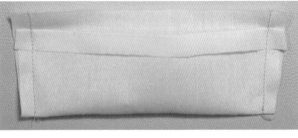

Fig. 4.18 *Cuff construction:* Cuff side seams are sewn, offsetting seam allowances in order for outside of cuff with pressed-under seam allowance to be slightly larger than other side.

sew up the open edge of the post, around the point, and down the other side by about 2cm ($^3$/4in). With the opening closed, sew at a right angle over the post.

### Joining the sleeves into the shirt body

With right sides together, pin the sleeve into the armhole, extending the sleeve seam allowance beyond the edge of the armhole by 1.3cm (½in); distribute the ease around the armhole.

Sew 6mm (¼in) away from the edge of the shirt armhole. Press the seam allowances towards the shirt. Wrap the longer seam allowance around the shorter seam allowance. Sew the seam close to the fold, creating a flat-fell seam on the shirt.

### Side seams and sleeve seams

With the wrong sides of the shirt together, join the side seams and underarm seams. Extend the back panel out from underneath the front by about 1.3cm (½in).

Sew 6mm (¼in) away from the cut edge of the shorter seam allowance. Press the larger seam allowance to cover the smaller one. Wrap the former around the latter and topstitch along the folded edge of the seam allowance to create a flat-fell seam. At the top of the tails make a bar tack over the seam.

### Joining the cuff to the sleeve

Pin the cuff to the sleeve with the right side of the cuff with the unfolded seam allowance to the wrong side of the sleeve.

Make some pleats to fit the volume of the sleeve into the cuff, ensuring the pleats of both cuffs are an opposing pair. For this shirt there are two pleats on the post side of the cuff opening and one pleat on the other side of the opening on the sleeve.

Sew the cuff to the sleeve. Turn the sleeve and cuff seam allowance to the inside of the cuff and top stitch along the folded seam allowance of the cuff just covering the first cuff-to-sleeve sewing line.

Alternatively, the unfolded cuff seam can be sewn to the right side of the

Fig. 4.19 *Sleeve opening and post:* From inside, rolled hem and right-angled topstitching are visible; finished post can be seen from outside.

bottom of the sleeve, the seam allowances turned to the inside of the cuff and the folded cuff seam allowance hand-sewn along the first cuff-to-sleeve sewing line; this method can be used on collars and cuffs if machine sewing on the outside of the garment is not desirable.

**Buttonholes**

Make a buttonhole on each side of the collar at the front. The collar stud will pass through the two holes and through the corresponding holes on the collar.

The bib front could have one or two buttons. It could also fasten with studs, which would require buttonholes on both sides.

On this style of cuff there are two buttonholes on each cuff; they are placed on the cuff in line with the post.

Fig. 4.20 *Sewing sleeves into armholes of shirt:* Sleeve on right is sewn in; sleeve on left has had welt formed.

## Drawers

Drawers are utilitarian garments and seldom considered worth preserving, so there are few surviving examples of men's drawers. Fortunately there are written records and patterns. It is possible that not all men wore these garments, particularly early in this period when the long and voluminous shirt would form a washable layer between the body and the outer clothes.

Men's drawers can be many different lengths. Various names have been applied, including 'trouser drawers', 'knee breeches' and the rather prudish Victorian term 'linens', which referred to all the garments worn close to the body (Willett and Cunnington, 1992).

The patterns here can be lengthened to make long drawers; the leg can be tapered to the ankle or a drawstring, or elastic can be used to draw in the ankle, or a cuff with button fastenings can be attached.

### Drawers, 1870s

These drawers are based on original pattern drafting instructions from the *Glencross Scientific Guide to Cutting*, 1873, Plate 23, cited in Shep and Cariou (1999), and described as 'knee breeches with full tops'.

The overlapped front waistband fastening reduces the requirement for extra buttons on the front centre opening.

### Marking Up and Preparation

This pair of drawers has been cut with 1.3cm (½in) seam allowance and 2cm (¾in) hem. The balance marks are indicated. The waistband can be cut three times the finished width with a seam allowance; the middle layer then acts as a simple interfacing.

### Construction Instructions

#### Drawers front opening

On the two front pieces make a double rolled hem, with the roll getting smaller and continuing off the seam allowance at the balance mark for the bottom of

Fig. 4.21 1870 drawers, front and back views.

the fly. This method is also used for sleeve openings and hems on shirts earlier in this chapter.

#### Joining the leg pieces together

Joining the front legs to the back legs with French seams.

#### Hemming the legs

Press under a turning of 6mm (¼in), press under a second turning of 1.3cm (½in). Sew the hem close to the upper fold.

#### Joining the legs together

Join the two legs together through the crotch seam with a French seam. Make a bar tack at the base of the fly with the French seam towards the left leg.

---

### PIECES NEEDED

**Fabric:**

Cut two front legs and two back legs. The waistband can be cut in one or with a centre back join.

**To finish:**

Buttons.

### Waistband

Press a seam allowance under, roll and fold the remaining waistband fabric into three with the cut construction line in the centre of the roll.

Close the ends of the waistband, with the seam allowance not sewn into the seam. Turn through to the right side and press. (Fig. 4.23)

### Joining the waist onto the waistband

Make regularly spaced and sized tucks along the waist area of the drawers, pin to hold. Ensure that these tucks are spaced and lapped mirror images of each other and that they will fit the waist measurement.

Match the right side of the waistband seam allowance to the wrong side of the drawers, and sew together.

Fold the seam allowances into the waistband. Topstitch along the fold line of the waistband with the fold covering the stitch line to the legs. Continue topstitching around the waistband to secure the inner layer of interfacing fabric.

On this waistband there is a fairly large overlap at the centre front fastened with two buttons. Make buttonholes and sew buttons to suit.

Fig. 4.22 Front opening with rolled and sewn seam allowance reducing to tiny roll and running off edge of seam allowance at balance mark (seen from back and front).

## Drawers 1870s

1 Square: 2.5cm (1") No seam allowance included

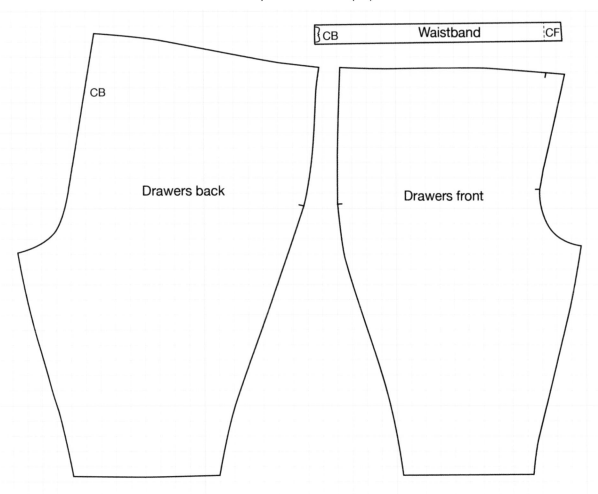

CB

Waistband

CF

CB

Drawers back

Drawers front

## Drawers 1890s

1 Square: 2.5cm (1") No seam allowance included

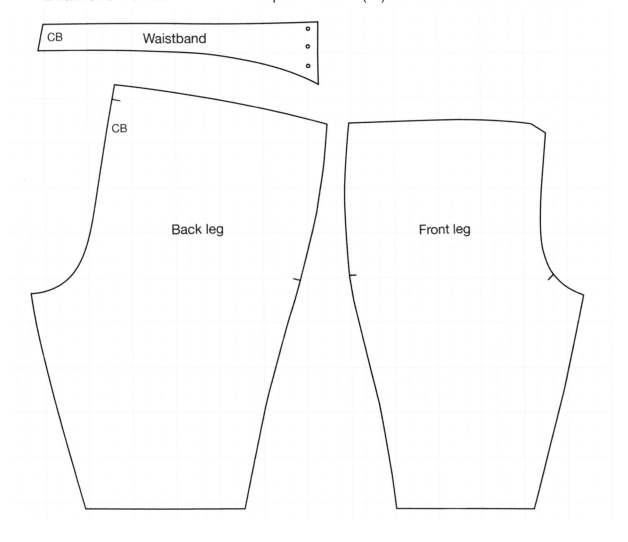

CB

Waistband

CB

Back leg

Front leg

## Drawers, 1890s

The basic shape is very similar to that of the 1870s drawers, but with the addition of a shaped waistband and a short opening at the centre back fastened with a cord to allow waist alteration. The pattern is based on a drawers draft from about 1895, in *The Keystone Shirt System*, plate 26 (cited by Shep and Cariou, 1999).

### Marking Up and Preparation

These drawers have been cut with 1.3cm (½in) seam allowance and 2cm (¾in) hem; the balance marks have been indicated.

### Construction Instructions

Use the instructions for the 1870s drawers. Construct the short back opening using the same rolled hem method as the front opening.

### Shaped waistband

Fuse or flat tack the interfacing into the waistband. Press a seam allowance under along the shaped side of the interfacing on the band. Bag out the waistband along the top and sides. Turn the waistband through to the right side and press.

Fit each side of the waistband as outlined for the 1870s drawers.

This pair of drawers is fastened at the centre front waistband with three buttons. There is enough fullness to give a small overlap below the

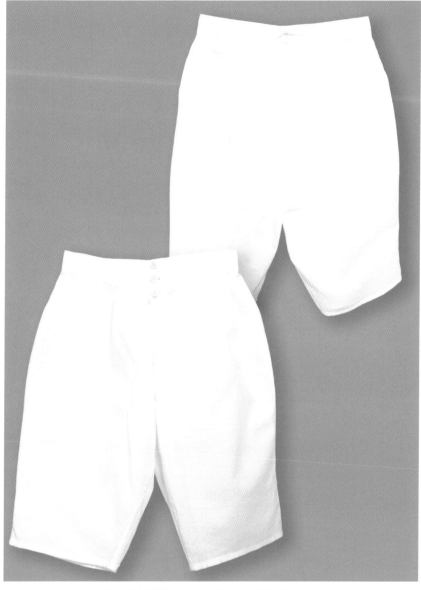

Fig. 4.24 1890s drawers, front and back views.

Fig. 4.23 1870s Drawers. Top: waistband is cut three times finished width plus seam allowance and pressed. Bottom: waistband is pinned with right sides together ready to sew.

### PIECES NEEDED

**Fabric:**

Cut two front legs and two back legs. Cut two waistbands folded along the straight edge or cut four waistband pieces and seam accordingly.

**Interfacing:**

Cut interfacing suitable for the waistband.

**To finish:**

Buttons, cord.

waistband: this may be fastened with a button placed midway along the opening.

## Back waistband opening

These drawers have three hand-worked eyelets on each side of the centre back waistband.

Mark the eyelet position. Make a hole by forcing the threads apart with a tailor's awl, then whip stitch around the hole two or three times, pulling the thread tight to keep the hole open. For a more decorative finish use a buttonhole stitch around the whipped hole.

Use a cord or tape to close the centre back waist to the right size.

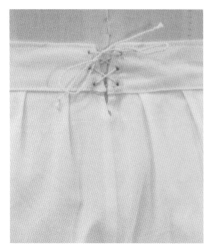

Fig. 4.25 *Back waist size adjustment:* Short centre back opening below waist, three hand-worked eyelets on each side of waistband and cord or tape used to fasten back.

## FRENCH SEAM

This is a neat and strong seam finishing method that is very useful for cotton or linen underwear which may have to stand up to vigorous washing. It is effective in joining straight seams and curves of the same shape.

### CONSTRUCTING A FRENCH SEAM

Begin by putting the wrong sides of the fabric together; sew together leaving a small seam allowance or trimming the seam allowance close to the stitch line after sewing. Press the seam allowance open or to one side, then press the seam back on itself, wrapping the body of the fabric around the raw edges. Press carefully along the fold. Sew parallel to the folded edge, trapping the raw edge of the seam allowance in the seam. Press to finish.

Fig. 4.26 French seam construction process, with two pieces of fabric sewn together and wrapped around seam allowance.

## LINEN BUTTONS

These were extremely widely used on washable garments after handmade Dorset buttons fell out of favour. Linen buttons also started by being handmade but were quickly brought into mass production, being based on a fabric-covered wire ring. They were highly practical as they could stand up to the rigours of washing, whereas more expensive mother-of-pearl buttons would break when garments were passed through the wringer (mangle).

Fig. 4.27 Linen and mother-of-pearl buttons; linen buttons were often sold on decorative cards.

# Chapter 5
# Early Victorian Frock Coat, Waistcoat and Trousers

### Frock Coat, 1840s

Frock coats belong to the group of the garments Victorian tailors called body coats: a body coat is closely fitted in the waist area, as are the morning coat and evening dress tailcoat later in this book. The chief difference between the coats shown here is in the cut of the skirt.

Victorian men's jackets and coats were rarely fully lined. Partial linings were used to cover and support padding which was quilted onto the lining to achieve the fashionable shape. Often the lapel facing would extend across the whole inside front of the garment, with the padding attached to it; a wide range of quilting techniques were employed to decoratively hold the padding in place. The skirts of tailcoats or morning coats were often finished by being partly or fully faced or lined in the outer fabric. At the very least the centre back skirt panel was faced in the top fabric, which could be wrapped around the centre back edge and joined to the pleat; this method enabled the whole skirt back to be used as a long pocket.

Frock coats were worn shorter and with less padding than in the previous decade.

In this example, all the pieces cut from the outer fabric are backed onto a cotton fabric. Backing fabrics can add an extra dimension to the qualities of the main fabric: firmness, thickness, body, depth or strength. The use of backings is fairly common practice in costume making.

The backing allows the use of fusible canvas. Using fusible canvas is not normally advisable on period garments; the outer layer of fabric must appear to be independent from the canvas. If a fusible canvas is really necessary, apply it to a backing so that it is less obvious and can be treated as a separate layer.

The main fabric has a slight pile and possible nap (where the pile lies in one direction). The pattern pieces have been cut following the grain and not 'topped and tailed' (cut in both directions to use less fabric). Although the fabric is a plain weave with no obvious wrong or right side, only one side of the fabric has been used and the 'wrong' side is indicated with chalk marks at the cutting stage.

The velvet used for the collar is a thick cotton velvet. Cotton velvets are usually the best behaved velvets; they 'creep' a lot less than silk or certain synthetic velvets. Cotton velvets can be more robust than other velvets; the pile on some velvets can be damaged very easily with heat or steam from the iron and some velvets are so delicate that the pile can be spoiled during routine garment making. Try to avoid using velvet for your first projects.

The pattern pieces for the main fabric have been cut with an allowance

Fig. 5.2 Frock coat, rear view showing centre back skirt opening and side back pleats, both of which were regular features until late in the century.

Left: Fig. 5.1 Frock coat based on an 1840s style, front view, single-breasted with velvet collar.

43

# Frock Coat 1840s

1 Square: 2.5cm (1") No seam allowance included

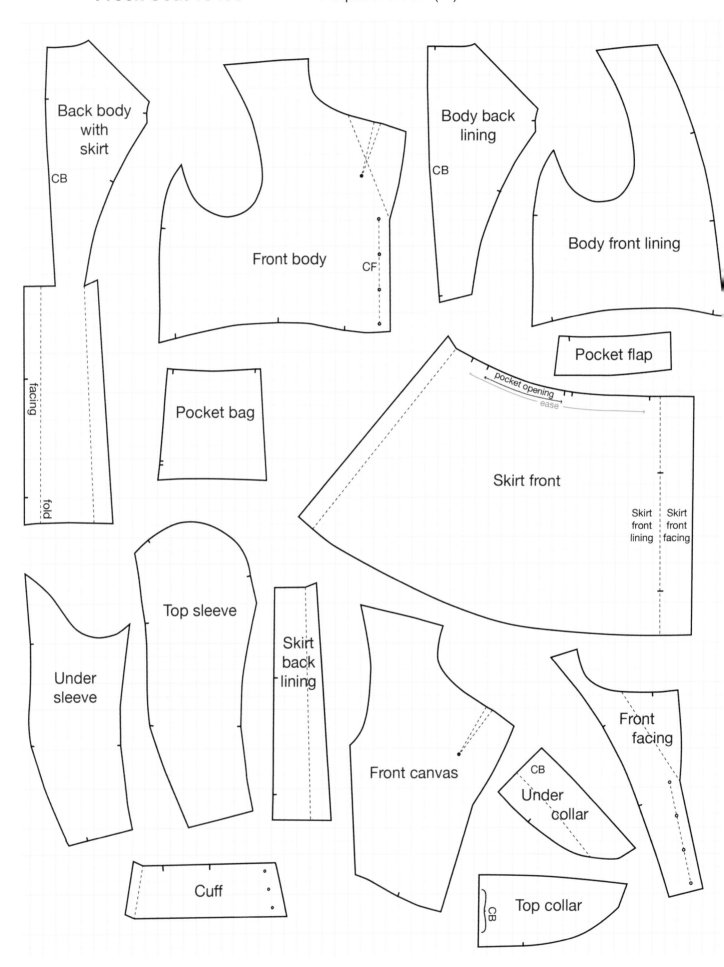

### Main and backing fabrics:

Cut two front bodies, back bodies with skirt, skirt fronts, top sleeves, under sleeves, cuffs, pocket flaps, front facings with lapel, skirt front facings (from the right-hand edge of the skirt front as far as the dotted and notched line).

The contrasting coloured top collar has been cut in one piece on the straight grain. The velvet used is substantial and has not been backed.

The under collar is a wool fabric cut on the bias with a centre back seam and seam allowance.

### Collar Canvas:

Cut the under collar on the bias in one piece without seam allowance.

### Lining:

Cut two front bodies, back bodies, skirt fronts (from the left edge of the skirt front as far as the dotted and notched line), skirt backs, cuffs, pocket flaps.

### Sleeve lining:

A cream-coloured imitation silk dupion was used here; the upper and under sleeves are cut using the same pattern as for the sleeves cut from the main fabric.

### Plain cotton fabric:

Cut two pairs of pocket bags; note that the pocket opening has been indicated and towards the bottom back of the pocket a mark has been made.

### Fusible hair canvas:

Covering the front of the body from the shoulder to waist, run the canvas from the lower front armhole narrowing to the waist (check the pattern illustration). This piece of canvas has a 2.5cm (1in) seam allowance on the shoulder and 1.3cm (½in) around the armhole; the rest has no seam allowance.

The skirt front canvas is the same width as the front body canvas at the waist, cut without seam allowance or hem allowance.

### Woven fusible interfacing:

Cut two panels on the bias to cover the shoulder and neck area at the top of the back body, stopping just below the armhole. This can be cut freehand; work on the bias and add a seam allowance. The lower back skirt is covered by the same interfacing cut with the grain of the skirt.

The pocket flaps and cuff interfacing are cut without the seam allowance; the pocket flaps have a seam allowance above the top edge of the pocket flap.

The top edges of the pairs of pocket bags are stabilized with a strip of fusible interfacing.

### Lightweight synthetic fusible knit interfacing:

Cut two cuffs; these are bonded onto the wrong side of the cuff linings fabric to make the cuff area a little more substantial.

### To finish:

Buttons.

---

of 1.5cm (⅝in) except on the front shoulder seams, which have 2.5cm (1in) allowed, and the coat hem, which has 5cm (2in) allowed.

Most seam allowances on the lining have been cut at 1.3cm (½in), except the hem of the skirt pieces which have only a 6mm (¼in) allowance.

### Marking Up and Preparation

The lining does not need construction lines marking; in this example, balance marks have been indicated with a very small snip.

All the pattern information, such as construction lines and balance marks, is marked on the backing or over the interfacing.

All the fusible interfacings should be fused onto the appropriate pieces of backing fabric before construction starts. Carefully match the edges of the canvas or interfacing where the canvas has been cut without seam allowance to the marked construction lines on the backing. Pin or weigh down to hold the pattern in place before marking the construction information on the backings, canvas and interfacing where the edge of the interfacing or canvas cannot be used as a guide.

For the collar canvas under collar, mark on the collar fold line.

### Construction Instructions

#### Flat tacking

Flat tack the backing to the fabric with the interfacing and canvas uppermost, tacking along all the construction lines and balance marks.

Flat tack along the edge of the woven interfacing on the cuffs.

Flat tack the pocket flap following the construction lines for the sides and bottom and the marked top construction line.

#### Skirt pleat lines and back opening

Using matching thread, backstitch along the skirt pleat lines and the fold of the skirt back opening; the stitch should be barely visible on the outside.

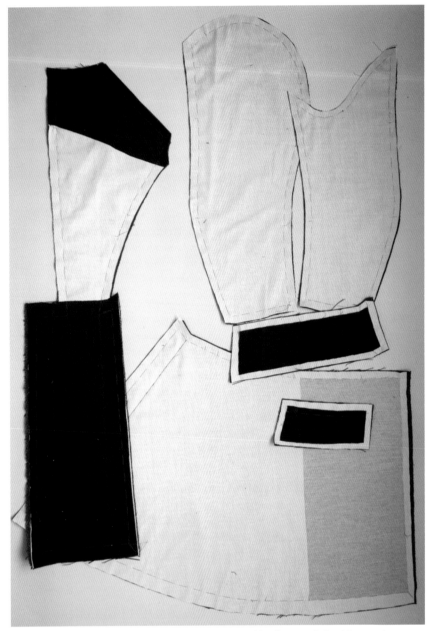

Fig. 5.3 Frock coat pattern pieces cut in fabric and backing with fusible interfacings applied and flat tacked together. Back body has interfacing on yoke area and skirt; cuff and pocket flap have woven cotton cut without seam allowances; front of skirt has fusible hair canvas cut without seam allowance.

### Flat tacking the backing and canvas to the front body

Flat tack around the front body, avoiding the shoulder area. Leave the shoulder seam and a strip of 5cm (2in) width along the neckline and the armhole separate from the backing.

Transfer the construction lines from the shoulder of the backing and canvas to the main fabric and tack the lines onto the main fabric.

Do not flat tack the lapel or break line; the dart has to be closed and pressed separately on both layers. The two lapel layers also need to be kept separate for the lapel pad stitching.

### Lapel darts

Tailor tack the end of the lapel dart from the canvas to the main fabric. Mark the dart construction lines on the canvas. Machine sew closed the dart on the main fabric. Cut along the centre of the closed dart as far as is easily possible. Press the dart open.

Cut the dart shape out of the canvas and backing fabric. With the cut edges of the dart meeting, iron a piece of fusible interfacing over the join. Machine zigzag over the join and interfacing.

Continue the front flat tacking to the break line.

Draw a straight line on the canvas joining the top of the break line to the bottom. Tack along the break line.

### Pad stitching the lapels

Starting at the break line and working parallel to it, fill the lapel area with pad stitching. (Before starting, look at the description of pad stitching a lapel in the Glossary.)

When both lapels have been pad stitched, press the pad-stitched area flat from the canvas side.

### Reinforcing triangles

Sew reinforcing triangles on the back body skirt at the top of the fold line for the side back pleat; make the point of the triangle touch the top of the pleat fold line. (Check the Glossary on this technique.)

Sew reinforcing triangles on the left back body at the centre back waist with the point touching the conjunction of the centre back seam and the hook right angle above the skirt back opening.

Both back panels need a reinforcing triangle on the side back waist with the point touching the side back to pleat join.

### Offsetting the seams on pocket flaps

Take the fabric pocket flaps with their backing and the pocket flap linings. With right sides together, pin the lining to the pocket flap along the side seams, exposing 6mm (¼in) of the lining under the side seams of the pocket flap and thus offsetting the side seams. Sew the side seams 3mm (⅛in) away from the side construction lines. Trim the seam allowance. Press the seam allowances towards the lining.

Pin the bottom edge of the pocket

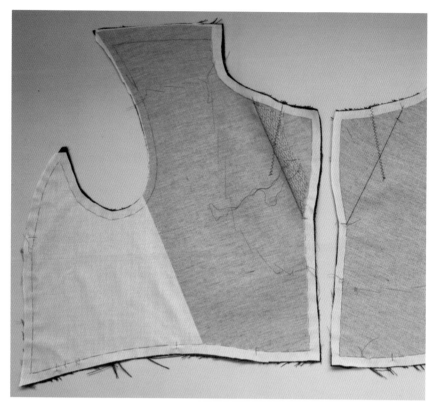

Fig. 5.4 *Frock coat front viewed from inside.* Backing and hair canvas have been flat tacked to main fabric except for shoulder area which has been secured below shoulder with pad stitch tacking. Front area around break line has been pad stitch tacked prior to closing darts, after which tacking up to and along break line has been completed. Left front lapel is being pad stitched and lapel is beginning to roll.

flap, pinning with the sides folded on the side construction line, the side seam allowance folded towards the lining and the bottom lining showing 6mm (¼in) under the edge of the main fabric. Sew the bottom edge from the construction line at the side, within a few stitches moving out into the seam allowance, to 3mm (⅛in) away from the construction line and back to the construction line near the other side seam. Trim off excess seam allowance and turn the pocket flaps through to the right side. Press the pocket flap from the inside to avoid iron damage. Tack the fabric to the lining along the tack line at the top of the pocket flap.

Putting the pocket into the coat skirt With right sides together, match the balance marks on the pocket bag with the reinforced top to the balance marks on the skirt waist. There is some ease along the waist of the skirt, which means that the length of the skirt along the pocket bag is bigger than the pocket bag and the fullness needs to be

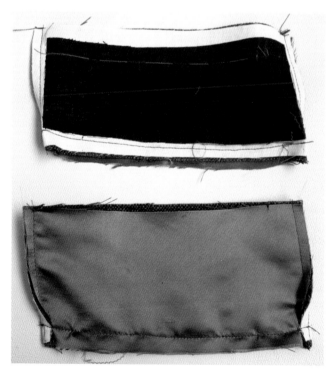

*Pocket flaps viewed from each side after sewing:* Tack line for top of pocket is visible, as are side and bottom sewing lines; offset lining is evident at bottom of top pocket flap.

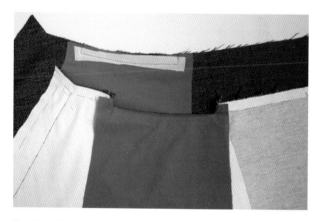

Fig. 5.6 Top: Sewing line for pocket opening on coat skirt can be seen. Bottom: pocket has been snipped to corners and seam allowance trimmed back, then turned through, bluff stitched and pressed; a very small amount of main fabric is visible around opening.

distributed along the top of the pocket bag without stretching it.

Sew the pocket mouth from the edge of the seam allowance at the pocket balance mark, working along the pocket opening construction line and back to the seam allowance at the second balance mark. Trim off excess seam allowance and snip to within a thread of the stitches at the angle of sewing at the balance marks.

Bluff stitch along the pocket bag fabric with the seam allowance towards the pocket bag, sewing from the edge of the seam allowance close to the join with the main fabric.

Turn the pocket to the inside of the skirt and press the pocket opening, ensuring the pocket bag cannot be seen from the right side of the skirt.

Sew the remaining pocket bag pieces onto the pocket bag on the inside of the skirt, sewing the pocket bags together along the pocket bag side seams and bottom.

Place the pocket flaps over the pocket opening, matching the balance marks and ensuring the construction line of the waist of the skirt matches that at the top of the pocket flap. Pin or tack the top of the pocket flap in place.

### Joining the body to the skirt

Pin the front body of the coat to the skirt front at the waist. The skirt waist is longer than that of the body waist. The ease on the skirt therefore has to be distributed along the body waist between the balance marks; it should be possible to disperse this without the need for gather stitches. (Use the quartering technique described in the Glossary.)

Sew the body and skirt waists together, stopping and securing at the point of the reinforcing triangle on the skirt pleat at the point where it joins the side back seam. Cut the reinforcing triangle open. Press the waist seam open with the seam allowance for the pocket flap towards the body. Carefully press the ease flat, avoiding making any pleats or tucks along the waistline.

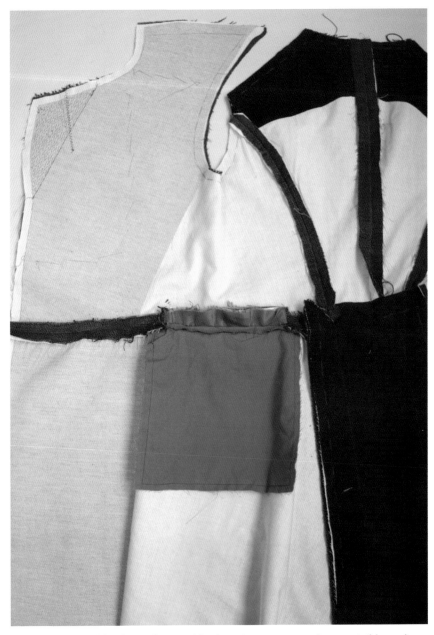

Fig. 5.7 Inside of frock coat front and back, with seams pressed open, visible pocket bag and flap.

### Bar tacking either side of the pocket flap

At each side of the pocket flap make a small bar tack. Sew along the side of the pocket flap with a stitch or two straddling the waist seam, sewing through all the layers of fabric and the pocket bag.

The bar tack reinforces the join at the waist and encourages the pocket flap to lie down over the skirt covering the pocket opening. Some original garments have substantial areas of top

stitching holding the pocket flap in place.

### Joining the coat centre back seam

Sew the two back body pieces together along the upper centre back seam, stopping and securing at the point of the reinforcing triangle at the waist. Press the back seam open.

### Joining the side back body seams

Pin the front body to the back body along the side back seam. Working with the front body uppermost, fit the seam to the side back seam of the back body, matching up the construction lines and balance marks. Sew together, stopping at the point of the reinforcing triangle and the top of the pleat at the waist, then secure the layers firmly.

Curved seams can be difficult to sew together, so working from the smaller curve can be helpful. Pin carefully and always check the sewing line is through the construction line on both pieces; unpick and resew if necessary.

Trim the side back seams as needed; trimming the seam down to 1.3cm (½in) is usually enough to allow the seam to be pressed open neatly. Do not snip into seams. Press the side back seam open to the waist.

### Joining the side back pleat seams

Match the pleat construction lines of the back body skirt to the front skirt and sew the two together. Trim down the pleat seam to 6mm (¼in). Press the pleat open at the hemline only.

Cut open the reinforcing triangles to allow the pleat to lie flat. With the seam allowance and pleat facing towards the front on the wrong side, press the pleat fold on the front skirt.

### Constructing the back lining

The lining for the body back has a pleat in it to allow for movement. It is also longer at the centre back to allow some extra length to cover the hook construction sewing (always make the back lining slightly long for this reason).

Sew the centre back seam of the body back lining. At the neckline, starting at the balance marks, sew another line parallel to the previous seam but stopping after about 2cm (¾in). Press the short seam to one side, pressing the fold to meet the seam at the waist, thus creating the pleat.

### Joining the front facings to the lining

Sew the body front facing with its lapel to the body front lining. Press the seam allowances towards the lining.

Sew the skirt front facing to the skirt lining. Press the seam allowance towards the lining.

### Joining the body lining to the skirt lining along the waist

Pin the body to the skirt along the waistline, matching facings and balance marks. As with the main fabric, there is some ease along the waist of the skirt lining; distribute the ease across the waist area of the body. Sew the waists together, stopping and securing at the back waist balance mark; this will allow the skirt pleat to lie flat. Press the waist seam open.

### Joining the front body lining to the back

Sew together the front body and the back body between the armhole and the waist. Press the seam open.

### Joining the skirt linings together at the pleat

Sew the front skirt lining to the back skirt lining along the construction line. Press the pleat seam open.

### Joining the coat lining with its facing to the coat

Pin the two panels together from the

Figs 5.8 and 5.9 Top: Sewn hem of coat seen from inside with facing distorted to allow sewing line to run onto lining. Bottom: Pressed hem seen from outside with mitred facing edge.

collar notch balance mark at the top of the lapel, continuing to the hem. Match up the centre front construction lines of the coat and the coat facing, ensuring all the points and balance marks match. There is some ease on the lapel above the break line on the front facing; keep the main area of ease towards the point of the lapel. This will allow the lapel to fold over without pulling the underside of the lapel into view.

Sew from the collar notch balance mark on the gorge where the collar will join the lapel, make one blunt stitch at an angle to the construction lines at the point of the lapel, and continue sewing to the hem.

Check both lapels are the same shape. Trim off the excess seam allowance, grading the seam allowances to reduce bulk. Press the front edge; it can be helpful to press the seam open from the inside first. Below the break line press from the inside facing of the coat, making a thin strip of the outer fabric visible along the edge of the facing when viewed from the inside. At the lapel press on the coat side of the lapel so that a small amount of the lapel facing can be seen around the edge of the coat lapel. The break line is the most difficult area to press as the seams above and below are going in different directions.

### Centre back skirt opening

With right sides together, join the lining to the main fabric along each side of the skirt back opening (Figs 5.8 and 5.9). Trim down the seam allowance as needed. Press the seam allowance towards the lining. Press in the folded edge of the back opening.

### Hem

For this coat's main fabric a 5cm (2in) hem has been allowed; the lining has a 6mm (¼in) hem allowance. With right sides together, fold back on the front fold with the seam allowance towards the lining. The hem edge of the facing has to be distorted; the facing is moved so the hem of the lining (which is shorter) is brought to meet the coat hem at the edge of the facing. The skirt

Figs 5.10, 5.11 and 5.12 *Creating hook on centre back opening.* Top: Cut to allow left top edge to outside. Centre: Attaching left back flap, leaving spike to fold to inside. Bottom: Hook topstitched across to under wrap. Stitch lines highlighted.

back opening has a small grown-on facing where the facing is included as one piece on the back skirt piece. The back opening is folded back along the fold and pinned at the fold. The hem of the facing has to be twisted to bring the lining hem to the coat hem at the edge of the facing. Pin the two hems together with pins placed at right angles to the hem. Because the skirt is circular and the main fabric hem is longer than the lining hem, the former will have to be eased onto the latter without stretching it (Figs 5.8 and 5.9).

### Sewing the coat and lining hems together
Starting on the front hemline, sew from the centre front hemline across the facing to 1cm (⅜in) from the cut edges of the hems. Continue along the hem with 1cm (⅜in) seam allowance. At the facing for the split, sew back to the hemline.

Turn the coat right way out. Gently press the hem up along the tack line and pin it in place with pins at right angles to the hem. At each facing, with the coat and hem lying flat and the facing uppermost, carefully flatten the facing area towards the hem; a mitred-type corner is thus created. Ensure the coat outer is lying flat, then press. Hand sew the mitred fold on the facing to the hem. The lining will be quite loose but will not show beneath the hem.

The hem can be hand sewn to the backing fabric or fused using short lengths of paper-backed fusible hemming tape.

### Back waist hook
Cut open the left back reinforcing triangle; this will allow the top edge of the left side opening to move out to the outside of the coat and lie flat. The seam allowance of the right back will also need to be cut into; cut slightly above the centre back and hook join but do not snip all the way to the sewing line.

Pin the centre skirt back opening evenly closed. Fold the hook so that it is at a right angle to the centre back seam, pin the hook seam allowance to

the back of the coat, mark the hook fold line, then sew close to the fold line on the seam allowance of the hook through to the coat back, but not the coat lining. Trim away the seam allowance, leaving a spike of fabric cut along the fold of the back edge and cutting close to the hook right angle seam line. Fold the spike back in line with the hook fold. Topstitch parallel with the hook trapping the seam allowances, continuing the topstitch across to the left back to the edge of the right back underwrap (Figs 5.10 and 5.11).

### Joining the coat linings at the waist
Lay the coat flat with lining uppermost, then match and pin together the waistlines of the coat and the lining, ensuring that the pocket bags are pushed down into the skirt. Roll back the body lining to expose the waist seam allowances of the coat and the lining. Hand sew the two seam allowances together; a large buttonhole stitch is ideal. Sew from the front facing to the side seam.

With the skirt area lying flat and the lining uppermost, the centre back waist of the lining is open, wrap the skirt lining around the pleats at the waist. At the top of the pleat seam allowance,

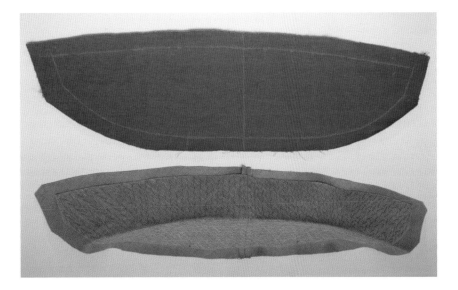

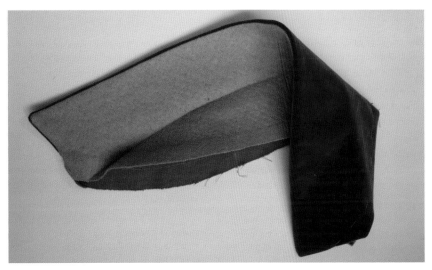

Figs 5.13 and 5.14 Top: Wrong side of top collar with marked construction lines and under collar canvas and wool pad stitched and pressed. Bottom: Completed collar bagged out and pressed, with strip of top fabric visible around edge of under collar.

tack the lining to the pleat and the pleat to the coat waist seam allowance.

The waist area of the upper body lining can be pinned to the waistline of the skirt lining. The centre back of the upper body lining is longer than the side back lining pieces; keep as much of the length as possible to avoid later tightness in the upper back. Hand sew the upper body lining to the waistline, sewing through the main fabric seam allowances for extra strength.

**Shoulder seams**

Join the front and back shoulder seams without including the front shoulder backing and canvas at this stage. There is some ease in the back shoulder area; distribute this ease over the length of the front shoulder seam. Sew the shoulder seams together with the construction lines matching. Press the seam open.

Smooth the front shoulder backing and canvas over the shoulder seam. Turn the coat to the right side with the canvas and backing over the open shoulder allowance. Pin through the shoulder seam to the canvas on the inside of the coat, then tack the backing and canvas to the back shoulder seam.

Continue the tack line of the armhole and neckline through the fabric and canvas.

**Starting the collar**

Sew the wool under collars together at the centre back, trim down the centre back seam and press the seam open (Figs 5.13 and 5.14).

Place the collar canvas onto the wrong side of the under collar, matching up the centre back, with the seam allowance of the under collar visible around the collar canvas.

Pin the canvas under collar along the collar fold line, using a few pins at right angles to the fold line. Hand sew along the collar fold line using a back stitch, which should be barely visible on the wool.

**Pad stitching the collar**

Working from the collar fold line towards the neck edge of the collar

## HERRINGBONE STITCH

Using a herringbone stitch to join the collar to the coat is a method that was used by Victorian tailors and continued to be employed by some tailors into the twentieth century. In this example the collar has been attached by machine, so the herringbone stitch is primarily decorative but it will hold the seam allowance towards the collar and give the appearance of the collar having been sewn on by hand. Alternatively, on the under collar the seam allowance can be held in place with a machine zigzag stitch.

stand, sew rows of pad stitches, sewing parallel to the neck fold line and continuing the lines until the edge of the canvas is reached.

Above the fold line on the outside or fall of the collar, starting at the centre back neck, make rows of pad stitching parallel to the centre back. At the sides of the collar make lines of pad stitching that run into the point following the grain of the collar canvas.

Press the under collar flat, ironing from the canvas side of the collar. Then press in the fold line along the collar.

**Preparing the top collar**

On the wrong side of the top collar fabric mark the construction lines; for this velvet collar the lines were marked with chalk. Tack the neckline and balance marks.

**Joining the top collar to the under collar**

With right sides together, match the edge of the canvas on the under collar to the construction line on the top collar. There is some ease on the top collar; keep the ease towards the side points of the collar.

Sew the collars together. Working close to the collar canvas, start sewing and secure at the neck edge of the edge of the collar where it will join to the gorge or neckline of the coat. Make one

blunt stitch at an angle to the construction lines at each collar point. Check both the points look the same. Trim away the excess seam allowances from near the sewing lines. Turn through to the right side, check the points and shape of the collar are as intended. Press with a small amount of the top collar fabric visible around the edge of the under collar.

For this collar a needle ironing mat was used to avoid damaging the velvet. Care was taken not to put the iron directly onto the velvet and all the ironing was done from the underside of the collar.

**Joining the collar onto the coat**

Pin or tack the hair canvas in place along the neckline at the shoulder.

Pin the under collar to the neck edge of the coat, matching up balance marks and the break line to the collar fold line. The front of the collar joins to the balance mark on the edge of the lapel. The edge of the collar canvas along the neck of the collar matches the construction line on the neck edge of the coat. Sew with the canvas uppermost. Stitch close to the canvas, securing the ends and ensuring the sewing is on the coat neck construction line and that the canvas and neckline are lying smoothly.

Snip into the coat neckline seam allowance at the balance mark for the lapel, close to the join to the collar.

Trim down the neck edge seam allowance of the under collar to 6mm (¼in) and trim down the neck line seam allowance to 1cm (⅜in). Press the seam allowance towards the collar. On the outside, herringbone stitch the seam allowance of the collar towards the collar.

Fig. 5.15 Under collar attached to coat and finished off with herringbone stitch.

Fig. 5.16 To finish gorge line, top collar fabric is tacked to collar fold and lapel seam is turned under and snipped after break line. After snipping, seam allowance is turned towards the neckline.

Smooth the top collar fabric from the outside edge over the collar fold line, ensuring it lies evenly over the collar. If necessary, pin through the fold line to hold the top collar fabric in place. Tack the top collar fabric to the under collar with a pad stitch tack, sewing along the back neck of the fold line, stopping 7–10cm (3–4in) before the edge of the neck fold.

### Joining the shoulder seams of the lining

Sew the front lining to the back lining at the shoulder. There is some ease along the back shoulder seam. Press the shoulder seam allowances towards the back.

### Finishing off the gorge, collar and back of the neck

Turn under the seam allowance of the coat facing from the edge of the lapel where it joins to the collar. Keep the fold level with the under collar and coat seam. About 2.5cm (1in) past the break line, snip into the seam allowance and allow the seam allowance of the facing and back lining to lie flat towards the collar. The turned-under portion of the lapel seam allowance could be tacked in place, through all the layers.

Before sewing the back neck lining check the lining is not tight down the back. If it is tight take out the pins at

the back of the neck, move the lining down and re-pin; ideally the lining should be slightly loose. Either tack the facing and back lining along the neck line or back stitch from the outside along the collar to neck seam.

### Top collar neck edge

Fold under the neck edge seam allowance of the top collar. Check if the tacking on the neckline of the collar is flush with the turned-under seam allowance on the lapel. The line may change; the seam of the collar must cover the snip in the facing and cover the sewing line from back stitching the lining along the back neck without excess collar fabric or creating tightness along the collar.

Trim down the collar neck edge seam allowance. The folds of the seams of the lapel and collar must meet neatly until past the break line. Pin or tack the seam allowance back.

Use a ladder stitch to join the lapel to the collar. Continue the ladder stitch to the snip after the collar fold break line; from the snip secure and sew the collar to the neckline just covering the back stitch. Where practical along the back neck area, sew through the lining to the under collar seam allowance.

### Cuffs

Bag out the cuff to the lining along the cuff underwrap. On the overwrap side of the cuff, offset the cuff and lining seam allowances; with right sides together the lining should be visible by 6mm (¼in) under the main fabric seam allowance. Sew the seam about 3mm (⅛in) outside the construction line at the side of the cuff. Trim down the seam allowances. Press the seam allowances towards the lining.

At the bottom of the cuff, fold along the side construction lines with the seam allowance towards the lining. Offset the seams along the bottom of the cuff and pin with the lining exposed from beneath the main fabric along the bottom of the cuff.

Sew the bottom of the cuff closed. Start sewing at the side construction line and in a few stitches move out to sew outside the construction line by

Fig. 5.17 *Finishing collar:* left side has been ladder stitched; on right, top collar seam allowance is turned under and pinned ready to be sewn.

3mm (⅛in), then finish sewing back at the side construction line. Trim the seam allowance and turn through to the right side.

Press the cuff flat, ensuring the folds are along the construction lines. From the lining side there should be some top fabric visible along the bottom and along the overwrap of the cuff.

With the cuff and lining flat, tack the cuff to the lining along the top construction line.

### Cuff buttonholes

On the cuff overwrap, mark the position of the three buttonholes and sew them.

### Closing the cuff

Wrap the buttonholes over the cuff to join at the balance mark indicating the button stand, Tack the cuff closed with the buttonholes towards the outside and tack on the seam allowance at the top of the cuff.

### Making the sleeves

This coat has an area of gather on the sleeve head. On the top sleeve in both main fabric and lining, run a gathering stitch between the balance marks on the sleeve head. Consider a zig zag machine stitch over a strong thread for the main fabric but a large straight stitch will be satisfactory for the lining.

On the main fabric sleeves, match the front arm seams together of the top and under sleeves and sew the panels together.

The front arm seam is curved and will need to be trimmed down to avoid distortions along the seam when it is turned through to the right side. Trim the seam down to about 1cm (⅜in) to 1.3cm (½in). If seams have a very deep curve the seam allowance may need to be reduced. Do not snip into curved seams; trim away excess seam allowance instead. Press the front arm seam open.

Match up the back arm construction lines on the top and under sleeves. Sew the sleeves together and press the seams open.

Construct the sleeve linings as an opposing pair. Press the seams open.

### Joining the cuff to the sleeve

With right sides together, attach the cuff to the bottom of the sleeve, matching construction lines, seams and balance marks. Sew the cuff onto the bottom of the sleeve.

### Attaching the sleeve lining to the cuff

Make an opposing pair of the sleeve and lining. With the right side of the lining to the cuff lining, pin the lining to the bottom of the sleeve using a small seam allowance. The smaller seam allowance is to ensure the sleeve lining is very slightly longer than the sleeve. Sew the lining to the sleeve and cuff, sewing along the same stitch line that joined the cuff to the sleeve.

### Securing the sleeve lining to the sleeve

Between the shoulder and elbow on each hind arm seam, join the seam allowances of the sleeve and sleeve lining. Use a few machine stitches or a strong back stitch towards the edge of the seam allowances. These few stitches are to stop the lining falling out of the bottom of the arm should the hand sewing holding the sleeve lining into the armhole come undone.

### Fitting the sleeves into the coat

Pin one sleeve into its armhole. Pin with right sides together, matching the construction lines and balance marks. The pins must be in line with the construction lines and must pass

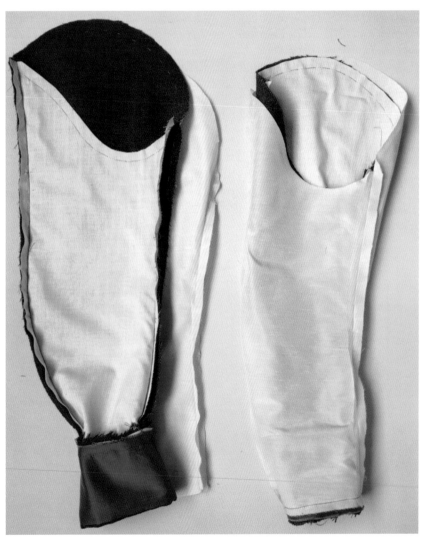

Fig. 5.18 *Sleeve and sleeve lining.* L: Sleeve with cuff attached. R: Right side sleeve lining is joined at cuff.

through the construction lines of both the armhole and sleeve. Stop at the gather threads.

Pull up the gather threads to fit the sleeve head to the armhole. Pin from the sleeve side with all the pins in the same direction for easy removal when sewing the sleeve in place.

### Checking the hang of the sleeve

The sleeve should hang down and slightly forward in a natural relaxed arm position. The hang of the sleeve can be checked in several ways: use a mannequin to support the shoulders or a coat hanger with wide supportive shoulders. Alternatively, the shoulder of the coat can be supported on an outstretched hand with the palm down; it can then be viewed either by holding it away from you with fingers pointing towards you or by looking at it in a mirror.

When the first sleeve position is accurate, pin in the other sleeve. It must be symmetrical with the first one; use seams and balance marks as a guide. When pinned, check that the sleeves are hanging in precisely the same way.

Machine sew the sleeves in, following the construction lines and pulling the pins out as the machine needle nears each one.

When both sleeves are sewn in, check that they still look the same. Look at the sewing and construction lines and check that they match. If they are in any way unsatisfactory, make alterations.

Make a second line of machine sewing on the seam allowance, 6mm (¼in) away from and parallel to the first line of sewing.

Trim the seam allowance close to the second sewing line, leaving a 1.3cm (½in) seam allowance or slightly less.

### Joining the lining to the coat at the armhole

Match up the seams and pinning in place at an angle to the armhole. Check the lining has not become tight anywhere – it must not pull or distort the coat in any way. If there appears to be any tightness, push the lining away from the armhole towards the body until the tightness is released. Hand sew the lining to the armhole using a back stitch, sewing between the two sewing lines around the sleeve.

### Sleeve lining

Fold back a small seam allowance around the sleeve lining armhole and pin it to the coat lining around the armhole, matching the seam allowances. Pull up the gather threads to fit the lining sleeve head to the armhole.

Hand sew the sleeve lining to the armhole, just covering the back stitch sewing line holding the coat lining in place.

### Buttons and buttonholes

On the coat front make four buttonholes; the top one is level with the end of the break line and the bottom one is just above the waist seam.

Sew four buttons at the front, one at the top of each back pleat where the seams intersect and three onto each cuff.

Fig. 5.19 Sleeve lining pinned around armhole, covering back stitches which hold body lining to armhole.

Figs 5.20 and 5.21 *1840s roll collar waistcoat:* Front has two welt pockets, back has eyeletted jiggers fastened with a cord.

## Early Victorian Waistcoat with Roll Collar

Roll collars on waistcoats continued to be a popular style throughout most of the Victorian period, with the width, length and depth of the collar and opening changing with fashion.

During the years of Victoria's reign, a wide variety of methods were used for drawing in the back of the waistcoat to give a smooth fit across the front. Jiggers with eyelets were popular, with different numbers of eyelets. The width of jiggers varied: they could be broad bands sewn in line with most of the side seam from armhole to waist, or they could be so narrow that they needed only a single eyelet on a small tab on either side of the lower back. Tape, cord or ribbon was used, then elastic in later years, and even fine springs in fabric casings to give a more flexible fit.

Formerly, waistcoat back fabric was not intended to be seen and therefore

### PIECES NEEDED

**Main front fabric, cut with a 2cm (¾in) seam allowance:**

Cut two fronts and lower front facings. The welt pockets have a small seam allowance included on the pattern.

Cut, in one piece, the front facing and collar with the centre back neck on the fold.

In our example the following pieces have all been cut with 1.3cm (½in) seam allowance.

**Back fabric:**

Cut two outside backs, four jigger pieces.

**Lining:**

Cut two backs and two fronts.

**Woven cotton fabric:**

Cut two pocket bags for the welt pockets; cut two under collars on the bias.

**Woven fusible interfacing:**

Cut two under collars on the bias; cut two welt pocket shapes without seam allowance.

**Fusible domette:**

Cut two front panels.

Non-woven sew-in interfacing has been used for the collar area of the front facing piece and backing for the jiggers.

**To finish:**

Buttons, eyelets, and a lace, cord or tape to draw the jiggers together.

# Waistcoat 1840s

1 Square: 2.5cm (1") No seam allowance included

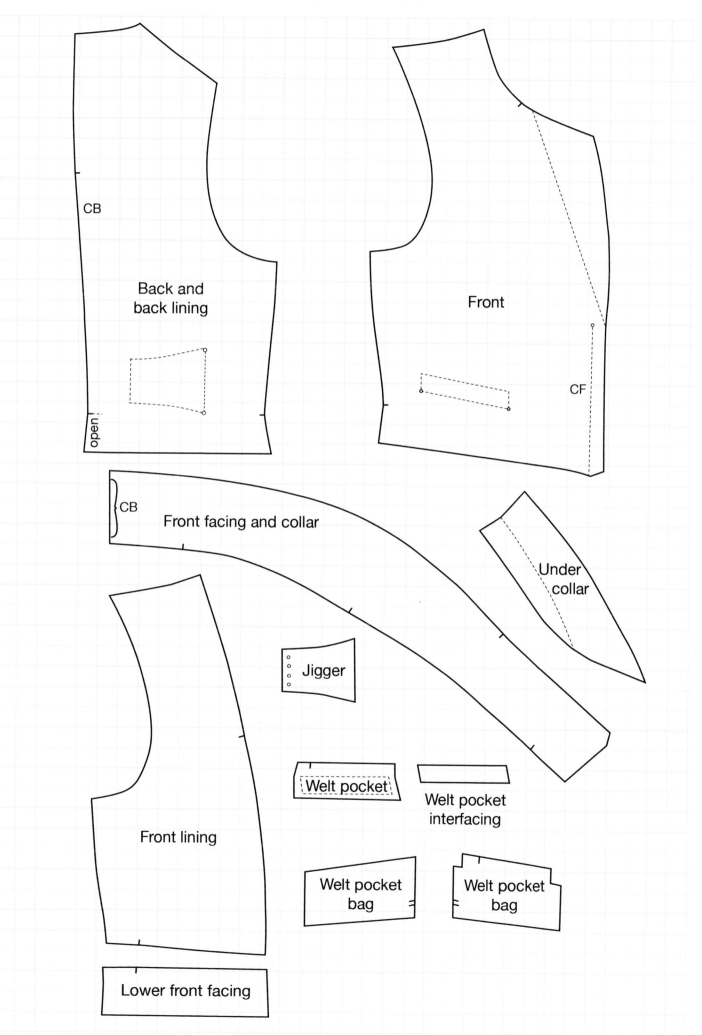

CB

Back and
back lining

open

Front

CF

Front facing and collar

CB

Under
collar

Jigger

Front lining

Welt pocket

Welt pocket
interfacing

Welt pocket
bag

Welt pocket
bag

Lower front facing

could be made from an inexpensive plain fabric. Plain cotton or linen began to be replaced by coloured satin-weave cottons coordinated to the front fabric and by the end of the century matching lining fabrics of sateen or twill weave were commonly used.

The front of this sample waistcoat front is made from red, white and blue fabric with a geometric pattern. The waistcoat back fabric is the reverse side of a shot (or two-tone) silk duchesse satin and the lining is a cream-coloured synthetic dupion.

The front facing and collar have been cut in one piece without a centre back seam. Cutting the collar and facing in one is neither historically accurate nor an economical method of cutting out this section. The collar could also be cut with a centre back seam, with the grain direction chosen to suit the part of the pattern that would work well on the lapel. If further fabric economy were necessary the facing could be joined below the collar break line opposite the top button.

To make the welt pockets stand out they have been cut with the straight grain along the opening.

The combinations of interfacings have been chosen to work with the fabrics and outlined to provide guidance; however, they will not be suitable for all fabric combinations.

## Marking Up and Preparation

Fuse the domette onto the inside of the fronts. Mark all the construction lines and balance marks on the domette, including the welt pockets. In this case all the construction lines and the welt pockets have also been tacked through to the outside: this is not completely necessary; the fronts could be cut with a consistent seam allowance rendering the marking and tacking unnecessary. Mark the two bottom corners of the welt position with tailor tacks, which are the only essential marking for the welt pockets.

Fuse the woven fusible interfacing to the under collar pieces and mark all the collar construction lines and the collar fold onto the interfacing of the under

Fig. 5.22 Waistcoat lining with non-woven interfacing is flat tacked onto wrong side of fabric to support collar; most of seam allowances have been pressed towards lining at join with lower front facing, and seam has been pressed open.

collar.

Fuse the welt pocket shapes cut from woven fusible interfacing onto the welt pocket pieces corresponding to the pattern, with a 6mm ($^1$/4in) seam allowance at the bottom; the top of the interfacing should be the same distance from each side of the welt.

If the main fabric being used frays easily, also fuse a lightweight interfacing to cover the whole area of the welt pocket.

Mark construction lines on the non-woven interfacing of the collar and front facing. Flat tack the interfacing onto the wrong side of the of the collar and facing, and mark the construction lines onto the lower part of the facing below the interfacing.

For the jiggers, mark the construction lines for the jiggers onto the non-woven interfacing. Flat tack the non-woven interfacing onto a pair of jiggers.

The outside edge of the jigger position is marked with tailor tacks on the waistcoat outside back pieces.

## Construction Instructions

### Welt pockets
Make up the welt pocket following the instructions in Chapter 9 for the working man's waistcoat.

### Centre back seams
Sew the back seams on the outer fabric back and the back lining, stopping and securing at the balance mark above the hem. The centre back has a short split from waist to the hem.

### Shoulder seams
Join the front and back shoulder seams; there is some ease in the back shoulder seam. Press the seam allowance towards the back.

Join the front linings to the back lining along the shoulder seams. Press the seams open.

### Joining front lining to lower front facing
Sew the lower front facing to the bottom of the front lining (Fig. 5.22). Press the seam allowance towards the lining.

### Joining collar with front facing to the lining
Pin and sew the collar and facing to the lining. Trim the excess seam allowance.

Press the seam allowance towards the lining. Along the back neck press the seam allowance towards the collar. To spread the bulk of the main fabric seam allowances at the lower front facing join, snip into the front facing seam allowance and press open the seam at the lower front facing.

### Under collar
Sew the centre back seam of the under

collars together, matching the construction lines and collar fold line. Trim off the excess seam allowance. Press the back neck seam open. Machine sew along the collar fold line from the edge of the seam allowance.

### Joining the under collar to the waistcoat neckline
Match the centre back balance marks and the edge of the neck of the collar to the edge of the neck on the waistcoat front. Sew together, ensuring the construction lines match. Trim off excess seam allowance. Press the seam allowance towards the collar.

### Joining the front to the front facing through the collar and under collar
Distribute the ease from the top collar evenly along the under collar. Sew together from the bottom of the waistcoat front. Trim the seam allowance by grading: the non-woven interfacing can be trimmed back close to the stitch line; trim the seam allowance fused with interfacing fairly short as the fusible will stabilize the cut edge.

Press the front edge and collar; the under collar must not be visible from the outside and the facing must not be seen along the centre front edge. The most difficult area to press is at the break line or top button where the two areas are being pressed in different directions.

### Finishing the armhole
Pin the armhole seams of the outer fabric and lining together, offsetting the seams. Offsetting makes the waistcoat lining slightly smaller than the outer. The lining is made slightly smaller by exposing it to be seen from under the edge of the outer fabrics by 6mm (¼in). Ease the seams together and sew together just outside the main outer fabric construction line. When turned through it will fold on the outer construction line.

Trim the armhole seam allowance back to 6mm (¼in). Turn through to the right side by drawing the front body of the waistcoat through the shoulder area.

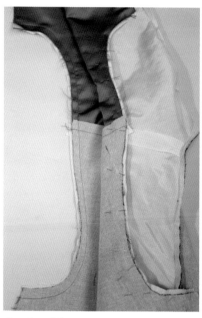

Fig. 5.23 *Waistcoat armholes with offset lining seam allowance.* R: Seam pinned ready to be sewn. L: Side armhole sewn prior to trimming down seam allowance.

Fig. 5.24 Shoulder seams of waistcoat armhole from outside and inside; thin strip of main fabric can be seen along side lining fabric.

Press from the inside; a thin strip of the outer fabrics will be visible at the edge of the lining around the armhole.

### Collar and back neck

Smooth the top collar over the under collar from the outside edge. Fold the collar over and pin or tack along the collar fold. Make a small back stitch along the join of the outer back collar through to the inside neckline to hold the collar in place.

### Hem

Ensure the fronts are lying flat. Turn through to the right side. Trim the hem seam allowances of the outer and facing to the same length.

With right sides together, fold back along the front fold with the seam allowance facing towards the lining. Offset the hem seam allowances to make the lining slightly smaller. Sew from the centre front construction line, then move off the construction line and sew parallel with the offset lower front facing. Turn through and press along the construction line.

### Back split and hem

Offset and sew together the back lining and outer fabric at the hem on both sides of the centre back seam. Press the seam allowance towards the lining.

At the centre back seams, match the end of the sewing and balance marks of the outer fabric and lining. Sew from the end of the sewing at the centre back, joining the outer to the lining with the seam allowance of the hem towards the lining. Turn through to the right side. Press the hem and centre back opening.

Make a bar tack just above the centre back opening, straddling the centre back seam.

### Joining the fronts to the back at the side seam

Lay the fronts of the waistcoat flat and tack the outer to the lining along the side seam allowance.

With right sides together, pin a front to a back along the side seam. Bring the pinned seam through the back and out through the open side seam; this will allow the side back of the waistcoat to wrap around the front side seam. Sew together. Turn the side seam back through to the outside and press.

On the remaining side seam, with right sides together, sew the waistcoat back to the front. Wrap the back lining around the armhole, sandwiching the front between the outer back and lining. Sew on top of the side seam sewing line, working from the armhole along about a third of the seam. At the hem wrap the back lining around the front, sew along the side seam stitch line for about a third of the seam.

Turn through to the right side. Hand sew closed the opening on the inside side seam. Press.

### Jiggers

Join the backing to the lining along one curved side seam, sewing close to the construction line. On the other curved side seam offset the lining seam, making the lining visible by 6mm (¼in) at the side of the fabric with the backing. Sew the remaining side seam close to the construction line. Trim down both side seams. Press the seam allowances towards the lining.

Pin closed the short end of the jigger with the side seam allowances towards the lining, then sew closed.

This jigger is going to have eyelets along the short edge and needs some stiffening to support the eyelets. This jigger edge was stiffened with a piece of plastic boning sewn to the seam allowance. Turn through and press.

Tack closed the open side of the jigger. If the fabric frays readily machine tack closed close to the construction line. Trim down the seam allowance and finish off the cut edge.

There are four eyelets on each jigger. Mark the positions and attach the eyelets.

### Attaching the jiggers onto the waistcoat back

With the back lying flat, pin or tack the outside back to the lining in the area around the marked jigger position. With right sides together and the eyelets towards the side seam, pin and sew the jigger to the waistcoat back. Fold back the edges of the jigger seam allowance at an angle and fold the jigger over the seam allowance to face the centre back seam. Topstitch the jiggers to the back by hand or machine, sewing parallel to the fold line, trapping in the seam allowance.

### Buttons and buttonholes

Mark the buttonhole positions on the wearer's left side and make the buttonholes. Attach the buttons opposite the buttonholes on the right waistcoat front.

Fig. 5.25 Jigger with tab of seam allowance pinned back at angle; when jigger is folded along stitch line towards centre back and sewn, all seam allowances will be hidden. Also visible: part of welt pocket, centre back hem split and strengthening bar tack.

## Early Victorian Trousers

Men's legwear from the 1840s had an assortment of silhouettes, from very narrow fitted trousers with fall front openings (sometimes called pantaloons) to tapered ankles with voluminous wide waists pleated onto a waistband. The fly front opening grew in popularity throughout the century. The ankle area often had exaggerated shaping or was slit at the centre front to flare and fit over the foot; around this time a stirrup or strap under the foot was used to hold the trouser leg taut and in place.

Figs 5.26 and 5.27 *1840s trousers*. L: Front waist pleated into waistband. R: Trouser back with peaks on waistband on either side of centre back.

# Trousers 1840s

1 Square: 2.5cm (1") No seam allowance included

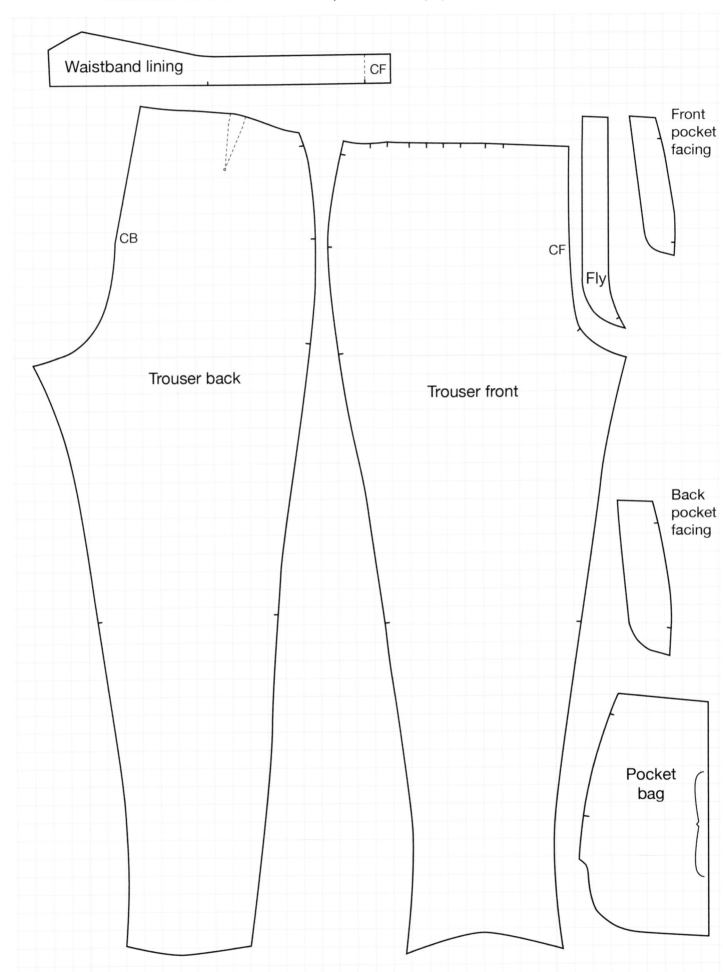

Waistband lining

CF

CB

Trouser back

Trouser front

CF

Fly

Front pocket facing

Back pocket facing

Pocket bag

The main constructional difference between this pair of trousers and others in the later chapters is these trousers have a separate waistband along with a button fly.

The fabric used for this pair of trousers is a fairly heavy, lightly felted wool. Because the wool is felted it does not need to have its seams finished off to stop the cut edges fraying. Although the fabric does not need to be finished a bias tape has been used to cover the fly seams and the side seams next to the pockets; this has been incorporated into the construction procedure. Other fabrics will need to be treated appropriately.

The centre back seam of the trousers and waistbands have been cut with extra-large seam allowance to allow future alteration. On the trouser centre back seam the large seam allowance at the waist narrows to merge with the seam allowance above the crotch curve.

## Marking Up and Preparation

On the wrong side of the fabric mark up the front and back legs with construction lines and balance marks. Place balance marks on the pocket bags and facings. Tack in the hemline.

## Interfacing

Fuse a fly shape onto the wrong side of the left front trouser leg fly area, then apply fusible interfacing to the two opposing fabric fly pieces. The woven fusible interfacing is fused along the centre of the waistbands; the lightweight fusible with seam allowance is applied over the top of the

---

### PIECES NEEDED

**Main fabric:**

Cut two front legs, back legs, waistbands, pocket facings for the front and back of the pocket bags, fly pieces.

**Woven cotton:**

Cut two pocket bags and waistband linings. Cut three fly pieces. Cut bias strips to make into bias tape.

**Woven fusible interfacing:**

Cut two waistbands without top and bottom seam allowances.

**Lightweight fusible interfacing:**

Cut three fly shapes; cut two waistbands with seam allowances. For lighter weight or delicate fabrics, a pocket stay of fusible or sew-in interfacing over the pocket area may be advantageous.

**To finish:**

Buttons for fly, waistband fastening and braces.

---

woven fusible on the waistbands. A strip of fusible interfacing can be bonded just past the balance marks for the pocket openings on the front and back legs; this is not essential in this case because the fabric is fairly substantial and the pocket bag helps to stabilize the area.

---

Fig. 5.28 Pocket bag viewed from both sides after facings have been finished off and sewn to bag.

## Construction Instructions

### Back darts
Close the back darts, then press the fold towards the centre back.

### Trouser side pocket
The pocket facings are different sizes in order to spread the bulk; the smaller facing is for the front of the pocket and the larger facing joins to the back seam where it is the most likely to be seen when the pocket is opened.

Finish off the long curved seams on the pocket facings. Place the facings onto the pocket bags matching the pocket opening balance marks to make an opposing pair.

---

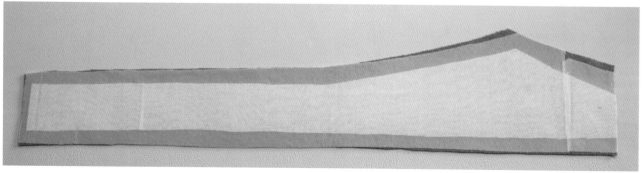

Fig. 5.29 Waistband with woven fusible interfacing (cut without top or bottom seam allowance) and lightweight fusible applied over top; front edge and centre back are marked.

## VICTORIAN TROUSER POCKET OPENINGS

Trouser pocket openings often had topstitching around the pocket mouth. If a topstitch detail is required it should be sewn while it is relatively easy to access the pocket.

Alternatively, the pocket bags can be cut as two pieces rather than one, which would make sewing around the pocket mouth easier. The pocket bags can be joined together with a French seam at the same stage as closing the bottom of the pocket.

Machine the facings onto the pocket bags along the long curved seam.

### Joining the pockets to the front and back legs
Match the balance marks and construction lines for the pocket opening; the short facing goes to the front leg. Machine between the balance marks of the pocket opening; do not sew beyond the balance marks. Secure each end.

Press the pocket opening seam allowance on the back leg towards the back. On the front press the front and pocket bag so that the seam allowance is trapped between the two layers of trouser front and pocket bag with facing; the pocket facing should not be visible from the outside.

On the front pocket to leg seam, trim down the seam allowance between the balance marks for the pocket opening.

### Trouser leg side seams
Sew the trouser side seams together above and below the pocket, securing close to the balance marks for the pocket opening.

Press the leg side seams open above and below the pocket.

On the front leg pocket opening, bluff stitch the pocket facing to the seam allowances close to the join with the front leg, sewing between the balance marks. This is slightly awkward

as the sewing has to be done through the pocket opening.

### Closing the bottom of the pocket
Take the bottom of the pocket through the pocket opening. With right sides together, sew together the bottom of the pocket close to the seam allowance. Put the pocket bag back through the opening. Press the bottom seam. Sew parallel to the fold trapping the seam allowance and thus making a French seam.

### Closing the side of the pocket
Snip into the pocket front seam allowance at the pocket opening balance marks, cutting carefully through the front pocket bag and facing. The pocket bag side seam allowances will lie together and can be sewn together along the pocket bag side seams.

### Binding the back leg and pocket bag seam allowances
Using the bias tape, bind the back leg side seam and the side seam of the pocket bag together; continue the bias binding just past the bottom of the pocket bag.

### Pleats
Pin or tack the marked front trouser pleats in place.

Pin or tack the pocket bag to the front of the trousers along the waistline; the waistband will hold the pocket in place.

### Bar tacking the pocket opening
Make a bar tack at the top and bottom of the pocket opening; sew from the outside with the pocket bag lying flat, stitching through all the layers of trouser seam allowance and pocket bag. The bar tack should straddle the side seam and be no longer than 6mm (¼in) long.

A straight stitch machine bar tack with matching thread is unobtrusive to reinforce the opening.

### Lining the left front fly area
Sew the fly lining onto the trouser left front. Start from the waist, sewing just outside the centre front construction line. At the bottom of the fly balance mark, sew at a right angle to the edge of the fabric on the seam allowance. Snip to within a thread of the corner of the right angle; trim the seam allowance. Turn the fly lining through to the right side; either press the fly lining ensuring no lining can be seen from the outside or bluff stitch along the edge of the lining through the seam allowances and press.

### Buttonhole stand
Sew the left front facing fly piece to a fly lining along the centre front line, slightly straightening the curve at the bottom of the fly piece. Press the lining back along the centre front line.

### Buttonholes
On the buttonhole stand mark the waistline and the bottom of the fly balance mark.

Fig. 5.30 Trouser side pockets, inside front; side seams have been closed and pocket on left has been trimmed and bluff stitched.

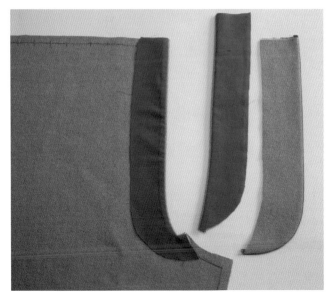 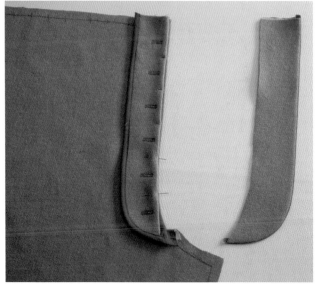

Figs 5.31 and 5.32 *Fly*. L: Trouser inside left front with fly lining sewn on, trimmed and snipped, then turned through and pressed. To right of same picture, buttonhole stand has been bagged out along centre front edge and button stand has been bagged out along long curved seam. R: Buttonholes have been placed, outside edge has been trimmed and bound and two bar tacks have been sewn.

Measure between the marks in centimetres and divide the measurement between the number of buttons to be used. Ideally, allow about 4–5cm (1$^1$/$_2$–2in) between buttons. If there is less space between the buttons they can be quite fiddly to use; more space between them might cause gaping.

Position the first buttonhole at half the calculated distance from the waistline. Each subsequent hole should be the full measurement apart. The final buttonhole will fall at half the measurement from the balance mark for the bottom of the fly.

Make the buttonholes at right angles to the centre front line; maintain the angle along the slight curve at the bottom of the fly piece. The buttonholes should start just over half the size of the button in from the folded edge. Cut the buttonholes open and check the buttons fit through them.

### Joining the buttonhole stand to the left front

Place the buttonhole stand onto the inside of the left front with linings together. The buttonhole stand must not be visible from the outside. Pin the buttonhole stand to the fly lining.

### Bar tacking between the buttonholes

Fold the left front fly lining away from the front, and bar tack at the edge of the buttonhole stand through the front fly lining and seam allowances. Do not sew beyond the edge of the buttonhole stand; the bar tack must not be visible on the outside of the fly.

### Finishing off the left front fly seam allowances

Trim the seam allowances of the left front fly level. Machine tack the three fly pieces together very close to the cut edge. Bind the outside edge of the fly with bias tape running off the bottom of the fly lining over the construction line of the crotch seam.

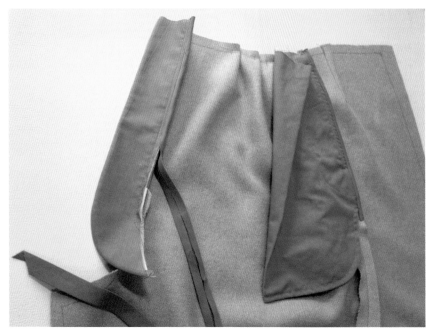

Fig. 5.33 *Trouser leg, right side, from inside:* Pocket has French seam closing bottom with bound side seam; button stand has been partially attached and bound.

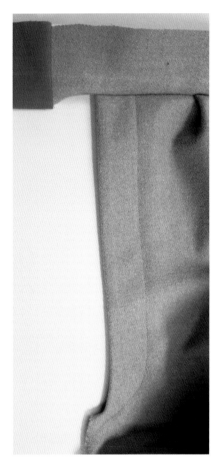

Fig. 5.34 *Right front fly area:* Waistband has been sewn to waist area and waistband lining is attached; fly shape topstitching is visible parallel to centre front and continuing into seam allowance at bottom of fly.

### The fly shape
Topstitch or stabstitch around the fly shape, sewing about 3cm (1$^1$/$_4$in) from the waist parallel with the centre front, following the fly shape and continuing below the bottom of the fly into the seam allowance. A hand stabstitch would be less obvious and give an authentic finish.

### Button stand
Sew the remaining fly and fly lining pieces together along the long curved seam, sewing close to the edge of the seam allowance. Turn through and press so that a small amount of lining can be seen from the fabric side.

Pin the right side fly piece to the right front. Sew together along the centre front; stop sewing 2.5cm (1in) before the balance mark for the bottom of the fly. Sew bias tape over the seam

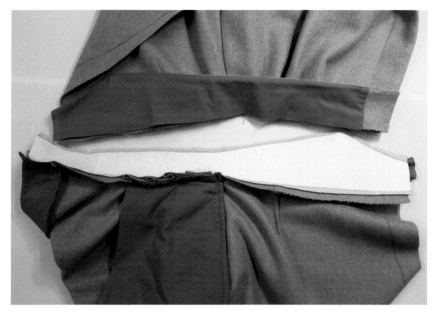

Fig. 5.35 Waist area of both trouser legs, inside and outside, with attached waistband and lining; upper part of picture shows left leg with fabric folded back across top of fly.

Fig. 5.36 Waistband wrapped round top of fly and pinned prior to sewing; fly is trapped into waistband (care must be taken when sewing not to catch fly into waist).

allowance, starting at the waist and stopping before the first sewing line stops.

### Waistband
Join a waistband to the waist area of each trouser leg. Press the seam allowance towards the waistband.

The fabric of the left front waistband wraps around the fly before joining to the waistband lining.

Remove from the front waistband lining the amount of the main fabric fold back, adding a seam allowance.

Ensure that the centre backs are in line. Sew the front waistband lining to the edge of the left front waistband.

On the right front waistband bag out the lining to the front edge of the waistband in line with the edge of the fly button stand.

Fold the waist back along the centre front. Sew the waistband to the lining along the top waist seam allowance, sewing close to the woven fusible interfacing. Trim away excess seam allowance from the top of the waistband. Press the seam allowances

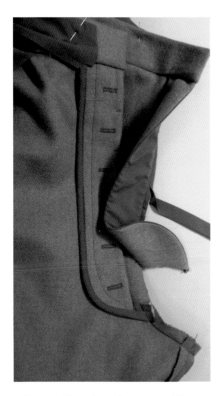

Fig. 5.37 Legs have been joined from angle at base of fly; next stitch line along crotch seam will also sew bottom of button stand over base of fly, seen here not sewn down.

towards the lining. Bluff stitch the lining to the seam allowances at the top of the waistband. Sew close to the join between the fabrics; the peaks at the centre back waist are tricky to bluff stitch. Sew as close to the centre front as possible.

At the centre front edge sew the waistband around the top of the fly. It is not possible to sew very far but gives a neat finish to the front of the waist. Trim off excess seam allowance, turn through to the right side and press the waistband.

### Inside leg

Sew front and back legs together along the inside leg seams. Press the seams open.

### Joining the two legs together

Pin the two legs together along the crotch line. Sew from the corner of the left front hook and balance mark and continue along the crotch seam through the centre back waistband and lining.

Pin the button stand over the bottom of the fly opening. Sew back along the crotch seam; starting at the waistband lining continue along the seam, sewing over the stitches at the bottom of the hook through to meet the stitches on the centre front and button stand.

Trim the seam allowance around the crotch and trim along the side of the fly so the seam allowances are level. The curved crotch seam allowance must not be longer than 1.3cm (½in). Leave the seam allowance above the crotch curve towards the back waist as long as possible for future alteration.

The bias binding along the fly can be continued down the fly seam allowance, covering the inside leg seams.

### Finishing the fly

Close the fly with the left front slightly overlapping the right centre front seam, then pin closed through the button stand. Make a small bar tack at the bottom of the fly opening through all the fly layers.

On the inside of the trousers sew the buttonhole stand to the button stand below the bottom buttonhole.

### Finishing the waist

Press open the centre back seam, waistband and lining.

Fold the waistband lining seam allowance at an angle towards the inside of the trousers. Sew the waistband lining over the waist seam allowances, either by hand on the inside or machine ditch stitch from the outside.

To prepare for the ditch stitching, fold the waistband lining seam allowance into the waistband and pin the lining to the waistline of the trousers, ensuring the edge of the lining extends slightly beyond the waistband stitch line. Place the pins along the seam at right angles to the waistband, with the pin heads towards the top of the waist. Machine from the right side along the 'ditch' between the waistband and the trousers, pulling the pins out when the machine needle is close to them.

### Fly buttons

Mark the position of the fly buttons on the button stand using the buttonholes as a guide. Sew the buttons slightly away from the centre of the buttonhole, towards the centre front seam, to reduce the chance of the button stand being seen while the trousers are being worn.

The waistband can be fastened with hooks and bars or with a button and buttonhole. The buttonhole can be made on either the outside or underside of the waistband with the button being placed correspondingly.

### Braces buttons

Suggestions for positioning the braces buttons can be found in the Glossary.

### Trouser hem

How to create a shaped hem can be found with the trousers in Chapter 8.

# Chapter 6
# Morning Dress

### Morning Coat, 1850s–60s

Originally a riding coat with skirts cut away from the waist, the name 'morning coat' arose from the custom of wealthy men riding out in the morning for exercise rather than travel. It became popular as daywear from the 1850s, and by the end of the century it superseded the frock coat as formal wear (Davis, 1994).

Although made originally without breast pockets, these became an occasional feature after about 1850.

Men's coats were frequently bound at the edges in contrasting or brightly coloured braid, such as plaited mohair braid. Such trims were common on contemporary military uniforms.

For this morning coat, a bias binding is cut and drawn through a bias tape maker.

Fusible chest felt has been used to pad the underarm area and front body below the shoulder: sew-in chest felt can be used. This type of padding can be used on any of the jacket or coats in this book.

All pieces have been cut with 1.5cm (⅝in) seam allowance except for the sleeve cuff hem which is 4cm (1½in) and is marked onto the pattern. Cut the sleeve lining without hem allowance.

All the edges to be bound will be trimmed back prior to binding.

## Marking Up and Preparation

Mark with tailor tacks the button positions on both front body pieces and the end of the lapel dart.

Tailor tack mark the end of reinforced triangles as follows: on the back body and back lining, at the conjunction of the centre back seam and right angle

**PIECES NEEDED**

**Main fabric:**

Cut two front bodies, side backs, back bodies with skirt, skirts, top sleeves, under sleeves, front facings and pocket flaps. Cut one top collar on the fold.

**Lining:**

Cut two front linings, side back linings, back linings, skirt linings, cuff linings, pocket flaps.

**Satin lining:**

Cut two top sleeve and two under sleeve linings from a satin lining fabric, to allow shirt sleeves to slip easily into the arms of the coat.

**Woven cotton fabric:**

Cut four pocket bags for the skirt pockets.

**Wool fabric:**

Cut two wool under collars on the bias.

**Collar canvas:**

Cut two under collars on the bias without seam allowance.

**Paper-backed bondable web:**

Cut two under collars without seam allowance.

**Hair canvas for the fronts:**

Cut with a seam allowance along the armhole, shoulder and the part of the neckline closest to the shoulder; cut out the lapel dart shape.

**Fusible chest felt:**

Cut two pieces to cover the top of the shoulder and around under the front armhole.

**Woven fusible interfacing:**

Cut two pocket flaps without seam allowance; cut bias strip for the sleeve head.

**Lightweight fusible interfacing:**

For the cuff area, cut two pieces that extend slightly beyond the dotted line indicating the top of the cuff and into the hem and cuff opening of the top and under sleeve. The back yoke area fusible interfacing is cut on the bias; it extends over the neck and shoulder area of the back-body-with-skirt panels, stopping just below the armhole. The back skirt interfacing is cut with the grain. Note that fusible interfacing is suitable for the reversible double-woven morning coat fabric; for other fabrics a sew-in backing fabric may be more appropriate.

**To finish:**

Buttons.

Left: Fig. 6.1 Morning outfit consisting of cutaway coat with contrasting trousers and waistcoat.

Fig. 6.2 Morning coat back with pleats and hook-topped skirt back opening.

This morning coat has been bound using a bias tape made from a cotton fabric. Sewing binding on is not difficult, but finishing the corners neatly and consistently takes practice. As with all new techniques try out a sample or two to find the most appropriate method for the garment and the fabrics.

Cut the binding fabric on the bias, then use a bias tape maker to form the bias tape.

First find out how far from the edge to be bound to sew the binding in order for it to wrap around the edge, and decide how the other side of the binding will be sewn in place. Practise taking the binding around corners.

With right sides together sew along the tape fold to the conjunction of the sewing lines at the corner and secure with a back stitch or two. Make a tuck in the binding just large enough to reach to the corner and back to the construction line, start sewing again to secure on the other side of the construction line and tuck in any excess. Ensure the sewing lines start and stop close to each other at an angle to the corner, secure and continue sewing.

At the break line sew from the other side to ensure neatest sewing is viewed.

When wrapping the binding around the edge, the tuck at the corner can be manipulated into an even mitre shape.

The other side of the bias tape can be hand sewn to the back of the fabric or machine ditch stitched from the right side. At the underside corner, fold the tape to create a mitre or pleat.

for the hook; on the same pieces at the top of the pleat line; on the rear of the skirt at the top of the pleat line; on the under sleeve at the hind arm seam to the button stand join.

Fuse a small amount of interfacing over the tailor tack and seam allowance, then make reinforcing triangles to the tailor tacks.

Fuse the interfacing over the cuff areas of both the top and under sleeves. Fuse a strip of bias-cut fusible interfacing over the sleeve head into the seam allowance and straddling the construction line.

Fuse the yoke piece onto the yoke area of the centre back panels.

Fuse the interfacing onto the back skirt panel.

Tack the cuff line on the coat sleeves.

# Morning Coat 1850s to 1860s

1 Square: 2.5cm (1") No seam allowance included

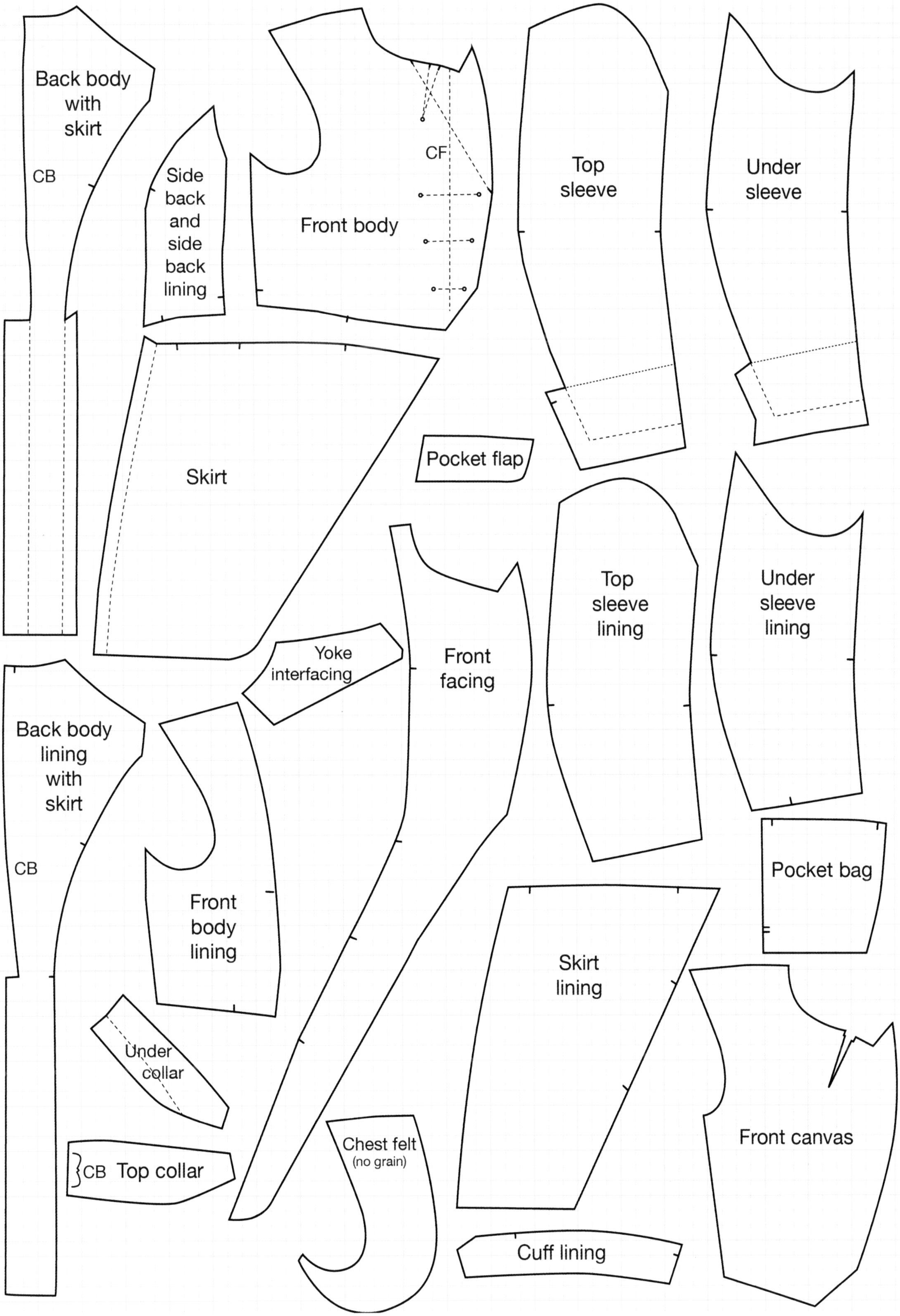

Back body with skirt

CB

Side back and side back lining

Front body

CF

Top sleeve

Under sleeve

Skirt

Pocket flap

Top sleeve lining

Under sleeve lining

Yoke interfacing

Front facing

Back body lining with skirt

CB

Front body lining

Pocket bag

Skirt lining

Under collar

CB Top collar

Chest felt
(no grain)

Front canvas

Cuff lining

## Construction Instructions

### Skirt pocket flaps

Fuse the interfacing cut without seam allowance to the wrong side of the fabric pocket flaps. Trim off the seam allowance from the sides and bottom of the pocket flap close to the interfacing; leave the allowance on the top edge.

With wrong sides together, lay the pocket flap lining onto the interfaced side of the pocket. Sew the pocket flap to the lining along the sides and bottom, sewing close to the edge of the pocket flap. Trim the lining seam allowance level with the cut edge of the pocket flap.

Bind the sides and bottom of the pocket flaps.

Insert the pockets using the instructions in Chapter 5 under the side heading 'Putting the pocket into the coat skirt' for the 1840s frock coat (Figs 6.3–6.5).

### Canvassing the front body

Close the lapel dart on the canvas and main fabric using the instructions in Chapter 8 under the side heading 'Lapel dart' for the short jacket (Fig. 6.8).

With the canvas uppermost, line up the two darts, check the canvas is an even distance from the front edge and pin the darts together.

Pin the canvas to the front along the centre front edge with the pin heads towards the centre front.

Turn the front over with right side up and carefully remove the pins from the front edge.

On the right side of the front body, with the canvas and fabric lying smooth and flat, pad stitch tack the top fabric to the canvas, starting about 5cm (2in) below the shoulder. Work down the front, back up in approximately the middle of the canvas and back down towards the edge of the canvas.

Fuse the shapes made from chest felt into the armhole and shoulder area.

On the outside chalk in the break line between the balance marks. Tack along the break line.

Pad stitch the lapel using the instructions in Chapter 5 for the 1840s frock coat under the side heading 'Pad stitching the lapels'. After completing the lapel pad stitching, press the lapel flat from the canvas side.

Trim the canvas along the bottom front to just inside the construction line. Fuse an edge tape over the bottom edge of the canvas and seam allowance.

### Bridle

Fuse a bridle tape next to the break line, continuing the tape into the seam allowances (Fig 6.8).

### Machine tacking the canvas to the front

Keeping close to the edge of the canvas, sew along the front and around the lapel to the gorge where the collar meets the lapel. The binding will cover

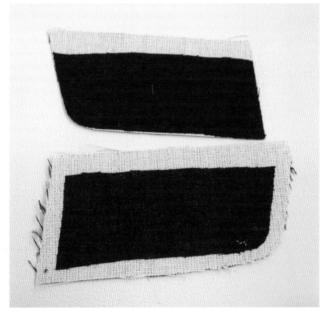

Figs 6.3, 6.4 and 6.5 Top Left: Pocket flaps with bonded interfacing, one with seam allowance trimmed. Bottom Left: Lining sewn to back, left flap lining trimmed and bias tape partially applied. Top Right: Flap with first stage of binding and underside of a bound flap.

Figs 6.6 and 6.7 *Fitting pocket into skirt*. Top L: Pocket bagged out around pocket opening. Top R: Pocket bag attached. Bottom: pocket flap positioned and tacked in place.

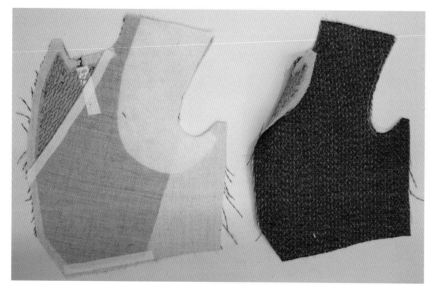

Fig. 6.8 Front bodies with canvas and pad stitched lapel. L: Bridle, chest felt and fused tape to hold canvas to waistline. R: Front not yet pressed.

the machine tacking.

Hand tack the canvas to the main fabric along the armhole seam allowance, stopping before the shoulder.

Sew the side back panel to the front body along the side seam. Press the seam open.

## Joining the skirt to the front body at the waist

Distribute the ease from the skirt along the front body waist seam, then sew the two together, sewing through the back of the pocket bag and pocket flap. Stop and secure the sewing at the conjunction of the side back seam and the top of the pleat. Press the waist seam open.

From the outside sew a bar tack straddling the waist seam and holding the pocket flap down.

## Joining the curved side back to the centre back panel

Pin and sew the side back seams together, securing at the conjunction of the construction lines at the waist. Snip the skirt waist reinforcing triangles open. Trim the side back seam allowances as needed and press the seams open.

Sew the skirt and the back together along the pleat construction lines. Snip open the side back reinforcing triangle. Press the pleat with the seam allowance towards the front. Tack the top of the pleat to the seam allowance.

## Assembling the lining and front facing

Sew the front body lining to the side back lining along the side seam. Press the seam open.

Sew the skirt lining to the waist of the front body and side back linings. Press the waist seam open.

Pin and sew the front facing to the front body lining and skirt. Press the seam allowances towards the lining.

Join the side back lining to the back lining. (There are no pleats in the skirt lining corresponding to the pleats on the skirt side back on the outer fabrics.) Sew the seam from the armhole through the waist to the hem. Press seam open.

Sew the centre back seams of the

Fig. 6.9 Half the constructed coat, inside and outside; reinforcing triangles opened to allow seams to be pressed open and pleat flat.

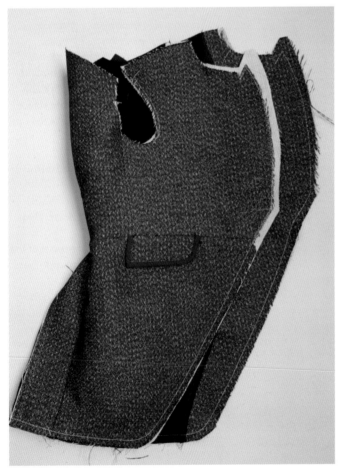

Fig. 6.10 Coat sewn to lining around lapel, front, skirt and back opening.

lining together, securing at the points of the reinforcing triangles. There is a small pleat in the upper back lining; sew from the neck notch down the back for about 2.5cm (1in) to secure the neckline and make the pleat. Press from the neck notch taking the seam allowances to one side, thus creating the pleat.

### Assembling the body of the coat

Join the coat's back body panels by sewing from the neck to the points of the reinforcing triangles marked. Press the seam open.

Fuse a small piece of interfacing onto the neckline at the join of the gorge and lapel.

With wrong sides together pin the lining and facing to the outer coat along the front edge and the hem, close the pleat and pin it to the lining and the pin together along the centre back opening.

### Sew the coat and lining together

Sew on top of the machine tack line around the lapel, along the front edge along the construction line, and continuing around the skirt, hem and centre back opening. Tack the lapel fabrics together and tack along the folded break line.

Trim seam allowances close to the stitch lines.

Snip the centre back reinforcing triangles on the main fabric and lining.

### Binding

The binding must be sewn to the outside or visible side of the coat first. This requires swapping the sides sewn at the break line: above the coat front break line the facing folds back and is seen from the outside; below, the coat front is visible. The change ensures the binding is sewn neatly where it will be seen on the outside of the garment.

Sew the binding to the top of the lapel facing, starting close to the gorge and lapel meeting point; do not secure at the start. Attach the binding around the lapel to the break line. Change to sewing the binding to the outside of the coat, Continue sewing the binding around the coat front, skirt, hem and back opening, running the binding into the seam allowance at the top of the back opening.

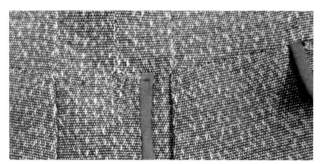

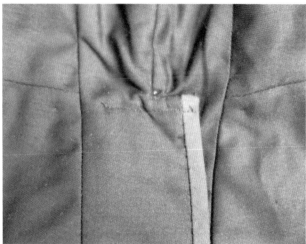

Figs 6.11, 6.12, 6.13 and 6.14 *Finishing hook at top of back skirt opening*. Top Left: Hook seam allowance sewn to coat back and trimmed. Bottom Left: Seam allowance folded back under hook; underside hook sewn to lining. Top Right and Bottom Right: Hook topstitched in place through both sides and lining.

### Centre back skirt opening

With the left back over the right back, pin the centre back opening evenly closed. Fold under the seam allowance of the hook along the construction line at a right angle to the centre back seam and press lightly. Pin the hook seam allowance to the back, sew the seam allowance to the back close to the pressed fold line but do not sew through to the lining. On the inside, fold the seam allowance of the hook under and hand sew the fold to the lining. Trim the seam allowance along the hook, leaving a spike to be folded towards the hook fold. Topstitch along the hook parallel with the hook fold,

then continue the sewing across the centre back to sew through the hook inside the coat, sewing through all the layers including the lining.

With the skirt lying flat, pin the waist seam allowances together; on the inside sew the coat and lining waist seam allowances together.

### Shoulder seams

Join the shoulder seams and fit the shoulder canvas using the instructions in Chapter 8 for the short jacket under the side heading 'Shoulder seam'. Join the lining shoulder seams and press the seam allowances towards the back.

### Collar construction

Start by constructing the under collar. Mark the collar fold line onto the canvas. Bond the canvas under collar to the wool under collar with paper-backed bondable web.

Sew the under collars together along the centre back seam, sewing close to the canvas. Trim the seam down and press it open. Make a machine zigzag stitch straddling the back seam.

Sew along the collar fold line from the seam allowance on the wool.

Machine pad stitch the collar. Starting at the collar fold line make a series of machine-sewn lines parallel to the fold line, working towards the neck

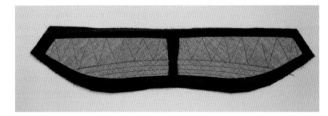

Fig. 6.15 *Collar*. Both sides of collar with machine pad stitching.

Figs 6.16, 6.17 and 6.18 Top: Collar fold pressed and curved; outer seam allowances trimmed off under collar. Middle: Under collar sewn to top collar, turning under top collar neck edge seam allowance. Bottom: Outside edges of collar bound, leaving binding unfinished at edges.

## Joining the collar to the coat

Pin the under collar to the coat neck construction line with right sides together, matching the centre backs and break line. Snip the coat front seam allowance between the neck fold and lapel. Sew the under collar to the coat neck, stitching close to the canvas. Trim the hair canvas close to the sewing, then trim the seam allowances on the lapel and mark. Using a zigzag stitch, sew the seam allowances toward the collar, starting and finishing the zigzag past the break line on the lapel.

## Closing the neckline

Pin the back neckline seam allowance of the lining to the coat neckline seam allowance, checking the lining is not tight or pulling the coat back.

Pin and tack under the seam allowances of the collar and lapel to past the break line; the folded edges of the collar and lapel should just touch. About 2.5cm (1in) beyond the break line, allow the facing seam allowance to go into the collar.

Back stitch along the join of the coat and under collar from around where the lapel seam allowance has been allowed to go into the neckline, sewing the lining and facing to the neck edge.

Ladder stitch the lapel and collar together along the gorge, continuing beyond the break line to where the seam allowance of the lapel is allowed to go into the neckline.

Fold under the neck seam allowance of the top collar and sew the top collar to the neck, just covering the backstitches holding the lining to the neckline.

Finish off the binding on the collar and lapel with both sides matching.

## Joining the top sleeve and under sleeve

Sew the top sleeve to the under sleeve along the front arm seam. Press the seams open.

## Cuff detail

Snip open the reinforcing triangle at the top of the button stand on the under sleeve. Apply the braid or detail to be used along the tacked cuff line.

seam.

Using a straight stitch make a large zigzag covering the top of the collar, making the two sides symmetrical.

Press in the fold, press the folded collar flat and curve the collar around the neck fold.

Trim the seam allowance level with the canvas on the sides and outside edge of the under collar, leaving the neck edge seam allowance.

### Top collar to under collar

With wrong sides together, pin the top collar to the under collar, smoothing it over the collar fold. A pad stitch tack could be used to hold the two collars together over the fold.

Fold the neck seam allowance of the top collar under at the sides, folding it in line with the neck edge of the canvas.

Sew the top collar to the under collar along the sides and outside edge, sewing very close to the edge of the trimmed canvas and wool. Tack the top collar over the under collar fold.

Trim the top collar seam allowance back to the canvas and under collar fabric along the sides and outside edge.

Bind round the sides and outside edge of the collar, leaving the binding on the area closest to the neck edge unfinished and a little longer than needed.

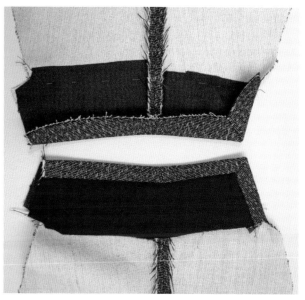

Figs 6.23 and 6.24 *Sleeve cuff and lining*. Top upper: Inside of sleeve with mitred seam between hem and cuff opening. Top lower: Lining joined to hem and above mitred seam. Bottom: Hem and lining have been bagged out along under sleeve cuff opening.

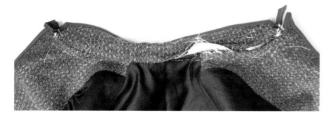

Figs 6.19, 6.20, 6.21 and 6.22 *Joining collar to coat*. Top: Under collar sewn to neckline; seam allowances zigzagged towards collar. Second: Back neck lining pinned to back neck seam allowances; seam allowances of lapel and collar folded under. Third: Back neck lining sewn in place; collar and lapel ladder stitched together. Bottom: Top collar sewn over back neck seam allowances.

Run the trim into the reinforcing triangle without closing it.

Make the top sleeve cuff opening using the instructions from Chapter 8 for the short jacket under the side heading 'Cuff opening'.

### Joining the cuff lining to the hem of the sleeve

Sew the cuff lining to the cuff hem, matching up the edges of the seam allowance and stopping and securing at the mitre.

Sew the side of the cuff lining to the cuff facing on the top sleeve, sewing as far as possible; a stitch or two by hand will be needed to secure the lining to the mitre.

Bag out the under sleeve button stand, hem and lining. Make a tuck in the side of the lining close to the hemline. Turn through to the right side and press.

### Hemming the cuff

Use the instructions for the cuff hem from Chapter 8 for the short jacket under the side heading 'Cuff hem'.

### Buttonholes

Mark and make buttonholes along the top sleeve cuff opening. Again, look at the section in Chapter 8 for the short jacket.

### Joining the hind arm sleeve seams

Matching up the cuff trim and balance marks, sew the seam from the corner of the reinforcing triangle on the cuff to the top edges of the sleeve seam. Press the seam open with the button stand lying flat with the opening of the top sleeve.

Pin or tack the sleeve button stand

and opening to keep it in place.

**Sleeve linings**
Make an opposing pair of sleeve linings, sewing the top sleeve to the undersleeve along the front and back seams. Press the seams open.

Join the sleeve lining to the sleeve at the cuff lining. With both the sleeve and sleeve linings inside out, make a pair of the linings and sleeve, slipping the sleeve lining cuff edge over the cuff lining and pinning the seam allowances together. Sew the sleeve lining to the cuff lining, sewing as close to the cuff opening as possible. Hand sew the remaining opening between the cuff lining and sleeve lining closed.

**Joining the seam allowance of the hind arm seams**
Match up the hind arm seam allowances of the sleeve and lining between the armhole and the elbow. Sew the seam allowances of the fabric and lining with a few hand or machine stitches.

**Fitting the sleeves into the armholes**
Use the instructions for fitting the sleeves from Chapter 8 for the short jacket.

**Buttons and buttonholes**
Check and mark the buttonhole positions. For this coat make the three buttonholes closest to the wearer's left front edge and make the top buttonhole only on the wearer's right front.

Sew three buttons on the wearer's left front edge to correspond to the buttonholes. Sew one flat inner button on the inside left front to suit the buttonhole, again making a very long shank. Sew the top button for the top of the other row, checking that you have positioned it so that the stitching for the inner button is concealed; this button only needs a short shank. Check for position and sew the two lower buttons, again with short shanks.

Sew buttons at the top of the back pleat at the conjunction of the side back and waist seams.

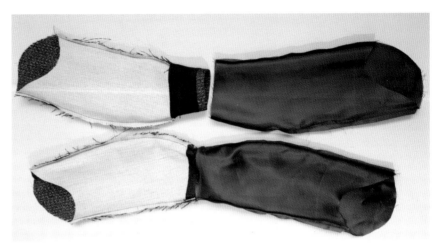

Fig. 6.25 Sleeves and sleeve linings joined at cuff lining.

Figs 6.26 and 6.27 Top: Sleeve head roll and coat sleeve with sleeve head roll pinned and back stitched along construction line. Bottom: Coat body lining positioned and back stitched around armhole; on left, sleeve lining has been sewn to body.

## Morning Dress Waistcoat, 1850s–60s

The purple corduroy fabric for this waistcoat, although not historically accurate, alludes to the popular Victorian colour and fabric. The purple colour is reminiscent of mauveine, one of the newly invented aniline dyes. Corduroy fabric was popular as a hard-wearing fabric for working clothing but from around the 1800s, when the wealthy began taking part in leisure activities in the countryside, corduroy become associated with equestrian activities and country sports.

The corduroy for this waistcoat has been cut with the pile running the wrong way to maximize the impact of the colour.

The metal eyelets along the edge of the jigger will be fastened with a lace or cord.

## PIECES NEEDED

**Main fabric:**

Cut two fronts, collar and front facings, bottom front facings and pocket blinds. Cut four jettings on the bias; these are strips approximately 4cm (1½in) wide and about 2.5cm (1in) longer than the pocket opening.

**Outside back fabric:**

Cut two waistcoat backs and four jiggers.

**Lining fabric:**

Cut two front linings and back linings.

**Cotton fabric:**

Cut two under collars on the bias; cut four pocket bags.

**Woven fusible interfacing:**

Cut two under collars. The jiggers have fusible interfacing cut to the size of the jiggers without seam allowance except for the side seam allowance. Cut fusible stay strips for the pocket opening areas.

**Sew-in non-woven interfacing:**

Cut two pieces for the collar area of the front facing, from the centre back to just beyond the top button.

**To finish:**

Buttons, tape to adjust jiggers.

Figs 6.28 and 6.29 Morning dress waistcoat front and back.

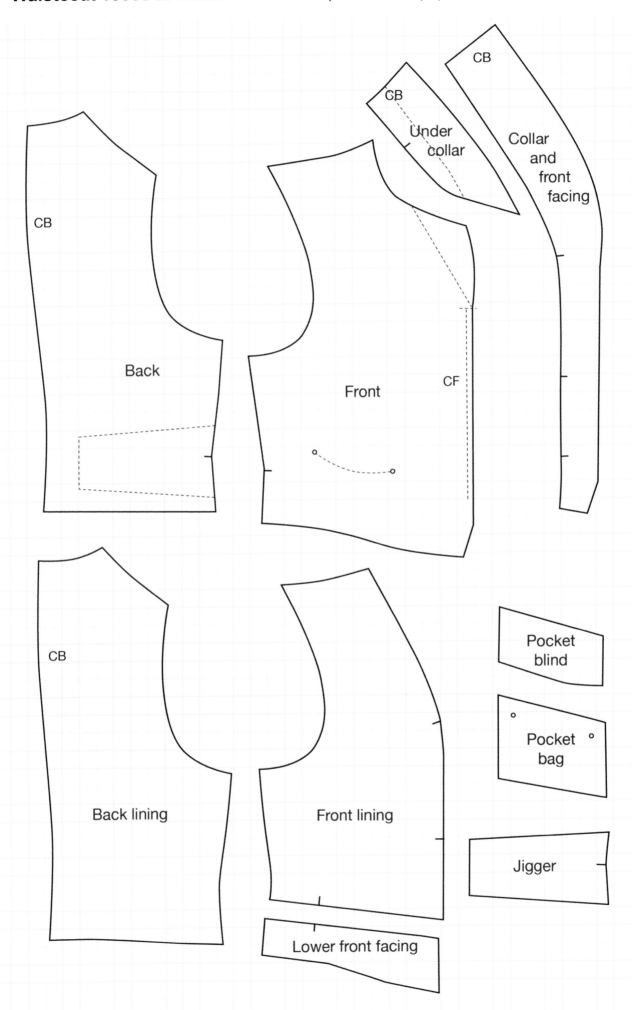

**Waistcoat 1850s to 1860s**

1 Square: 2.5cm (1") No seam allowance included

CB

Under collar

CB

Collar and front facing

CB

Back

Front

CF

CB

Back lining

Front lining

Pocket blind

Pocket bag

Jigger

Lower front facing

## PILE FABRIC FOR THE THEATRE

Corduroy, like velvet, is a pile fabric. Such fabrics can have a definite nap with the pile smoothing in one direction. For clothing the pile usually smooths downwards, which feels pleasant and the fabric wears better.

Light can have a very particular effect on pile fabrics and must be considered whenever using it. Before cutting out the garment try draping the fabric around something so that both pile directions can be seen at once and examine the difference; the pile facing and smoothing downwards can look faded whereas the pile facing upwards can look richer and deeper in colour. In the theatre, velvet and other pile fabrics are often cut the 'wrong' way because the colour looks more luxurious.

## Marking Up and Preparation

Because this waistcoat has been cut with a consistent 1.3cm (½in) seam allowance, construction lines are not needed, so just indicate the balance marks.

The pocket shape and position is marked with tailor tacks.

The fusible interfacing stay is applied to the wrong side of the pocket areas.

The non-woven interfacing is machine flat tacked close to the edge of the seam allowance of the collar area of the front facing.

Fuse the interfacing to the under collar and mark the collar fold line.

Fuse the interfacing onto one pair of the jigger pieces, leaving a seam allowance around the two long sides and the short side.

## Construction Instructions
### Making the curved jetted pockets

Pin or tack a pocket bag to the inside of each pocket opening; the pocket bag will act as an extra stay. On the outside of the waistcoat, use chalk to mark the pocket opening and the ends of the pockets in line with the grain.

For this type of pocket one side of the bias strips should be marked to ensure all the strips go in the same direction. The arrangement of strips must be considered and be placed intentionally as the shade changes due to the pile

Figs 6.30, 6.31 and 6.32 Top: Jettings sewn to either side of pocket opening; on inside, pocket has been cut open between stitch lines. Centre: Jetting fabric wrapped around seam allowances and pinned, ditch stitched, the triangle and jetting seam allowances secured. Bottom: Blind sewn onto remaining pocket bag, sewn to pocket opening and trimmed round.

Fig 6.33 Waistcoat with under collar; waistcoat lining with collar and facing.

can have an obvious and distinctive effect. Other fabric with patterns will need some consideration; a chevron effect can look striking.

As with a straight jetted pocket, lay the jetting next to the chalk line with right sides together. Sew from the chalk line in line with the pocket opening, stitching parallel to the pocket opening finishing in line with the marked opening. Place and sew the rest of the jettings in the same way.

From the wrong side, cut open the pocket in the centre of the two parallel sewing lines, stopping about 1cm (⅜in) from each end and snipping from the centrally cut line to within a thread of the last stitch of each line of sewing, thus creating a triangle.

Wrap the jetting fabric closely and firmly around the cut seam allowance of the jetting and the pocket opening and secure with pins placed at right angles to the jetting. Ditch stitch through all the layers and jetting seam allowance; the ditch stitching can be performed by hand or by machine.

Push the seam allowance of the jettings to the inside of the opening; the wrapped edges of the opening should finish evenly without overlapping.

With the right side of the waistcoat uppermost, fold back the side of the waistcoat along the grain line to expose the cut triangle from the pocket opening and the ends of the jettings. Check that the jettings are lying flat and have not overlapped each other. Sew across the widest part of the triangle and jetting seam allowance.

Sew the seam allowance of the bottom jetting to the pocket bag, using a machine zigzag or hand herringbone stitch to cover the cut edge.

Finish the bottom edge of the pocket blind as appropriate to the fabric used. Match the blind to the top of the pocket bag and sew it onto the pocket bag along the finished edge. Place the pocket bag with blind onto the inside of the pocket opening.

With the pocket bags pinned together and the right side of the garment facing up, fold back the side of the waistcoat to reveal the side of the pocket bag. Sew from the top towards the bottom of the bag, turn with the machine needle in the fabric, fold back the fabric along the bottom of the garment to expose the pocket bag and continue to the top of the other side of the pocket.

Sew the pocket bags together along the top curve of the pocket, sewing as close to the curve as is easily possible.

## Constructing the rest of the waistcoat

Construct the rest of the garment by following the instructions for the 1840s waistcoat from Chapter 5.

The main differences are that (a) this waistcoat does not have a split on the back between the hem and the waist, and (b) the jiggers for this waistcoat are sewn into the side seam, therefore need preparing and tacking onto the waistcoat back side seams before the front and back are sewn together at the sides.

### Jiggers

The jiggers are supported with a woven fusible interfacing cut without seam allowance. Sew the jigger pieces together along one long side seam, sewing about 3mm (⅛in) beside the interfacing.

On the other long side of the jigger piece, offset the lining by about 6mm (¼in). Sew together about 3mm (⅛in) beside the interfacing. Turn through and press the seam allowances towards the lining.

Turn back through to the wrong side, with the side seams folded towards the lining. Sew along the short end of the jigger, drawing the lining from under the main fabric in the centre of the

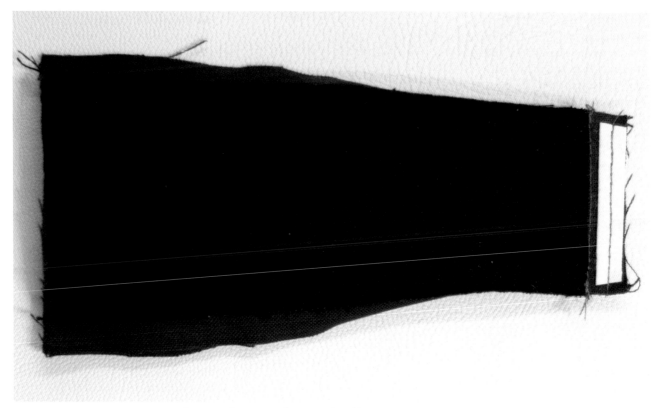

Fig. 6.34 Jigger, inside out, with stiffening on seam allowance.

## REINFORCING JIGGERS

When more than one pair of eyelets is being used to fasten or tighten, the eyelets must have some form of stiffening to stop the eyeletted area collapsing and all the holes folding towards each other. For this waistcoat a strip of a non-woven collar canvas has been sewn to the seam allowance where the eyelets will be attached. Other stiffenings can be used, such as plastic boning can be sewn onto the seam allowance. The Victorians would have used whatever seemed most effective and was accessible: whalebone, wood or metal or a stiffener such as starch, glue or lacquer could be applied.

short end and sewing slightly away from the interfacing.

A thin strip of stiff interfacing is sewn across the short end seam allowance to support the eyelets. The jigger can now be turned through and pressed. Attach metal eyelets or make hand-worked eyelets.

Place the jiggers on the outside back, matching the waist balance marks. Machine tack the jiggers to the side seams.

To close the side seams, use the instructions from the 1840s waistcoat in Chapter 5.

**Buttons and buttonholes**

Mark the buttonhole positions: you can either use the pattern as a guide or you can mark the top and bottom buttonhole, measure the distance between them and divide the measurement among the spaces between the buttons – there is one more button than there are spaces. Then make the buttonholes and attach the buttons.

## Morning Dress Trousers

Fashion plates of the 1840s show many different styles of men's dress; light-coloured trousers were combined with bright patterned waistcoats and morning coats of a darker colour.

In these trousers there is a back waist dart and the centre back peaks for the braces buttons are rounded. Around the ankle there is a slight flare and some shaping.

The trousers have been cut with a regular 1.3cm (½in) seam allowance except for the hem, which has been cut at 4cm (1½in), and the centre back waist, which has been cut with extra seam allowance starting after the crotch curve widening to the waist. The same amount is added to the centre back facing. The extra is to allow for future waist alteration.

The example shown here is made from reversible fabric.

### Marking Up and Preparation

Indicate all the balance marks.

Tack the hemline and indicate the dart with a tailor tack.

Fuse interfacing along the waistline; fuse a fly piece along the centre front inside of the left leg; fuse the remaining

**PIECES NEEDED**

- - - - - - - - - - - - - - - - - - - - - -

**Main fabric:**

Cut two fronts, backs and fly pieces. Cut two front pocket facings and back pocket facings.

**Lining fabric:**

Cut two front waistband facings, back waistband facings and pocket bags, all on the fold. Cut three fly pieces.

**Fusible interfacing:**

Cut two pieces for the waist area for the front and back waists. Cut three fly pieces. Consider fusing stays along the pocket openings.

**To finish:**

Buttons.

fly pieces to the fabric fly pieces.

Mark the shape of the back waist onto fusible interfacing.

### Construction Instructions

The fabric used for the sample trousers frays very little so the seam allowances have not been finished off. However,

most fabrics will fray, especially if subjected to hard wear, so the first step is to finish off the exposed seam allowances before the garment is constructed. Start by trimming the crotch curve to 1.3cm (½in) or less, then use the instructions for finishing trouser seam allowances in the evening dress trousers later in the book.

Close the back waist darts. Press the seam allowance towards the centre back.

### Pockets and side seams

Fit the pockets into the side seams of the front and back legs, following the instructions in Chapter 5 for the 1840s trousers. The sides of the pockets for this pair of trousers have been finished off with a machine zigzag stitch instead of the binding.

After snipping into the seam allowance of the front pocket bag at the pocket opening balance mark, let the front pocket side seam fold back to join the side back leg pocket bag. Sew closed the side of the pocket bags and finish off the seam allowance. On this pair of trousers, the side seam of the pocket bag and facing have been finished off together.

### Waist facing

Construct and fit the waist facing using the method used in Chapter 8 for the 1890s trousers. The instructions will need slight modifications to allow for the rounded peak on either side of the centre back waist on this pattern.

Continue through the trouser assembly guided by the 1890s trouser instructions in Chapter 8.

Fig. 6.37 *Morning coat trousers.* Completed pocket and side seam; right leg has button stand partially sewn on; right leg only has waist facing sewn on.

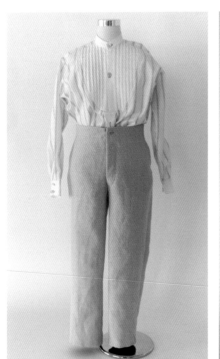 

Figs 6.35 and 6.36 Trousers for use with morning coat, front and back views.

**Trousers 1850s to 1860s**    1 Square: 2.5cm (1") No seam allowance included

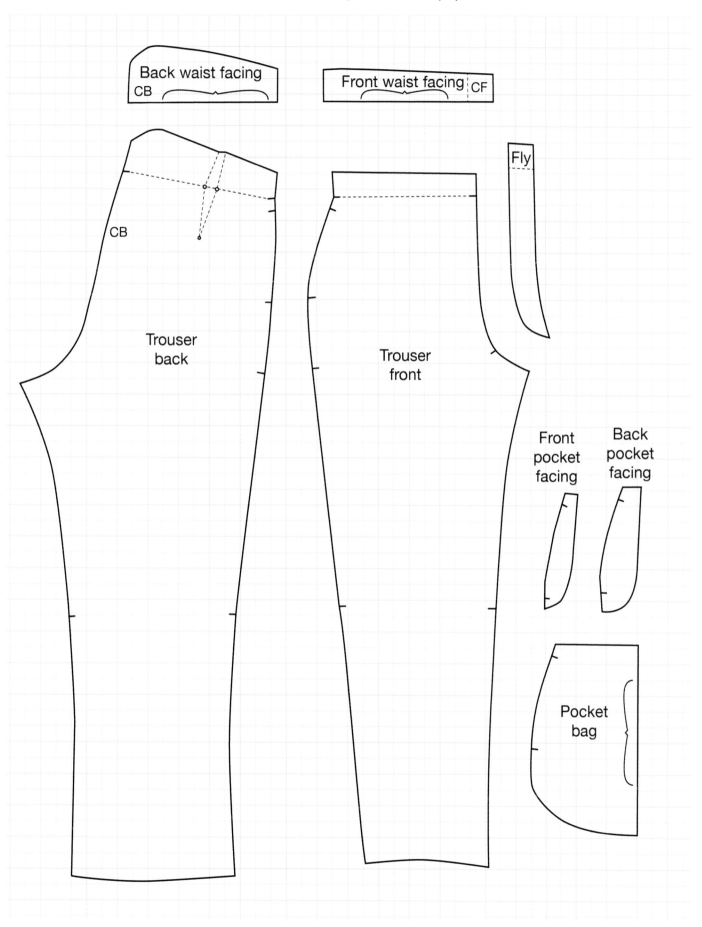

# Chapter 7
# Evening Wear

*For evening wear black started to replace colours from the early 1800s and by the 1840s black was ubiquitous. Long trousers were worn with the tailcoat from the 1850s. Until about mid-century ties could be black or white; after the 1860s white or ivory ties became customary.*

In the 1880s dinner (or lounge) jackets became usual; the tails had disappeared and the hem of the garment finished near the top of the thigh.

## Evening Dress Tailcoat, 1870s

This tailcoat has two lining pockets on the upper front body, extending from below the armhole into the facing. There is a skirt pocket in the lining; skirt pockets were often much bigger than this one, which might be large enough for a pair of evening gloves, but the size can be altered as needed.

For this evening dress tailcoat the seams have been cut to a consistent 1.3cm (½in) seam allowance; the sleeve cuff hem has been cut at 5cm (2in).

### Marking Up and Preparation

The sleeve cuff line is tack marked.

Balance marks can be indicated with a small snip or chalk mark.

Sew tailor tacks to mark the junction of the centre back construction line and the right angle of the top of the hook in the top fabric and lining. The top of the pleat line is tailor tacked on the skirt and side back.

The lining pocket is indicated with a tailor tack at each side of the opening, with one tack on the side front lining and the other on the satin front facing.

The top of the neck dart is marked with a small snip at the top of each construction line; the point of the neck dart is marked with a tailor tack.

The cuff line is marked on the outside of the sleeve.

The fold line of the side back pleat could be tacked, to help when pressing the pleat in place.

Start by backing the tailcoat skirt and yoke areas. The cotton backing pieces are sewn onto the inside of the appropriate pieces of fabric. In this case the pieces are machine flat tacked onto the wrong side of the main fabric, sewing close to the edge of the seam allowance.

Fuse a piece of interfacing over the centre back hook tailor tacks on the coat and lining and top of the pleat line on the back body and skirt.

Fig. 7.2 Evening dress, 1870s, rear view.

Left: Fig. 7.1 Late Victorian evening dress, 1870s: tailcoat, waistcoat and trousers.

## PIECES NEEDED

### Main fabric:

Cut two front bodies, back bodies, side backs, skirt fronts, top sleeves, under sleeves, lapels, front facings for the lapels and skirt front facings. Cut two under collars on the bias. Cut one top collar on the fold.

### Contrasting fabric in a satin weave or appropriate fabric:

Cut two contrast front facings.

### Lining:

Cut two side front linings, back body linings, side back linings, skirt front linings, top sleeves and under sleeves (cut the sleeve linings without hem allowance). Cut two jettings for each inside pocket and two facings for the skirt lining pocket.

### Cotton fabric:

Cut two skirt pocket bags and pocket bags for each inside pocket.

### Cotton backing fabric:

Enough for backing the skirt fronts, skirt backs and yoke areas.

### Hair canvas:

Cut two front bodies with cut-out lapel dart; seam allowance is included along the armhole, the neckline close to the shoulder (shoulder seam allowance of 2.5cm (1in)); all other edges have been cut out along the construction lines.

### Collar canvas:

Cut two under collars on the bias without seam allowance; fusible web to bond the collar canvas to the under collar

### Fusible interfacing:

Use to reinforce the lining pocket area and add firmness around the skirt seams and edges.

### To finish:

Buttons.

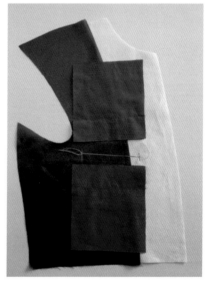

Figs 7.3, 7.4 and 7.5 Top: Pocket bag and lining jetting, both sewn to pocket bag. Centre: Pocket stay interfacing covering pocket opening and running into armhole seam allowance. Bottom: Pocket opening marked on right side between tailor tacks and pocket bags.

Fuse interfacing at the hem area of each sleeve. Fuse a strip of interfacing over the sleeve head seam allowance and construction line.

Sew reinforcing triangles to the tailor tacks at the bottom of the centre back hook on the fabric and lining and at the top of the skirt pleat on the side back and skirt.

For fabrics that fray excessively, fuse very lightweight interfacing onto the top of the front facing strip.

## Construction Instructions

### Lining pocket

Sew the side front lining to the contrast fabric front facing. Press the seam allowance towards the lining.

Fuse a strip of interfacing covering and joining the tailor tacks that indicate each side of the lining pocket.

Continue the interfacing into the armhole seam allowance to strengthen the pocket opening; it can be sewn into the armhole to provide additional stability.

On the right side, chalk a straight line between the tailor tacks to indicate the pocket opening; at each tailor tack make a chalk mark in line with the grain to mark the edge of the pocket.

### Preparing the jettings and pocket bags

Press under a seam allowance on the pocket jettings. Match up the unfinished edge of jetting to the top edge of the pocket bag and sew the lining to the pocket bag along the folded edge (Figs 7.3–7.5).

With right sides together place the pocket bag with jetting piece against the chalk line for the pocket opening.

# Evening dress tailcoat 1870s

1 Square: 2.5cm (1") No seam allowance included

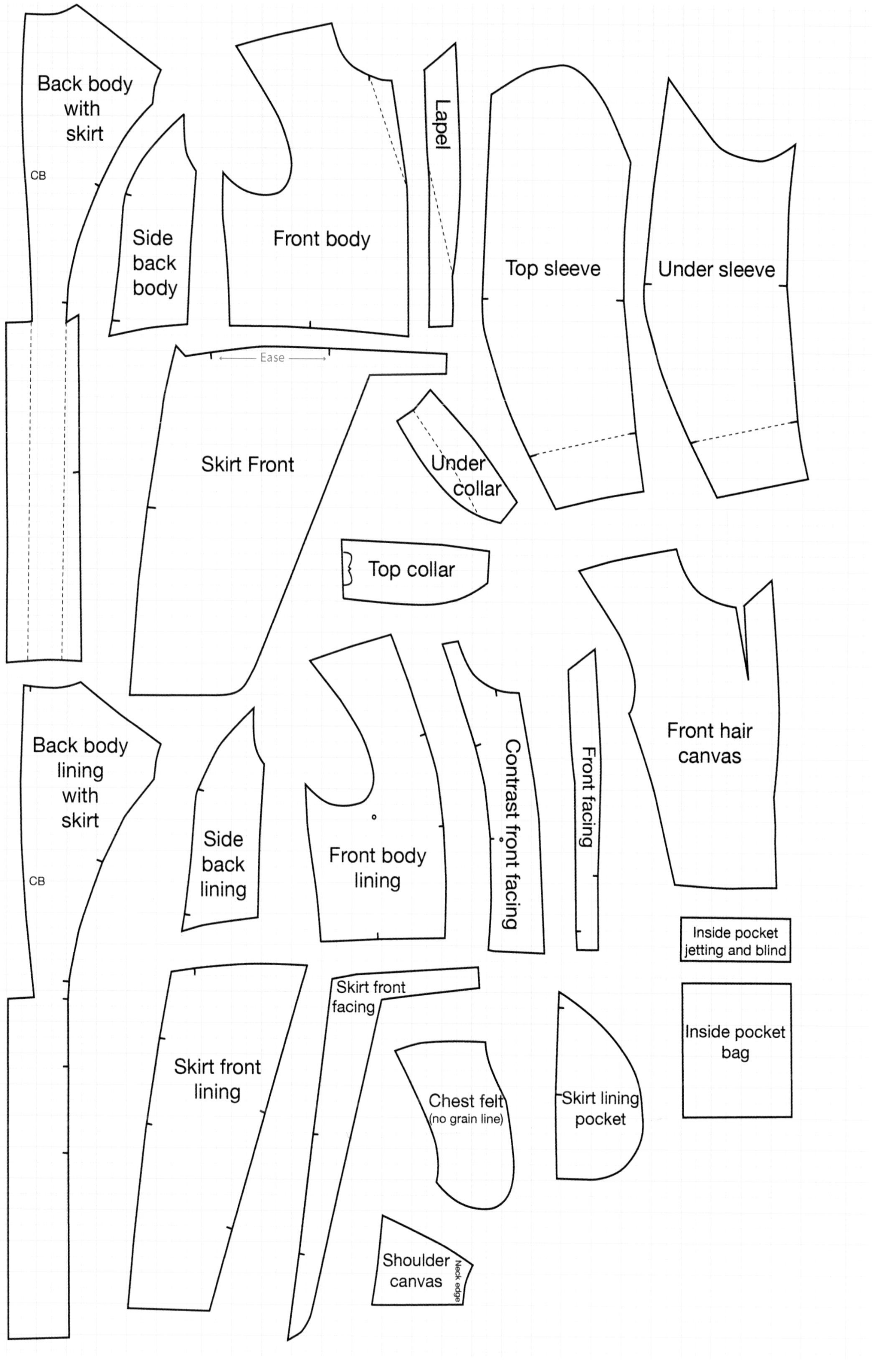

Back body with skirt

CB

Side back body

Front body

Lapel

Top sleeve

Under sleeve

Ease

Skirt Front

Under collar

Top collar

Front hair canvas

Back body lining with skirt

CB

Side back lining

Front body lining

Contrast front facing

Front facing

Inside pocket jetting and blind

Inside pocket bag

Skirt front lining

Skirt front facing

Chest felt
(no grain line)

Skirt lining pocket

Shoulder canvas

Neck edge

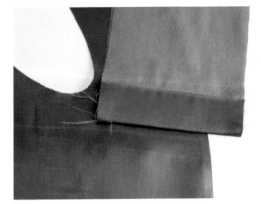

Figs 7.9, 7.10 and 7.11 Top: Jetting placed
against marked pocket opening. Centre:
Jetting sewn parallel to opening as far as
ends marked in line with grain. Bottom:
On wrong side, pocket cut open between
sewing lines; snipping into corners at
end of stitch lines.

Sew one pocket bag to either side of
the chalk line, making the sewing lines
the same distance from the pocket
centre chalk line and parallel to each
other. Each end must be finished
securely at the grain line chalk mark.

Cut the pocket open between the two
lines of sewing; towards each end cut
to within a thread of the last stitch of
each sewn line, creating a triangle.

Wrap the pocket bag with lining
jetting closely around all the seam
allowances, pin in place. Sew along the
join of the jetting to the front lining to
form the jetting.

Take the pocket bags through to the
inside of the pocket opening. With the
outside of the garment uppermost, the
pocket opening lying flat and the
jettings meeting, fold back the side of
the garment to expose the jettings seam
allowances and the cut triangle. Sew
over the triangle and jetting seam
allowances, sewing as close to the
widest part of the triangle as possible.
Press the pocket opening (Figs 7.16–
7.18).

Fold the top bag down to lie over the
lower pocket bag. Press the pocket

bags. With the front and pockets all
lying flat and the pocket opening
uppermost, draw back the side of the
lining or facing to expose the side of
the pocket. Sew down the side of the
pocket bag, turn at the bottom and roll
back the lower part of the lining and
facing to sew along the bottom, then
continue to the top of the pocket.

From the right side sew along the
sides of the pocket opening through
the jettings and pocket bag; for this
pocket a machine zigzag was used.

**Skirt lining pocket**
To strengthen and support the lining
seam allowance and pocket opening,
fuse a stay of lightweight fusible
interfacing on the inside of the lining

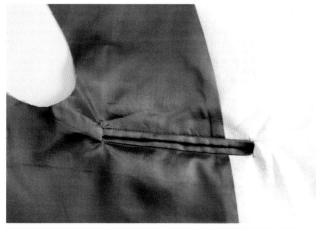

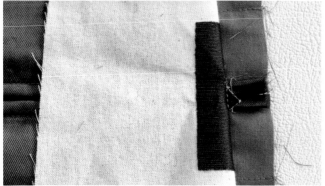

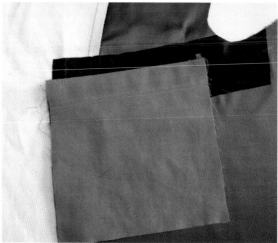

Figs 7.12 and 7.13 Top: Pocket opening with pocket bag taken through to inside. Bottom: Side of garment is folded back and triangle sewn to jetting seam allowance.

Figs 7.14 and 7.15 Top: Jettings pressed. Bottom: Top pocket bag folded down to cover pocket opening.

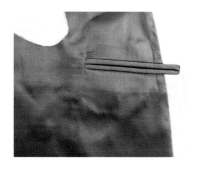

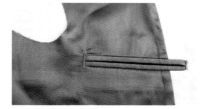

Figs 7.16, 7.17 and 7.18 Left: Finished pocket without strengthening sewing at sides. Above: Strengthening sewing added. Right: Pocket bag viewed from other side; side sewing joining pocket bags and side strengthening stitches can be seen.

from the waist downwards along the construction line, finishing beyond the balance marks for the bottom of the pocket opening.

Finish the pocket facing along the long curved edge. Sew the pocket facings to the pocket bags along the finished edge.

Sew the pocket bags to each side of the right back side seam on the skirt,

stitching close to the construction line along the edge of the pocket.

### Assembling the coat and lining

Sew the skirt front facing to the skirt front lining. Press the seam towards the lining.

Sew the lapel band to the contrast front facing. Press the seam open.

Join and sew the side backs to the

front bodies of the main fabric and the side back lining to the front lining sewn to the contrast fabric front facing. Press the side seams open.

### Skirt centre back opening below the hook

Offset the lining against the main fabric along the opening; the lining should be visible from under the main

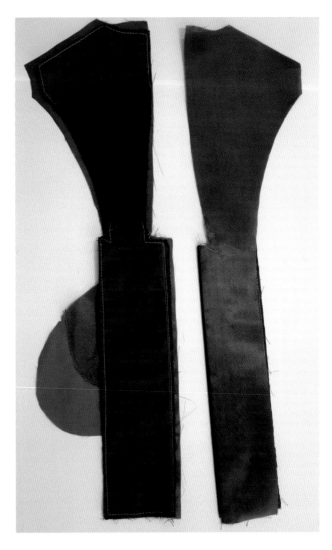

Figs 7.19 and 7.20 Left: Skirt front facing sewn to skirt front lining; attached lining pocket is visible. Right L: Inside of back body and back body lining, sewn together along back opening with skirt and shoulder area backing visible. Right: Right side back is turned through to right side and pressed, with strip of fabric visible along edge of back opening.

fabric by about 1.3cm (½in). Sew together, leaving a small seam allowance. Press the seam allowance towards the lining; press back along the construction line of the back opening.

### Joining the skirt to the body

The next steps relate to both the main fabric and the lining. Pin the waistlines together; there is some ease on the skirt so distribute the ease between the balance marks over the hip area.

Sew the body and the skirt together along the waistline, securing the lower side back construction line to the top of the fold line of the pleat. Snip the pleat fold line reinforcing triangle open. Press the waist seam open.

Sew the front facing band onto the front edge of the coat body, over the waist seam. Press the seam open.

### Joining the centre backs of the coat and lining

Snip to the end of the reinforced triangle at the centre back waist of both fabrics. Sew together the coat centre back seams and secure at the hook

Figs 7.21 and 7.22 Above: Assembled linings for front body, side back and skirt. Right: Assembled main fabric pieces.

right angle and points of the reinforcing triangles. Press the coat back seam open.

### Sew the lining centre back seam closed

Secure at the hook right angle and points of the reinforcing triangles. The centre back lining has a pleat; sew the back neck balance marks together, continuing for about 2.5cm (1in) down the back. Press the fold into the centre back lining between the neck balance marks and the bottom of the centre back.

### Creating the centre back hook

With this method of forming the hook the two opposing hooks are bagged out; the left hook will lap over the right side of the coat back.

With right sides together, place the lining to the main fabric and match up the tailor tacks at the base of the centre back reinforcing triangles.

Sew at a right angle from the centre back tailor tacks to the fold of the opening. Trim away excess fabric from the sewing line. Turn the hooks through to the outside and press, ensuring the lining on the left back hook is not visible from the outside. The left back hook will extend over the right back of the coat with the right back hook on the inside.

### Canvassing the front

The front body canvas pattern has been cut with a seam allowance at the shoulder, armhole and part of the neckline. There is no seam allowance on the waist, front edge, lapel or along the top of the lapel or close to the lapel on the neckline.

### Lapel dart

Close the lapel dart on the canvas and main fabric using the instructions in Chapter 8 for the short jacket under the side heading 'Lapel dart'. The dart on the main fabric is incorporated into the seam joining the lapel to the body front; the dart in the canvas should be in line with the lapel-to-body-front seam.

Pad stitch (or fuse) a piece of hair

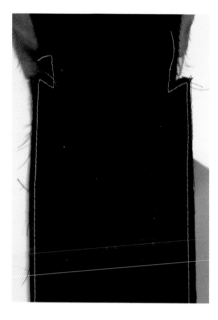

Figs 7.23 and 7.24 Top: Centre back hook, bagged out. Bottom: Same, finished and seen from right side.

canvas along the shoulder of the canvas, keeping the grain of this canvas in line with the shoulder line.

Fuse a piece of fusible chest felt down the chest area of the hair canvas; ensure the chest felt does not cover the break line.

Lay the front body with the right side down and place the front canvas on top. Match up the dart centre to the seam between the front body and the front facing strip; use two pins to hold the dart area. Smooth the canvas over the front body; ideally the cut edge of the canvas should not quite cover the front and lapel construction lines. Pin the canvas to the front body with the pin heads towards the front seam for easy removal; the pins are to hold the canvas to the front body when it is turned over.

Turn the front body right side up.

Using pad stitch, tack the front body to the canvas, starting about 5cm (2in) below the shoulder line near the neck. Keep the canvas and fabric separate along the shoulder line.

Take out the front edge pins, gently smooth the main fabric down the front and continue the pad stitch tack down the front edge. Do not tack beyond the break line onto the lapel. At the bottom edge tack back up the body to below the shoulder. From the shoulder, tack back down the body roughly along the side of the canvas.

Tack the main fabric to the canvas along the seam allowance of the armhole, stopping 5cm (2in) below the shoulder.

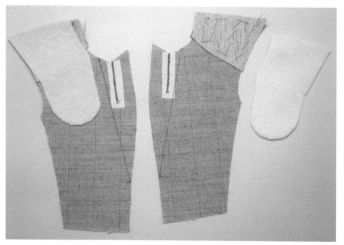

Fig 7.25 Front body; dart closed and shoulder canvas and chest felt attached.

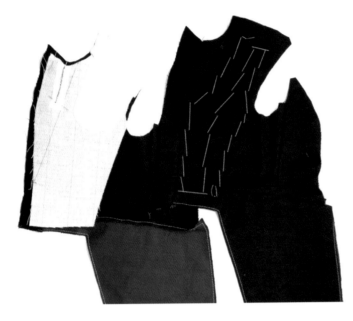

Fig. 7.26
Canvas placed
into inside coat
front and pad
stitch tacking
in position.

### Preparing and pad stitching the lapels

On the outside of the garment and using a straight edge, chalk a line connecting the top and bottom of the break line at the construction line.

Tack along the break line. From the inside, back stitch along the break line, using a matching thread; the stitch on the outside should be almost invisible. Pad stitch the lapels

Starting from the top or bottom of the break line, pad stitch along the break line, continue up and down parallel to the break line and rolling the lapel over the fingers of the non-dominant hand until the lapel is filled in. (Pad stitching is described in the Glossary.)

When both lapels are pad stitched press them flat from the canvas side.

Edge tape the neckline, lapel, front and waist.

Trim back any canvas that extends beyond the front construction lines.

Fuse edge tape around the neckline, lapel, front and bottom edges of the canvas, straddling the edge of the canvas and seam allowance. Fuse the tape along the neck canvas without seam allowance, continue around the front of the canvas and along the bottom edge, stopping just after the side of the canvas.

An edge tape can be sewn on or a fusible edge tape can be secured with hand sewing, using one of the methods described in the Glossary.

### Joining the side back to the centre back panels

Join the side back to the back body along the curved side back seams. Sew with the side back panel uppermost. Secure at the conjunction of the side back seam and the waist seam. Trim the seam allowances as needed but do not clip into seams; press the seam open (Fig. 7.27).

### Side back pleats

Join the skirt side seam of the back body to the side seam of the skirt front, matching the balance marks. There is an extension of 2.5cm (1in) on the skirt side seams to create a pleat. Press the pleat seam allowance towards the front. Tack the pleat closed just above the hemline. Tack the top of the pleat to the waist seam allowance.

### Lining side back seams and skirt pocket

Sew the side back lining to the back body lining, matching up the waistline and balance marks. The lining has no pleat; the construction line runs from the armhole through the waist to the hem.

For the skirt pocket, sew the side back seam securing at the balance marks at either side of the pocket opening. Press the seam open and press the pocket bag towards the front of the skirt. Sew the pocket bags together, sewing the pocket bag through to the seam allowance where possible.

### Joining the skirt to the lining and facing

Pin the waist areas of the tailcoat to the lining and facing, slightly offsetting the facing (Fig. 7.29). Place a pin diagonally through the construction

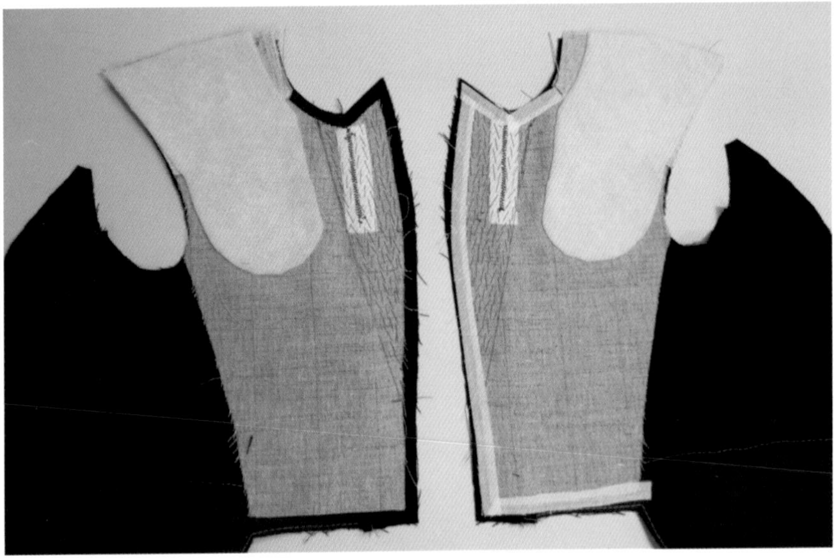

Fig. 7.27 Coat front, pad stitched and pressed lapels with (on right) edge tape fused to straddle canvas and seam allowance.

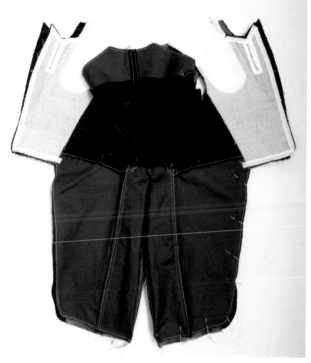

Fig. 7.29 Preparing and sewing skirt to facing and lining.

Fig. 7.28 Coat side back and skirt seams sewn together and pressed.

lines at the waist-to-skirt connection so the facing is slightly smaller; continue down the side front to the hem, fold the pleat up at the hemline and pin or tack close to the hem fold. This allows for the bulk of the pleat fabric going round the hem; without this the finished pleat will be distorted.

Sew together along the waist and down the front, stitching just outside the construction lines. At the hem sew from the side construction line to slightly outside the hemline; close to the centre back opening sew back onto the hemline.

Trim excess waist seam and side skirt seam allowances, then snip close to the corner stitch of the waist-to-side-skirt sewing line. Turn through to the right side and press. Press the hem up. Press the skirt side front and waist so that the facing cannot be seen from the outside.

**Lapel to lapel facing and front edge**
Pin the front body and lapel together (Fig. 7.30). There is ease along the outside edge of the lapel towards the top point and along the short side of the lapel point. Match the lapel band seams. Fold the seam allowance of the waist edge towards the lining.

Sew the front body to the facing, making one blunt stitch at the point of the lapel; secure close to the seams joining the contrast facing and the strip for the outside edge of the lapel.

Trim the seam allowance, especially the point of the lapel; as it is quite narrow the bulk of the seam allowances needs removing. At the dart and side of the lapel point, snip the dart open to

the sewing line and undo a few stitches along the join of the lapel edge strip to the sewing line joining the inside to the outside.

Turn through to the right side and press the front edge. Above the break line a thin strip of the lapel facing fabric should be visible from the coat front; below the break line a thin strip of the coat fabric should be visible along the edge of the inside of the coat.

Lay the coat flat with the lining uppermost and pin the lining to the coat along the waistline. On the inside, hand sew the waist seam allowance of the coat to that of the lining.

**Topstitching the hook**
Lay the coat flat with the outside of the coat uppermost and the left side of the back hook over the right back. Pin the skirt centre back opening closed with an even overlap along the length of the opening.

Sew across the top of the left hook, continuing over the centre back seam.

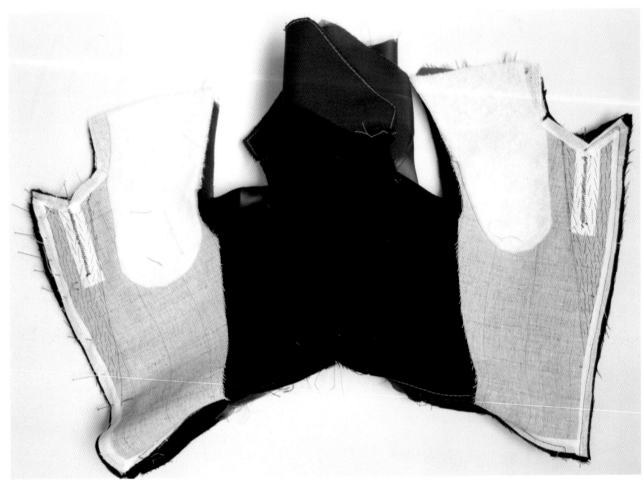

Fig. 7.30 Preparing and sewing lapel to facing and front panels.

Sewing through to the right hook, topstitch (Figs 7.32 and 7.33) by machine or use a hand stabstitch.

### Shoulder seams
Join the shoulder seams and fit the shoulder canvas using the instructions from Chapter 8 for the short jacket.

Join the lining shoulder seams. Press the seam allowance towards the back.

### Under collar
Machine pad stitch the under collar and use the instructions for the collar of the morning coat in Chapter 6 under the side heading 'Collar construction' up to pressing in the fold. (Ignore the paragraph about trimming the seam allowance.)

### Top collar to under collar
With right sides together, pin the top collar to the under collar, distributing the ease from the top collar towards the sides of the outside edge and along the sides. Pin the collars together close to the canvas at the side of the neck edge. Turn back the top collar neck edge seam allowance in line with the canvas.

Sew round the collar close to the canvas. Turn the collar to the right side and press. Pad stitch tack the top collar over the collar fold along the back neck area.

### Collar to coat
Join the under collar to the coat neckline, matching the dashed collar fold line to the break line on the neckline. The collar finishes at the body-front-to-lapel seam.

Continue by using the instructions in Chapter 6 for the morning coat under the side heading 'Closing the neckline'.

### Sleeves
Join the top sleeve to the under sleeve, sewing together along the front arm seam (Fig. 7.31). Press the front arm seam open.

Define the cuff line with a stitch line or braid. On lightweight fabrics interface the whole cuff area or the cuff line before applying the cuff line.

Sew the hind arm cuff seams together. Press the seams open.

Sew the top and under sleeve linings together along front and hind arm seams; press the seams open.

Lightly press the cuff hem allowance up along the tacked line.

With both sleeves inside out, slide the lining sleeve over the sleeve hem. Match the sleeve seams to make an opposing pair. Sew each sleeve to its lining at the cuff with a 1cm (⅜in) seam allowance.

Fuse paper-backed fusible hemming

Fig. 7.31 Top sleeves seamed to under sleeves along front seams, pressed, and cuff lines defined; hind arm seams joined and sleeve linings sewn together.

tape along the hemline between the seams, but not close to the hemline.

Sew the sleeve seam allowances together at the top of the hem.

On the hind arm seam sew the seam allowance of the sleeve to the seam allowance of the lining between the elbow and shoulder.

Remove the paper backing from the hemming tape and gently press the hem where the tape is to activate the glue. If hemming tape has not been used sew the hem up.

**Fitting the sleeves into the armholes**
Use the instructions for fitting the sleeves from Chapter 8 for the short jacket.

**Buttons and buttonholes**
Evening tailcoats of this time often had buttons arranged as if for a double-breasted style but which could not fasten, and were purely decorative.

Fig. 7.32 and 7.33 Top: Sleeve and lining sewn together at cuff, paper-backed hemming tape applied between seams along hemline and seam allowances sewn together at hem. Bottom: Hind arm seam allowance of sleeve and lining sewn together between elbow and sleeve head; hemming tape fuses hem up.

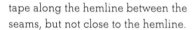

## Late Victorian Evening Dress Waistcoat

Evening waistcoats were generally made from wool if black; white or off-white waistcoats might be made in fine wool, cotton, linen or silk. Evening waistcoats could be quite decorative although the colour palette was usually restricted to self-coloured patterns or embroidery in similar shades. Buttons on black coats and vests were usually black, flat-fronted and covered with silk, either plain or patterned; white waistcoats usually had white buttons. Evening waistcoats exposed a large area of shirtfront, usually stiff and smooth.

This waistcoat has a shawl collar and a fairly short single-breasted opening with four buttons. The fabric is a white cotton damask, with a back in white twill-weave fabric. The back waist jiggers have three eyelets on each side which can be pulled in with a tape or lace.

### PIECES NEEDED

**Main fabric:**

Cut two fronts, welt pockets, collar and front facings, lower front facings.

**Back fabric:**

Cut two backs and four jigger pieces.

**Lining:**

Cut two front linings, backs, under collars (on the bias), jigger backings.

**Cotton:**

Cut two of each pocket bag.

**Lightweight synthetic knit fusible interfacing:**

Cut two each of the front and welt pocket. Cut two pocket stays.

**Non-woven sew-in interfacing:**

Cut two collar and front facings.

**Woven fusible interfacing:**

Cut two under collars and two finished welt pocket shapes.

**Stiff non-woven interfacing:**

Cut two small pieces to support the eyelet edge of the jigger.

**To finish:**

Buttons, ribbon or tape to adjust jiggers.

Fig. 7.34 Evening dress waistcoat, 1870s, front and rear views.

# Evening dress waistcoat 1870s

1 Square: 2.5cm (1") No seam allowance included

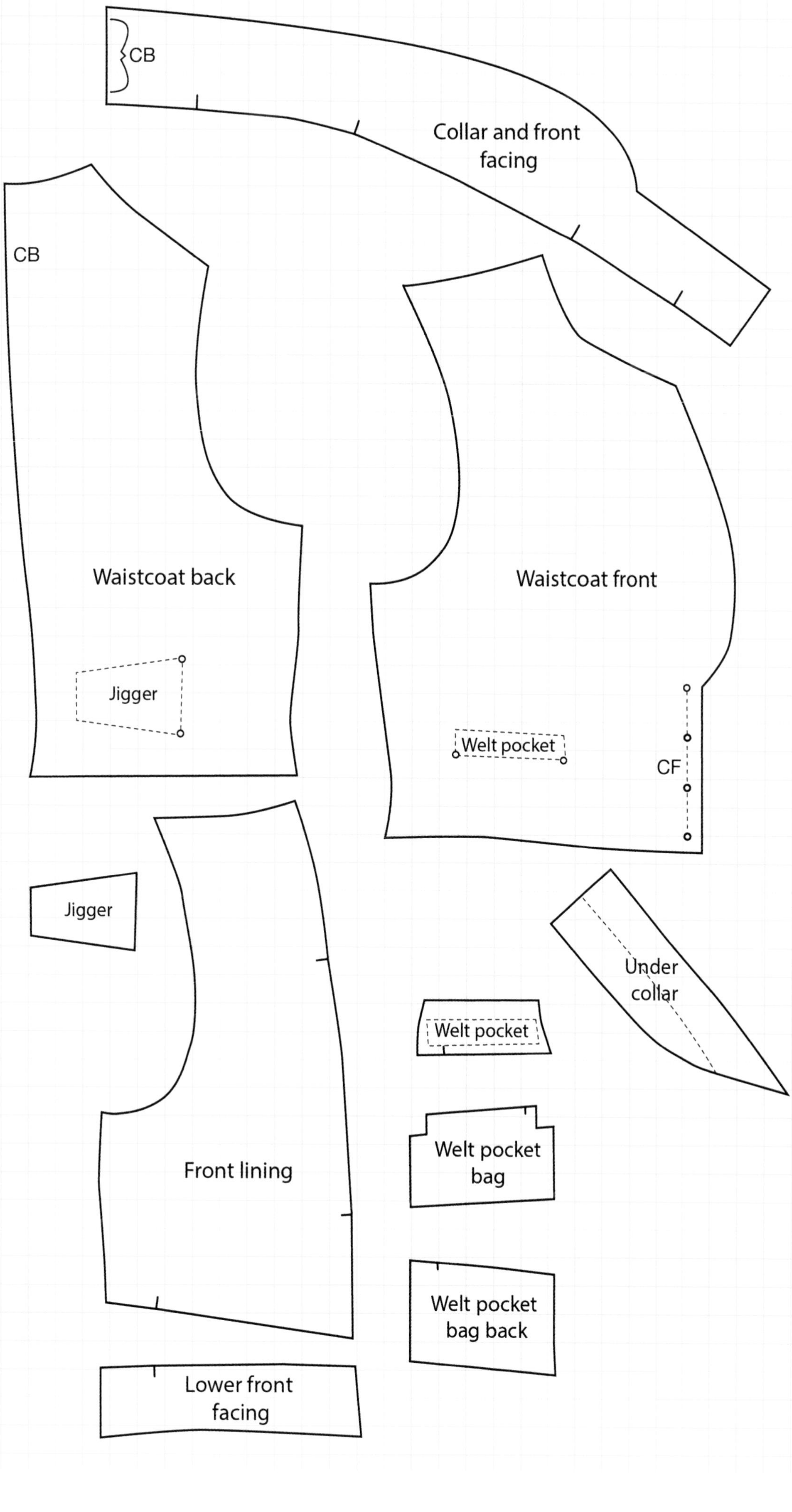

CB

Collar and front facing

CB

Waistcoat back

Jigger

Waistcoat front

Welt pocket

CF

Jigger

Front lining

Welt pocket

Under collar

Welt pocket bag

Welt pocket bag back

Lower front facing

The pieces of this waistcoat have been cut with a consistent seam allowance of 1.3cm (½in). The welt pocket pattern includes a 6mm (¼in) seam allowance.

## Marking Up and Preparation

Indicate the balance marks.

Tailor tack each side of the bottom of the welt pocket and indicate the jigger positions.

Back the front facing with the non-woven sew-in interfacing, machine tacked close to the edge of the seam allowance.

Fuse the fusible interfacing to the wrong side of the appropriate parts.

## Construction Instructions

### Welt pockets

Fit the welt pockets using the instructions in Chapter 9 for the working man's waistcoat.

### Rest of the waistcoat

Use the construction instructions in Chapter 5 for the early Victorian waistcoat with a roll collar.

There are two minor differences. This waistcoat has a machine topstitch close to the edge of the collar from the top button after the outside and inside are joined. The topstitch is continued down the front edge after the hem has been completed, helping to keep the under collar in place and adding interest.

The early Victorian waistcoat has a split from the back waist to the hem which this waistcoat does not.

### Jiggers

Machine tack the cotton backing pieces onto two jigger pieces.

Construct the jiggers using the instructions in Chapter 5 for the early Victorian waistcoat.

### Eyelets

Make three eyelet holes in the short end of each jigger. In this case the hole was made by pushing a tailor's awl into the fabric and forcing the threads apart. Hand whip stitch around the holes, pulling the sewing thread tight to keep the hole from closing up; sew round each hole twice.

Alternatively, metal eyelets could be used or a buttonhole stitch could be worked around the holes.

Attach the jiggers to the waistcoat (Fig 7.38) using the instructions in Chapter 5 for the early Victorian waistcoat.

### Buttons and buttonholes

Mark the position of the buttonholes on the wearer's left front, make the buttonholes and cut them open. Sew on the buttons.

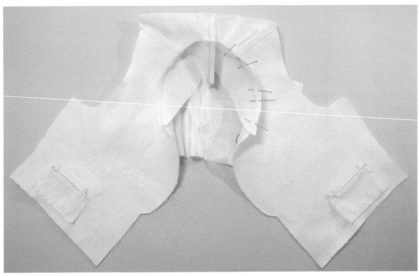

Fig. 7.35 After joining front and back at shoulders, under collar is sewn on.

Fig. 7.36 Offsetting hem allowances to make lining slightly smaller, construction line on front edge is sewn to just outside line on seam allowance. When turned to right side and pressed flat, fold should be on construction line.

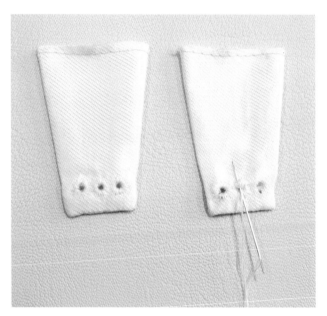

Figs 7.37 and 7.38 Above: Constituent parts of jiggers. Right: Hand sewing around eyelet hole made with awl.

Fig. 7.39 Evening dress waistcoat jiggers joined with ribbon.

### Late Victorian Evening Dress Trousers

Evening dress trousers often had a stripe down the outside leg, usually black silk satin braid, an echo of army uniform trousers. There is no stripe on these trousers; when fitting a stripe consider how to sew it to the outside leg and at what point in the pocket and side seam assembly to apply the stripe.

These evening dress trousers have a centre back waist opening above the waistline, there is no back dart and the ankle area of the pattern has some shaping.

The pattern pieces have all been cut with a 1.3cm (½in) seam allowance, except for the trouser hem which has 5cm (2in) on the back trouser legs. On the front legs at the side seam there is a 5cm (2in) cut straight across to permit turning the hem with a fish dart sewn along the hemline. The back legs have extra seam allowance at the centre back

waist, narrowing to join the seam allowance above the crotch curve. The back waist facings are cut with the

same extra centre back seam allowance as the trouser back waist, allowing for future alteration.

---

**PIECES NEEDED**

**Main fabric:**

Cut two fronts, backs (the back leg hem is 5cm (2in) and follows the hem shape), narrow pocket facings (for the front trouser legs), wide pocket facings (for the back trouser legs). Cut two opposing fly pieces.

**Woven cotton:**

Cut two pocket bags, front waist and back waist facings. Cut three fly linings.

**Interfacing:**

As the fabric for these trousers is relatively light, some extra support has been provided by a fusible lightweight synthetic knit interfacing. Interface the trouser back and front waist area, the two fabric fly pieces and the left front fly area of the trousers.

**To finish:**

Buttons.

Fig. 7.40 Evening dress trousers, front view and back waist detail.

# Evening dress trousers 1870s

1 Square: 2.5cm (1") No seam allowance included

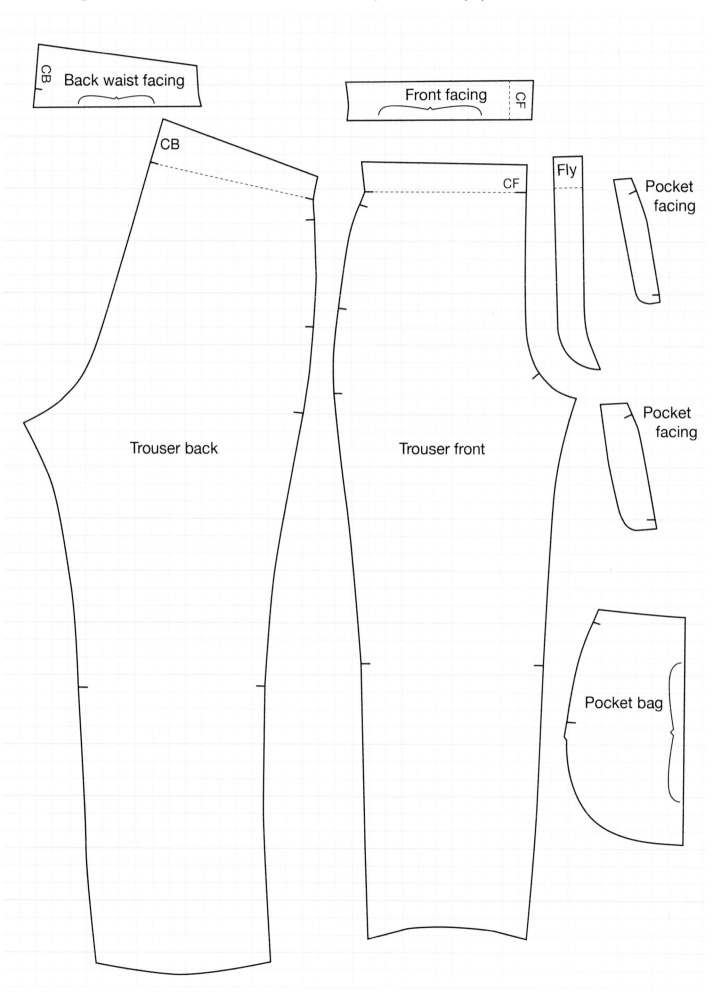

CB
Back waist facing

CB

Front facing
CF

CF

Fly

Pocket facing

Pocket facing

Trouser back

Trouser front

Pocket bag

## Marking Up and Preparation

Tack the hemline and waistline. Indicate the balance marks.

Tailor tack to indicate the top of the centre back seam and bottom of the back waist opening; this mark is particularly important because of the larger seam allowance at the back waist.

Fuse the interfacing along the front and back waist areas; each edge of the waist interfacing will be secured in place with the construction sewing.

Fuse a fly-shaped piece of the interfacing into the inside of the left front fly area. Fuse interfacing onto the wrong side of the two fly pieces cut from fabric.

## Construction Instructions

### Finishing the seam allowances

Finish off the cut edges of the seam allowances; whenever possible it is easier to finish these edges before they are sewn together. Finish the inside and outside legs and crotch seam allowances; the front crotch finishing does not need to go much beyond the fly balance mark as it will be covered or finished with the fly. Trim the curved crotch seam allowances down to 1.3cm (½in) or less before finishing the seam. Finish off the long curved seam of the pocket facings.

### Pockets and side seams

Use the pocket fitting instructions in Chapter 5 for the 1840s trousers.

The trouser pockets and side seams in Chapter 5 are finished off with a binding; for these evening trousers a machine zigzag is used to finish the pocket side seam allowances.

Continue assembling the trousers using the directions in Chapter 8 for the 1890s trousers but with the following variations. Also note that the centre back waist opening detail provides the main difference in construction.

### Joining the two legs

Pin the two legs together along the crotch line. At the bottom of the centre front fly opening, match the angle on the left front and the balance mark. Sew the two legs together, starting at the corner of the right angle and continuing along the crotch seam, following the construction line, to the centre back tailor tack which marks the top of the centre back seam and bottom of the back waist opening.

Pin the button stand over the bottom of the fly opening. Sew back along the crotch seam starting at the centre back tailor tacks. Continue sewing over the stitches at the bottom of the hook through to meet the stitches joining the centre front and button stand.

### Back waist opening

With right sides together, sew the

Figs 7.41, 7.42 and 7.43 Top and centre: Centre back waist and waist facing bagged out along centre back waist from tailor tack marking bottom of opening. Bottom: Waist turned to right side with facing seam allowance folded in and pinned.

centre back waist of the trouser to the waist facing, sewing from the tailor tack at right angles to the edge of the waistband.

Turn through to the right side and fold the facing seam allowance under the facing. Lightly press the back waist opening and press the centre back seam open.

For this pair of trousers, the facing is pinned to the trouser to secure. To mark the waistband pins are placed following the edge of the waist facing. On the right side the pin line is marked with chalk, the waistline pins removed and the line checked and straightened.

Topstitch along the marked waistline (Fig. 7.44).

### Hem

Hem the trousers using the instructions in Chapter 8 for the 1890s trousers.

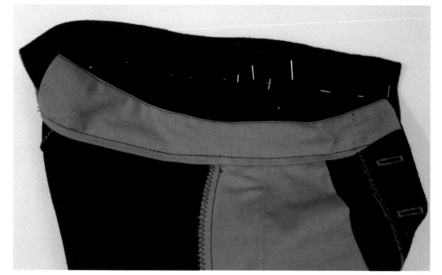

Fig. 7.44 Waistline of trousers sewn through to the waist facing.

# Chapter 8
# The Suit with Short Jacket

*The short jacket came about partly because of the advances in railway travel that reduced the need to travel by horse. A less demanding type of clothing was needed for informal occasions, so the short jacket, devised to aid movement, started to be worn for leisure or in the countryside in the 1850s (Willett and Cunningham, 1992). 'The Tweedside' was an early and popular short jacket. As with all Victorian garments the silhouettes and names varied, ultimately becoming the 'lounge jacket'; other names included the 'ditto suit' and the 'sack suit'.*

## Late Victorian Short Jacket, 1890s

Although the individual pieces of men's outfits had intermittently all been made from the same fabric, it is this style of short jacket, trousers and waistcoat that are recognizable as a suit.

Jackets frequently had topstitching or stabstitching details which can provide an interesting feature and control the facing and lapel.

The collar construction method for this jacket uses a method similar to that in traditional tailoring; this is straightforward, effective and neat. It can be used for any of the coat collars in this book, but requires an extra seam allowance adding onto the sides of the collar.

Seam allowances vary: check the suggested seam allowances in the pieces needed box.

### Marking Up and Preparation

Apply the fusible interfacings to the wrong side of the fabric: at the hem straddling the hemline and on the sleeves, cuff hem, button stand and top sleeve head.

Mark all construction lines onto the wrong side of the pieces on top of the fusible interfacing.

Tack mark the neckline and top of the lapel; tack the front, hem and armholes; on the sleeves tack the cuff hem and armholes.

Mark on the collar canvas the centre back seam and the neck fold line.

Mark the dart and pocket positions with tailor tacks.

On this jacket the front and back lining have the construction lines marked onto them with dressmaker's carbon paper.

### Construction Instructions
#### Side front darts
Sew closed the side front dart. Cut the dart open as far as is possible. Press the dart open.

#### Welt pocket
Fuse a stay over the welt pocket position on the left front.

Fit the welt pocket following the instructions for the working man's waistcoat in Chapter 9.

#### Jetted pocket with pocket flap
Jetted pockets are also known as bound or double piped pockets.

Jetted pockets with flaps nearly always come as pairs although some

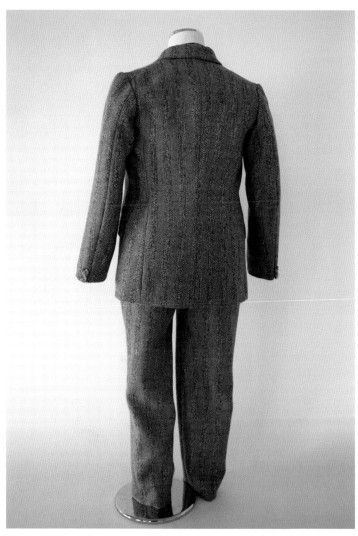

Fig. 8.2
Short jacket
with
trousers,
rear view.

Left: Fig. 8.1 Short jacket, waistcoat and trousers, 1890s.

**Main fabric:**

Cut two fronts, backs, top sleeves, under sleeves, front facings, pocket flaps (cut with a small seam allowance around the sides and bottom and 2.5cm (1in) at the top), pocket blinds, under collars cut on the bias (under collars are often cut from a wool Melton).

Cut one top collar on the straight grain with an extra-long seam allowance of 2.5cm (1in) allowed at each side of the collar at the collar notch, a welt pocket for the left front breast. Cut two narrow and two wide pocket jettings.

The main fabric seam allowances are 1.3cm (½in), the hem of the coat has been cut with a 5cm (2in) hem and the sleeves have been cut with a 4cm (1½ in) hem at the cuff.

**Lining:**

Cut two fronts, pocket flaps cut the same as the main fabric. Cut one back lining on the fold.

**Striped sleeve lining:**

Cut two top sleeves and two under sleeves, omitting the cuff button stands on both.

All the linings have been cut without hem allowance; the rest of the seams have been cut with a consistent 1.3cm (½in) seam

allowance, as noted above.

**Woven pocketing:**

Cut two jetted pocket bags and one of each pocket bag piece for the welt pocket.

**Hair canvas:**

Cut two fronts with no seam allowance except the shoulder, which has 2.5cm (1in); the neckline has a short area of seam allowance towards the shoulder and on the armhole.

**Collar canvas:**

Cut two under collars on the bias with no seam allowance except for a centre back join.

**Lightweight fusible interfacing:**

Needed for the hem of the coat, on the sleeve cuffs and around the cuff opening button stand; a strip is fused along the top sleeve head and at the back neck and shoulders.

**Woven fusible interfacing:**

Used for the pockets stays, the pocket flaps and welt pocket, all cut without seam allowance.

**To finish:**

Buttons.

opening. Fuse the interfacing (cut without seam allowance) onto the wrong side of the pocket flap. Tack a line to indicate the top of the pocket flap.

Cut the pocket flap and lining exactly the same size as each other.

**Offsetting the seams**

With right sides together, pin the centre bottom of the flap and lining together. Place the pins at right angles to the stitch line with the pin head towards the outside and the point towards the centre of the flap. On each side seam move the fabric back towards the centre pin exposing the lining by about 6mm (¼in); pin diagonally through the corners to hold, then distribute the fullness from the top fabric between the pins and secure.

Offset and tighten the side seam of the lining. Move the fabric down from the top edge, exposing the lining by a little less than at the sides. Pin at the top of the interfacing on the tack line and distribute the fullness along the side of the pocket flap.

**Joining the fabric and lining**

Sew the sides and bottom of the pocket flap by machining 3mm (⅛in) beside the interfacing, blunting the corner by sewing one stitch at a 45-degree angle across the corner. When making two flaps check that they are identical after sewing.

Turn the pocket flap through to the right side and press carefully. The top fabric should be visible around the lining; the lining should not be visible from the right side of the flap (Fig. 8.3).

Victorian and, indeed, more modern jackets and coats occasionally have three jetted pockets with flaps; the third pocket is often a smaller pocket set above the right front pocket.

After making a sample pocket prepare all the parts required for the pockets in order to work on both pockets at the same time.

Assemble the pieces needed to make the pockets: jettings and blind, pocket flaps, pocket flap linings and woven

interfacing and pocket bags

A tailor tack marks each end of the pocket opening; on the inside cover the pocket area with a fusible stay.

On the right side join the pocket tailor tacks with a straight chalk line, indicate the tailor tacked ends with right angle chalk mark.

**Pocket flap**

These need to be made first; they need to be slightly wider than the pocket

**Preparing the pocket opening**

Check the size of the pocket flap compared with the distance between the tailor tacks for the pocket opening; the pocket flap must be slightly larger than the opening by up to 6mm (¼in); re-mark the outside of the pocket accordingly (Fig. 8.4).

**Jettings**

The 5cm (2in) deep jetting is for the lower opening and the 4cm (1½in)

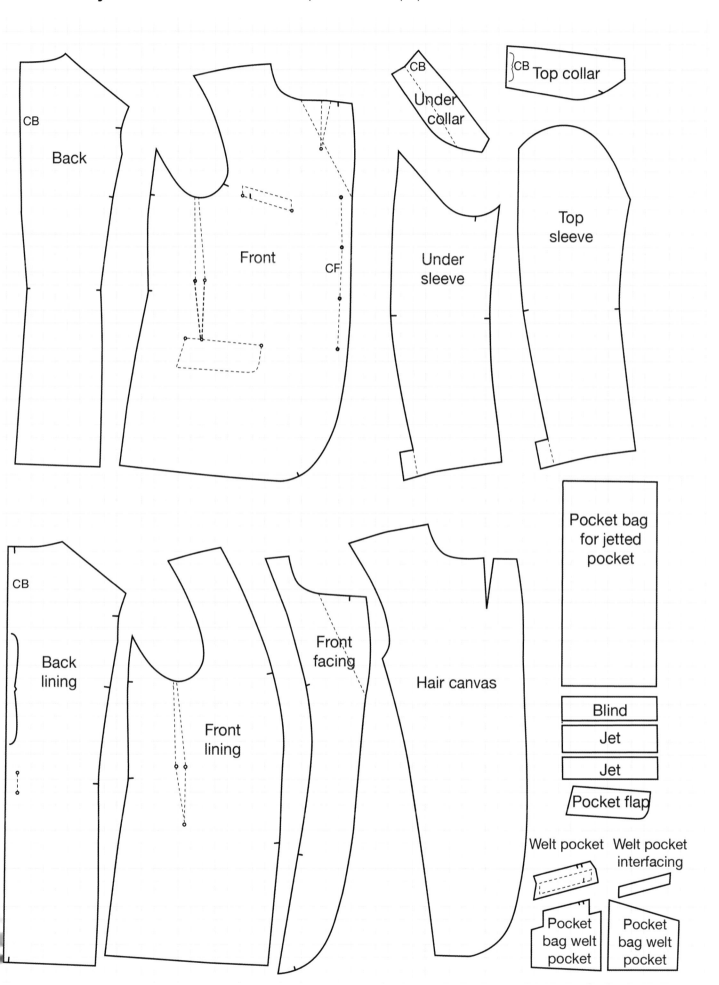

**Short jacket 1890s**    1 Square: 2.5cm (1") No seam allowance included

CB

Back

CB

Front

CF

CB
Under collar

CB Top collar

Under sleeve

Top sleeve

CB

Back lining

Front lining

Front facing

Hair canvas

Pocket bag for jetted pocket

Blind

Jet

Jet

Pocket flap

Welt pocket    Welt pocket interfacing

Pocket bag welt pocket    Pocket bag welt pocket

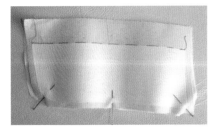

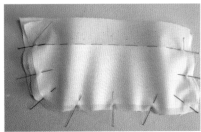

Fig. 8.3 *Pocket flap construction stages: Pinning, offsetting seams, joining, turning and pressing.*

jetting is for the top.

Lay a jetting with right sides together to the marked opening. Sew along the jetting, sewing 6mm (¼in) from the chalked line and edge of the jetting; secure each end in line with the tailor tack.

Place the other jetting just touching the sewn jetting, over the top of the marked opening. Mark the end of the stitch lines with a pin. Sew with the stitch lines parallel, starting and

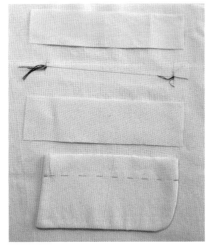

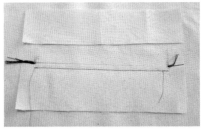

Fig. 8.4 *Constructing pocket opening: Stay fused behind pocket opening; tailor tacks marked and joined with straight line; jetting sewn at each side of line; cut made between sewn lines and to last stitches.*

finishing exactly opposite the tailor tack.

### Cutting the opening

On the inside of the garment cut between the two lines of sewing stopping about 1cm (⅜in) from each end (Fig. 8.5). From the centre cut, cut to within a thread of the ends of each sewing line to make a triangle.

Depending on the resilience of your fabric, press the seams of the jetting and garment open, or just wrap the jetting around its seam allowance. Pin through the stitch line at right angles to the jetting to hold.

Ditch stitch along the join between the jetting and garment; this can be done by hand or by machine.

Push the jetting seam allowance to the inside of the pocket.

### Securing the sides of the pocket opening

With the right side of the opening uppermost, fold back one side of the garment so that the sides of the jettings and the cut triangle can be seen. Sew over the triangle and jettings close to the fold and widest part of the triangle.

### Pocket bag

Sew the pocket bag onto the lower jetting seam allowance.

### Blind

Finish off the seam allowance of one long seam of the blind; for this example the seam allowance has been pressed under (Fig. 8.6). On the inside of the pocket lay the right side of the blind over the pocket opening with the finished edge towards the bottom of the pocket.

Take the free end of the pocket bag, bring it to the top of the pocket covering the blind and jettings. The bottom of the pocket bag should finish at least 2cm (¾in) above the hem. Pin the pocket bag to the blind and sew the blind to the pocket bag along the finished bottom edge of the blind.

### Fitting the pocket flap

Place the pocket flap into the pocket opening with the tacked line level with the bottom jetting. Pin or tack the flap in place. With the fold of the outside of the pocket uppermost, pull back the top of the garment to expose the jetting and the flap seam allowances. Sew along the seam allowance through the jetting and pocket flap.

### Finishing off the pocket bag

Place the pocket bag with the blind over the pocket opening, pin the sides of the pocket bag. With right side of

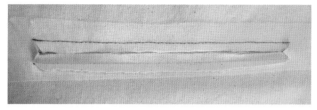

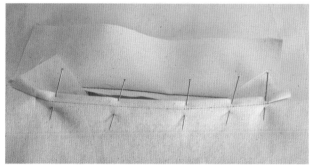

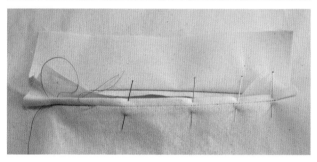

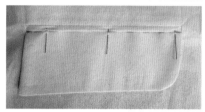

Fig. 8.5 *Jettings:* Open seam between jetting and pocket opening; jetting fabric wrapped around jetting seam allowance; ditch stitching between jetting and garment; jetting seam allowance taken to inside of pocket; jettings secured and triangle made inside pocket opening.

Fig. 8.6 *Fitting blind and pocket flap.* Top: Right side of blind placed over inside of pocket opening and blind sewn onto pocket bag. Centre: flap placed into pocket opening. Bottom: flap pinned in place and sewn to seam allowances.

the garment uppermost, fold back the garment until the side of the pocket is exposed, sew down the side of the bag, then repeat the process for the bottom and the other side. This method keeps the pocket flat as it is sewn.

Close the top of the pocket in the same way, sewing close to the sewing line used to attach the pocket flap.

## Lapel dart
Start on the main part of the garment by sewing closed the lapel dart on the jacket front. Cut the dart open as far as possible and press it open.

Cut the darts out of the canvas, cutting along the construction lines, leaving a V-shaped void. Close the sides of the V by fusing a strip of fusible interfacing over the join. Machine sew a zigzag stitch straddling the fused join.

## Canvassing the front of the jacket
Lay the canvas onto the inside of the jacket front, matching up the darts and lining up the edge of the canvas with the front edge and hem tack line. Pin the dart centres together and put a couple of pins down the front to hold the canvas in place during the next step. Turn the jacket front over.

Carefully take out the pins holding the canvas to the front but leaving in the dart pins.

Gently smooth the fabric over the canvas, working down from the pinned dart.

## Pad stitch tacking the front to the canvas
Starting about 5cm (2in) below the shoulder seam, work down the centre front. Do not sew beyond the break line onto the lapel. At the bottom work back towards the top. When nearing the shoulder turn and continue pad stitching back down the jacket side front close to the edge of the canvas but do not sew through the jetted pocket or pocket bag. Make a double back stitch to start and finish sewing.

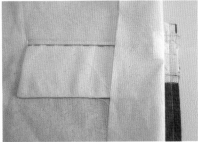

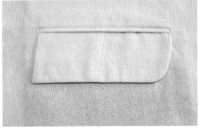

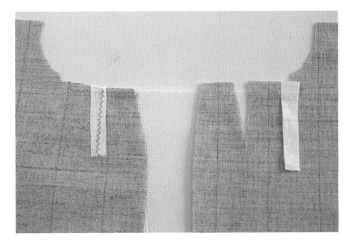

Fig. 8.7 *Finishing off jetted pocket:* Pocket flap placed with blind over pocket opening; sides of pocket bag sewn; top of pocket bag closed.

Figs 8.8, 8.9, 8.10 *Lapel dart and canvassing front.* Top: Close lapel dart with fusible interfacing and zigzag sewing. Centre: Pad stitch canvas to inside of jacket. Bottom: Pocket shapes cut out of canvas, canvas fitted round jetted pockets and secured with herringbone stitch.

### Fitting the canvas around the lower pockets

Cut out a rectangle of canvas slightly larger and corresponding to the opening of the pocket. Fit the canvas around the pocket jettings. Herringbone stitch the pocket jetting seam allowance to the canvas; under the pocket catch the canvas to the stay supporting the pocket opening.

### Mark and tack the break line

On the outside of the jacket chalk a straight line joining the top and bottom of the break line. Tack the fabric to the canvas along the break line.

### Pad stitching the lapel

Pad stitch the lapel using the instructions in Chapter 6 for the morning dress frock coat.

Press the lapel area flat.

### Joining the canvas to the jacket front edge

With the canvas side up, check the edge of the canvas is close to the front edge construction line but does not cover it. Trim off any canvas that covers the tack line from before the collar notch on the neck edge, around the

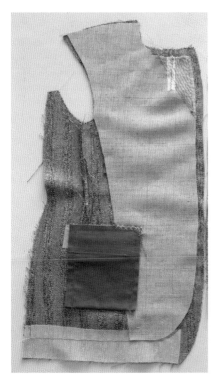 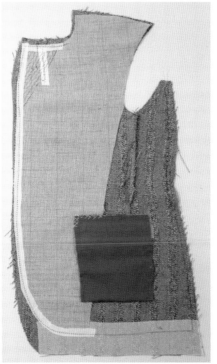

Fig. 8.11 *Jacket fronts*. L: Lapel pad stitched. R: Lapel pressed, edge tape applied and construction line marked onto tape.

tack line and balance marks through onto the edge tape.

## Constructing the body of the jacket

Sew the backs together along the centre back. Press the centre back seam open.

Sew the side front to the side back. Press the seam open.

## Constructing the lining and front facing

Sew the front lining side darts closed. Press the darts towards the back.

Sew the front facing to the front lining. Press the seam allowances towards the lining.

## PLEAT IN THE CENTRE BACK BODY LINING

Incorporating a pleat or some fullness into the back lining is important because the outer fabric often has a small amount of stretch whereas most lining fabrics have no 'give' or elasticity in them. The pleat allows for flexing of the back and shoulders but prevents the back lining seam from splitting as less stress is put on the seams joining the linings of back and sleeve.

lapel down the front and around the curved edge of the edge of the canvas.

Starting at the seam allowance on the neck of the canvas, fuse an edge tape half on the canvas and straddling the front of the jacket seam allowance with its centre on the construction line. Bond the stay tape along the top of the lapel and along the front lapel over the break line, continuing along the front

edge and around the bottom curve, finishing just past the end of the canvas on the hem. An edge tape can also be hand sewn (see information in the Glossary).

## Mark the front edge through onto the edge tape

Using a tracing wheel and dressmaker's carbon paper, mark the

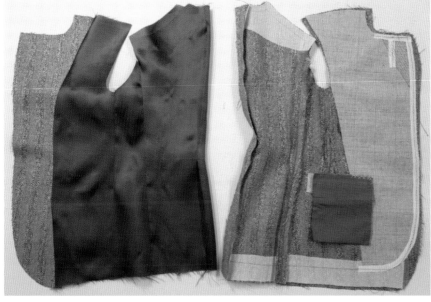 

Fig. 8.12 Constructed inside and outside parts of jacket joined together from collar notch through fronts and hem.

### Centre back lining pleat

Sew centre back seam and the pleat at the neck, waist and seat line of the back lining. Press the fabric to one side between the sewn areas to form the pleat.

Sew the lining side back seam to the side front seam. Press the seams open.

### Joining the outside of the jacket to the lining and facing

With right sides together carefully match construction lines and balance marks. From the collar notch on the jacket and facing, match the corner of the lapel on both layers and pin through the corner at an angle. Ease has been included on the front facing lapel from the collar notch around the lapel; this allows the lapel to roll back over the front of the jacket without pulling the underside of the lapel into view. Join the lapels together to the break line and down the front to the end of the lower front curve.

Where lining and facing join on the lower front curve, the seam has to be manipulated slightly to line up the hem of the jacket and lining.

Machine the jacket to the facing and lining, starting and securing at one of the collar notch balance marks. Sew to the outside corner of the lapel; at the corner make one blunt stitch at an angle over the corner, then continue sewing down the lapel and front of the jacket following the construction lines. At the balance mark at the bottom of the front curve sew across the facing and jacket to the hem allowance to the coat and lining hem. Using a 1cm ($^3$/8in) seam allowance, continue sewing around the jacket and finish securely at the other collar notch balance point.

Trim off or grade the excess seam allowance from the front facing area. A snip can be made close to the collar notch sewing on the jacket front seam allowance only; do not snip into the facing seam allowance.

Fuse paper-backed hemming tape to the jacket hem between the seam allowances. Do not fuse the tape over the seam allowances or apply the hemming tape close to the hemline.

### Turning the jacket through

Turn the jacket through to the right side. Press open as much of the facing seam allowance as is possible. Ideally, press the lapel area from what will be the jacket side and the rest of the front edge on the facing side; make a thin strip of facing visible along the edge of the lapel and a thin strip of the jacket visible from the facing side below the break line. The most difficult area to press is the conjunction of lapel and front edge at the break line because above the break line the facing is seen on the outside and below it the facing must not be seen.

Lightly press the hem.

Between the edge of the lower front curve and the edge of the facing, lay the front flat and press. A fold is created on the facing towards the hem; hand sew the fold to the jacket hem.

If a paper-backed hemming tape is not being used pin the hem up and sew up the hem on the inside of the jacket and lining, making sure the stitches do not show on the outside of the jacket.

Sew the seam allowance together along the hem. Remove the paper backing from the hemming tape and press lightly along the hemline to activate the glue.

Fig. 8.13 Jacket and lining sewn together, trimmed along front edge and paper-backed hemming tape fused along hem.

Fig. 8.14 Jacket turned through to right side and pressed. At curve between bottom of facing and hem, with the outside flat, manipulate to create a pleasing join between facing and hems.

### Shoulder seam

Sew the front and back shoulder seams together without the canvas, dividing the ease from the back shoulder along the length of the front shoulder seam, Press the shoulder seams open.

Smooth the canvas over the joined shoulder seam. With the jacket the right way round ensure the canvas follows the shape of the shoulder. From the outside pin through the shoulder seam to the canvas. Sew the canvas to the back shoulder seam allowance by hand or machine.

Check the fabric is resting smoothly over the canvas and tack fabric to the canvas around the armhole.

With the whole neck area of the jacket lying flat tack the necklines together and shoulder seam allowance in place.

### Making the under collar

Overlap and sew the centre back seams on the under collar canvas with the construction lines matching.

Sew the under collars together at the centre back neck. Trim down the seam allowance and press the seam open.

Lay the collar canvas onto the inside of the under collar, matching up the centre back seams; there should be an even seam allowance of fabric visible around the edge of the canvas.

Tack the canvas to the collar along the marked fold line.

### Pad stitching the collar canvas to the under collar

Pad stitch along the fold line and continue pad stitching parallel to the neck fold, filling in the neck/collar stand area with lines of pad stitching. Starting at the centre back seam, pad stitch parallel to the centre back seam above the collar fold. Close to the side of the collar change the direction of pad stitching so that the sewing runs parallel to the short end of the collar for a few lines.

Press the under collar flat. Press in the marked fold line.

### Joining the top collar to the under collar

Match up the centre backs of the under collar and top collar on the outside edge, pin and match the two layers evenly to about two thirds of the way along the collar from the centre back, pinning at right angles to the construction line. On the remaining third of the collar create some ease by sliding the top fabric back towards the centre back by about 6mm (¼in) to 1.3cm (½in) depending on the fabric being used; distribute the fullness evenly over the last third of the collar.

There are no marked construction lines on the top collar because the collar canvas on the under collar is used to indicate the construction lines. The top collar is a little deeper than the under collar to allow for the extra length of fabric needed to go over the collar fold. The sides of the top collar have a generous seam allowance to finish the collar similar to a traditional tailored collar.

Sew the collar layers together, machining close to the canvas along the outside edge.

Trim down the seam allowance. Press the seam allowance open, turn to the right side and press from the underside with an even narrow strip of the top collar visible.

### Joining the collar to the jacket neckline

Using the neck edge of the collar canvas as the construction line, match the under collar to the neckline, pairing the collar notch balance mark and canvas side.

Sew the collar to the jacket, securing the ends. Do not stitch beyond the collar notch balance marks. Check the shoulder seam allowances fit neatly into the neck curve.

Trim the seam allowance along the neck curve; the front canvas can be trimmed back close to the sewing line. Press the seam allowance towards the collar.

Machine a large zigzag stitch along the neck edge of the collar through to the seam allowances, sewing as far onto the lapel as is easily possible.

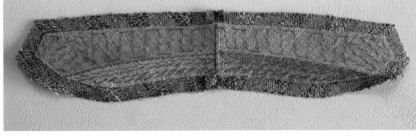

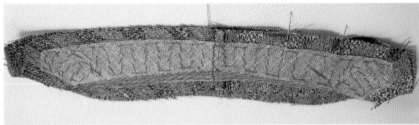

Fig. 8.15 *Collar construction.* Top: Collar canvas pad stitched to under collar. Centre: Top collar sewn to under collar with ease in top collar. Bottom: Collar turned through to right side and pressed with thin strip of top collar visible from underside.

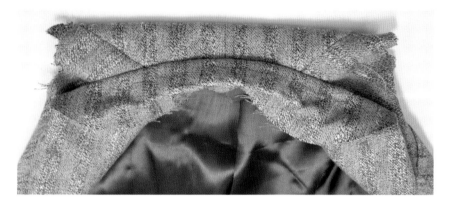

Figs 8.16, 8.17 and 8.18 Top: Top collar fabric tacked to under collar and facing fabric tacked to lapel. Centre: Seam allowances folded under along gorge line. Bottom: Collar and lapel are sewn together with ladder stitch.

Alternatively, for a more authentic look, herringbone stitch along the edge of the under collar. See the frock coat collar in Chapter 5.

Tack the top collar fabric to the under collar along the outside edge of the collar with a pad stitch (Fig. 8.15).

Pad stitch tack the top collar along the neck fold of the collar, starting and finishing the tacking about 4cm (1½in) from the gorge line, leaving enough space to fold the collar seam allowance under. Ultimately the top collar fabric must lie smoothly over the under collar.

## Joining the lining shoulder seams
Sew the front and back shoulder seams together. Press the seam allowance towards the back.

## Tacking the front facing to the lapel
The front facing fabric must lie smoothly, with the lapel rolled over at the break line. Tack along the break line but do not tack all the way to the gorge line; leave enough room to turn the facing seam allowance under.

## Joining the top collar to the lapel along the gorge
Fold the seam allowance of the lapel and collar under and pin with the folder edges of collar and lapel seams just touching, continuing past the break line by about 2cm (¾in) (Figs 8.19–8.21).

Ladder stitch the collar to the lapel along the gorge line, starting at the balance mark for the collar notch and continuing to beyond the break line. From a point about 2cm (¾in) after the break line, sew the collar to the neck to collar seam allowance and backstitch along the join.

From the edge of the ladder stitching, turn the lining seam allowance under. Check that the centre back lining is not tight and pulling or distorting the hem. Sew the lining over the top of the collar backstitching holding the top collar to the neck line.

## Finishing the collar notch
At the collar notch at the sides of the collar, fold back the excess fabric along the edge of the collar canvas. Pin the

Figs 8.16, 8.17 and 8.18 Top: Lining neck edge seam allowance turned under. Centre: Seam allowance is sewn to cover sewing holding top collar to neckline. Bottom: Collar notch side seam allowance folded under along collar canvas edge and herringbone stitched to under collar.

Fig. 8.22 Finished and lightly pressed collar with tacking threads still in place.

excess fabric in place, checking both sides of the collar look the same. Sew the raw edge to the underside of the collar with a herringbone stitch.

### Pressing the collar and lapel

With all the tacking still in place give the collar and lapels a gentle press, firming in the break line and collar fold (Fig. 8.22). Not all fabric is suitable for pressing with tacking in; some fabrics will retain impressions of the tacking stitches.

### Sleeves

Make a reinforcing triangle on the under sleeve back seam, with the point of the triangle touching the intersection of the back arm construction seam line and the right angle at the top of the button stand.

Join the front seam of the top sleeve and undersleeve. Press the seam open.

### Cuff opening

Making the top sleeve cuff opening mitred seam between the opening seam allowance and hem (Figs 8.23–8.25).

With right sides together, fold from the hem and hind arm seam intersection, join the edge of the hem and edge of the button stand seam allowance.

The sleeve pattern can be used to mark the correct angle; place the bottom of the sleeve pattern along the fold with the hind arm seam of the pattern to the folded intersection of cuff and back seam on the sleeve; mark the pattern's back seam line on the fabric.

Sew from the intersection of the seams to the edge of the hem and edge of the button stand seam allowance; the line should be approximately at right angles to the fold.

Fold the corner through to the right side and check the hem and button stand back seam line will be on the fold when the sleeve is lying flat.

With right sides together and folded along the hemline, bag out the edge of the button stand extension to the hem. Turn through to the right side.

### Cuff hem

Press the sleeve hem edge and button

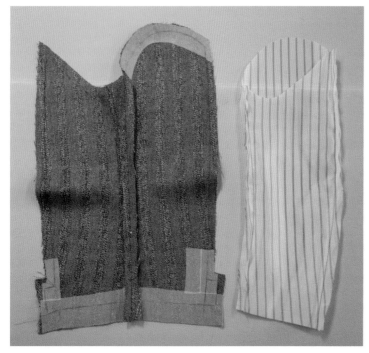

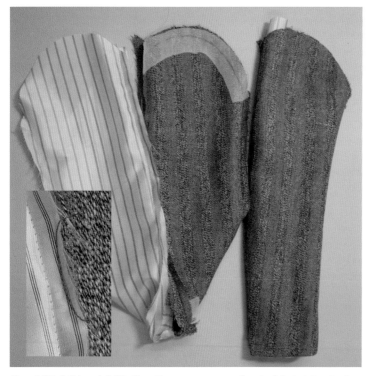

Figs 8.23, 8.24 and 8.25 Top: Front arm seams of main fabric joined, also top and under sleeves of lining. Centre: Top sleeve cuff opening finished with mitred corner and button stand bagged out. Bottom: Seam allowances of hind arm seams joined.

stand lightly.

Apply fusible paper-backed hemming tape to the hem between the seam allowances; do not fuse it close to the hemline as this would create a hard line. Leave the backing paper on.

Sew the front arm seam allowances together at the hem fold.

The hemming tape and sewn seam allowance, in combination with the button stand, are quick and easy methods to keep the cuff hem up. The cuffs could be hand hemmed after the lining has been attached.

### Buttonholes for the cuff buttons

This jacket has only two cuff buttons. The cuff buttonholes are not essential. The buttonholes do not need to work and often they are not obvious because the button covers most of the buttonhole. The buttons can be sewn through the cuff opening to give the impression of working buttons. Alternatively, buttonholes can be sewn but do not need to be cut open; if they are not cut open, the stitches can be removed in future alterations. Some cuffs did not have an opening or buttons at all.

Where practical, hand-worked functioning buttonholes on a jacket cuff are an elegant detail.
Mark and make the buttonholes. Ensure they are not too close to the top of the button stand as this will make sewing the back seam closed difficult.

### Closing the hind arm seam

Snip to the point of the reinforcing triangle.

Sew the hind arm seams of the top and under sleeves together to the top of the cuff opening. Press the seam open. The snipped open triangle will let the undersleeve button stand lie over the cuff opening. Pin or tack the cuff opening closed.

### Sleeve linings

Sew the top sleeve lining to the under sleeve lining. Press the seams open.

### Joining the sleeve lining to the sleeve

With the sleeves and sleeve linings

inside out, slip a sleeve lining cuff over the sleeve cuff, matching up the seam allowances.

Machine the lining to the edge of the cuff hem using a 1cm (⅜in) seam allowance. Sew around the cuff, sewing as close to the button stand as possible, and hand sew the remaining lining to the hem.

### Joining the seam allowance of the hind arm seams

On the hind arm seam between the armhole and the elbow, join the seam allowances of the fabric and lining with a few hand or machine stitches. This is to stop the lining from falling down the sleeve should the hand-sewn armhole finishing come undone.

Take the paper backing off the hemming tape. Press the hem lightly to activate the glue and fuse the hem up or hand-sew the cuff hems up at this stage.

### Buttons

Sew on the cuffbuttons to the button stand or through all the layers of the cuff opening.

### Fitting the sleeves

Pin in one sleeve matching the construction lines and balance marks and distributing the ease in the sleeve head area over the shoulder and towards the back of the sleeve. Pin in line with and through both construction lines.

### Easing in the sleeve head

How much ease can be distributed along the sleeve head depends on the fabric. Wool has a lot of movement in it and much of the 5cm (2in) can be eased away. Other fabrics may need to have less ease; for example, some cotton weaves, silks and synthetics do not have much flexibility and consequently need to have less ease. Too much ease will result in tucks or a gathered look around the sleeve head.

When one sleeve is pinned in place, check it is hanging properly. The sleeve should hang down and be angled slightly forward in a natural relaxed arm position.

Check the arm position on a tailor's dummy or on a coat hanger with wide formed shoulders or support the shoulder over an out-stretched hand with fingers spread wide and palm facing downwards. Look at the sleeve and ask yourself if the hang or angle of the sleeve looks natural. If it is not, decide what needs to be changed. Alter the pinning until the arm position is right. The whole sleeve may not need to come out; sometimes moving the ease around can have a significant effect.

When the first sleeve is pinned in satisfactorily, pin in the other sleeve and check that they are hanging the same way before sewing.

Sew both sleeves in following the construction lines. Sew from the sleeve side, checking the sewing carefully for small tucks and that the construction lines have stayed in line during sewing. Sewing sleeves in can be fiddly; take your time and do not be afraid of

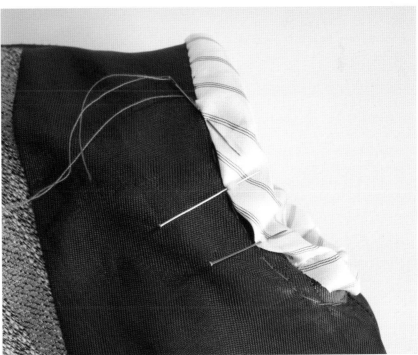

Figs 8.26 and 8.27 Top: After checking sleeve 'hang', sleeve double-sewn into jacket and excess seam allowance trimmed. Bottom: Lining positioned round armhole and backstitched in place (pink thread); sleeve lining positioned and sewn over backstitch (slip stitch at top of picture).

unpicking a few stitches or more and resewing where necessary.

When both the sleeves have been sewn into the jacket and you have checked that both sides look the same, sew a second line of sewing up to 6mm (¼in) away from the first.

Trim down the seam allowance close to the second stitch line. It is important not to have too much excess seam allowance around the armhole, particularly under the arm.

### Sleeve head roll

This is a strip of felt that pads out the sleeve head area of the sleeve; it runs from just above the front arm seam to just past the hind arm seam. Try different thicknesses of roll to suit the garment fabric.

Make the sleeve head roll from a wool or felt-type fabric, cutting it 2.5cm (1in) wide and slightly longer than the sleeve head area, rounding off the ends of the strip. Place the sleeve head roll along the sleeve head with the centre over the sleeve construction line, then back stitch it to the sleeve head, sewing close to the armhole sewing line.

### Shoulder pads

Although shoulder pads were not a commonly used element in Victorian tailoring, for costume purposes they may be used to supplement the performer's shape or suggest characteristics.

If the jacket has been fitted with shoulder pads sew them in now, pinning the pad centrally to the top of the shoulder with the straight edge of the pad to the seam allowance. Sew the pad along the seam allowance with a large buttonhole stitch.

### Joining the lining to the armhole

Pin the lining to the armhole, matching up the shoulder seams and the underarm dart.

Check that attaching the lining to the jacket armhole has not caused any tightness across the front with the lapel folded over on the break line, or between the underarm and the hem; the lining must be loose or it will distort the jacket.

Sew the lining to the armhole. Back stitch by hand between the two rows of machine sewing holding the sleeve in.

### Sewing the sleeve lining to the inside of the jacket

With the inside of the jacket armhole turned to the outside, pin the sleeve lining in around the armhole, turning under a small 1cm (⅜in) seam allowance and matching up the lining seams to the sleeve seams. Using a small stitch, sew the sleeve lining just covering the back stitches from sewing in the jacket lining.

### Topstitching

Jackets of this period often had topstitching or stabstitching outlining the lapels and fronts of the jacket. Topstitching can help control the coat edges and facings.

### Buttons and buttonholes

Check and mark the buttonhole positions; the top buttonhole is at right angles to the front at the bottom of the break line. Make the buttonholes and sew on the buttons

### Finishing off

Take out all the tacking stitching and give the garment a press. This is a good opportunity for quality control and to ensure everything is as you want.

Fig. 8.28 Finished jacket partly inside out, showing striped sleeve lining.

## Late Victorian Waistcoat

Waistcoats were often garments in which the individual could choose the details to express themselves; for example, the amount of pockets, what type of collar or lapel, how the back waist could be altered.

Back neck bands are not always used and seem to have been formed differently by each tailor; they were sometimes an extension of the front and were often cut on the straight grain. The version for this waistcoat is the shape of the back neck much like an external facing and can be omitted if preferred.

The pattern has no seam allowance included except for the welt pockets, where it is 6mm (¼in) with the welt side seams offset and cut at an angle to draw the seam allowance towards the back.

For this waistcoat the collar pieces have been cut with a small 6mm (¼in) seam allowance, except for the neck edge of the waistcoat front and collar which is cut with a 2cm (¾in) seam allowance.

All other pieces have been cut from the fabric with a regular seam allowance of 1.3cm (½in). A consistent seam allowance removes the need for marking construction lines.

### PIECES NEEDED

**Main fabric:**

Cut two fronts, front facings and lower front facings, bands for the back of the neck, collars, lapels and lower welt pockets. Cut one upper welt pocket for the left side.

**Outside back fabric:**

Cut two backs with the back neck area cut out, also two waistbelts and two collar lapel linings.

**Lining:**

Cut two front linings and back linings.

**Cotton:**

Cut two of each pocket bag for the upper welt pocket and two of each pocket bag for the lower ones.

**Fusible domette:**

Cut two fronts and two welt pockets cut to the shape of the welts.

**Lightweight fusible interfacing:**

Cut two front facings, two collars and stays for the pocket areas.

**To finish:**

Buttons, buckle for the back waistbelt.

Fig. 8.29 Late Victorian waistcoat, front and back views, showing welt pockets, collar and buckled back waistbelt.

# Waistcoat 1890s

1 Square: 2.5cm (1") No seam allowance included

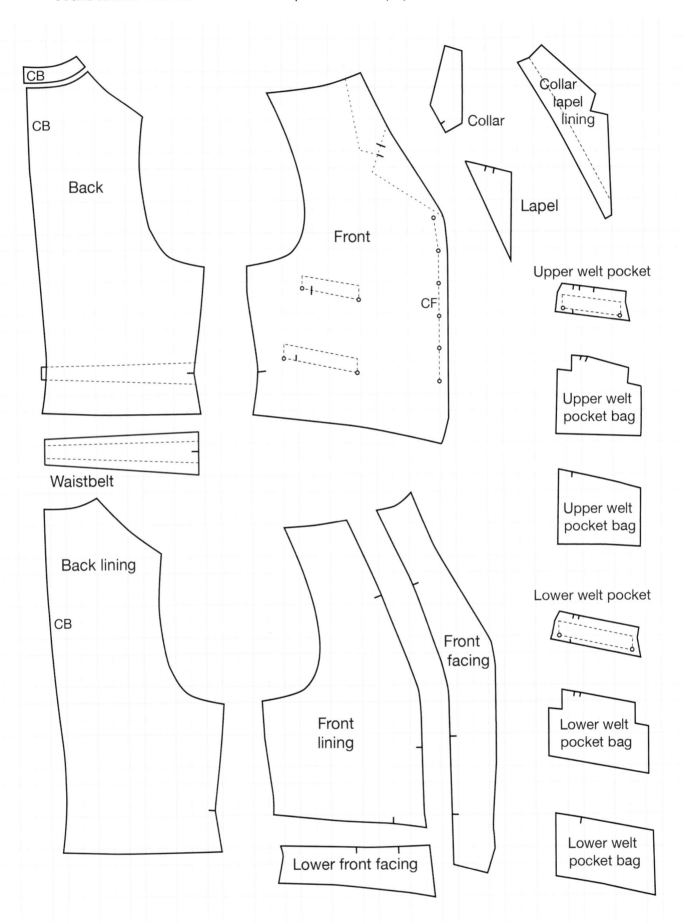

CB

CB

Back

Collar

Collar lapel lining

Lapel

Front

CF

Upper welt pocket

Upper welt pocket bag

Upper welt pocket bag

Waistbelt

Back lining

CB

Front lining

Front facing

Lower welt pocket

Lower welt pocket bag

Lower front facing

Lower welt pocket bag

## Marking Up and Preparation

Bond the fusible interfacing to all the appropriate pieces.

Mark all the construction lines on the wrong side of the fronts. Tailor tack both bottom corners of the welt pockets. Tack the front neckline and front shoulder seam.

Bond the fusible stays over the pocket opening.

Indicate the balance marks.

The collar pieces have had interfacing fused on to them. The construction lines and balance marks are then marked on the interfacing. The neck and shoulder line has been tack marked.

## Construction Instructions

### Facing and lining

Join the lower front facing to the front lining. Press the seam allowance towards the lining.

Join the front facing to the front lining. Press the seam allowance towards the lining. For thicker fabrics snip into the facing seam allowance at the join with the lower front facing, pressing the seam open next to the lower front facing, thus allowing the seams to lie flat.

### Back neck band

Join the neck band onto the neck area of the outside back. Trim, then press the seam allowance towards the neckband.

### Centre back seams

Join the centre back seams for the outside back fabric, also the lining centre back seam. Press the seams open.

### Welt pockets

To fit the welt pockets, use the instructions in Chapter 9 for the working man's waistcoat.

### Collar

Sew the collar and lapel together, stopping and securing at the construction line intersection. Lightly press the seam open.

With right sides together, pin the joined collar pieces to the one-piece collar lapel lining.

Sew the collar to the lining along the outside edges; stop and secure close to the seam joining the collar to the lapel, then start sewing at the other side of the seam. Trim down the seam allowance along the outside edge of the collar. On the lining only, snip close to the join of the collar and lapel. Turn the collar to the right side and press, ensuring the lining is not visible from the right side.

Fig. 8.30 *Collar and lapel.* Top: Construction lines marked and neck edge tacked, then joined together and sewn to lining. Bottom: Collar turned through to right side and pressed, both sides.

Fig. 8.30 *Completed parts of waistcoat*. Top row: Fronts with welt pockets and collar, front facing and lining, Bottom: Back with neckband and belt and back lining.

### Joining the collar to the waistcoat front

Tack the collar to the neckline along the construction line. Press the neckline seam allowance back along the tack line. Tack the seam allowances together.

### Shoulder seams

Join the outer fabric and lining backs and fronts together at the shoulders. Press the seams on the lining open. Press the seams in the outer fabrics towards the back.

### Joining the outside of the waistcoat to the lining and facing

Match the outside of the waistcoat to the lining from level with the bottom button, working along the fronts and neck. Sew together, stitching the facing to the collar neckline slightly inside the neckline fold and construction line.

Trim the excess seam allowance along the neckline. Turn through to the right side and press, making sure that the facing and inside back lining are not visible from the outside.

Bluff stitch along the back neck lining with the seam allowances

towards the lining, starting about 2cm (¾in) before the shoulder seam and sewing over the shoulder seams and around the neck. This under stitching is mainly to reinforce the joins on the shoulder seam and back neck where the seams have been trimmed down.

### Waist adjustment belt and buckle

Fold the waist belt pieces in half and sew the two long sides together (Fig. 8.31). Press the seam open using the point of the iron to avoid adding more creases. Flatten the narrow end of each belt and, with the seam in the centre,

Fig. 8.31 Waistcoat bagged out along front and hemline, then partially turned right sides out.

Fig. 8.32 Waistcoat armhole showing lining offset and sewn close to construction line, then seam allowance trimmed.

sew closed.

Turn the belt pieces through to the right side. Use a knitting needle or similar long tool without a sharp point to create neat corners. Press with the seam along the underside centre of the belt.

For this waistcoat a buckle with its prong removed was used to join the two waist belts. (It is possible to buy waistcoat buckles that resemble some of the huge variety of Victorian waistcoat buckle styles; they often have two sharp prongs which pass through the belt fabric to hold the belt securely.) The narrow end of the belt was passed over the back bar of the buckle and sewn to the belt around the bar. The other side of the belt is passed through the buckle and fastened, leaving a minimal extension.

Lay the closed belts across the back waist area with the buckle in the centre, matching the centre of the belts to the waist balance marks. Pin or tack the belts to the side seam allowances.

## Hems, back and front

Check the waistcoat front and back panels are exactly the same length; trim the hem allowances to be even.

Offset the hems of the waistcoat front and the back and sew the main fabric to the facing. Press the seam allowance towards the lining, then press the whole waistcoat front and back flat; with the fronts and back flattened the pressed fold should be the hemline.

Join the outside fabric to the facing in the area between the bottom button and hem, sew with the hem allowance folded towards the lining.

Trim off excess seam allowance. Turn the front edge through to the right side and press.

## Finishing off the armholes and closing the side seams

To finish off the armholes and close the side seams use the instructions in Chapter 6 for the 1840s waistcoat.

## Back waistbelt

With the back lying flat, pin the half-belts to the back through both the top fabric and the back lining about 10cm (4in) from the side seams; at this measurement from the side seam both halves of the belt should be the same distance from the hem. Topstitch across the width of each half-belt through the back and the lining.

## Buttons and buttonholes

Mark the position of the buttonholes. Make a sample buttonhole and check that the buttons fit through the hole. Make the buttonholes and sew on the buttons.

### Late Victorian Trousers, 1890s

The back waist detail was inspired by a pair of trousers from the V&A collection seen in *Nineteenth-Century Costume in Detail* (Johnston, 2005).

The seam allowance used was 1.3cm (½in), except for the crotch which was cut 1cm (⅜in) from the front fly area through the curve. Leaving a large crotch seam allowance makes the trousers appear to fit badly.

An allowance of 4cm (1½in) was added to the centre back, starting after the crotch curve where the back seam straightens and flaring to 4cm (1½in) at the top of the back waist. It was added to the centre back seam on the trouser leg, back waist detail and waist facings, in order to build in some scope for future waist alteration. There is a 5cm (2in) hem at the bottom of the leg. The front leg hem is cut straight across from the 5cm (2in) hem at the sides.

### Marking Up and Preparation

Fuse the interfacing onto the wrong side of the appropriate areas or pieces.

The trouser front, back and back waist detail pieces all have the construction lines and balance marks marked onto the wrong side of the fabric on top of the fusible interfacing.

Tack the waistline and hemlines.

### Construction Instructions

#### Finishing seam allowances

Finish off the cut edges of the seam allowances. Whenever possible it is easier to finish the edges of the pieces before they are sewn together. Finish the inside and outside legs and front crotch seam; the left front crotch finishing does not need to go much beyond the balance mark as it will be

---

#### PIECES NEEDED

**Main fabric:**

Cut two front legs and two back legs, back waist details, fly pieces, front and back pocket facings.

**Cotton lining:**

Cut two pocket bags, front and back waist facings cut on the fold. Cut three fly pieces.

**Fusible interfacing:**

Cut two front waist area, back waist detail, pieces for the side back waist on the trousers. Cut three fly pieces. Consider adding stays along the pocket mouth.

**To finish:**

Buttons.

---

covered by the fly; ensure the curved crotch seam allowance is trimmed down to 1.3cm (½in) or less before finishing the seam allowances.

Finish off the long curved seam of the pocket facings (the side that will be in the pocket).

#### Back waist detail

Sew the back waist detail to the back trouser legs. Trim and finish the back waist detail and trouser back seam allowance together. Press the seam allowance towards the waist detail. The centre back seam can be finished off through the back waist detail piece.

#### Pockets and side seams

Use the pocket fitting instructions in Chapter 5 for the 1840s trousers. There, the trouser pockets are finished at the sides with a binding; for these 1890s trousers a machine zigzag finishes the pocket side seam allowances (Fig. 8.34).

#### Waist facing

Sew the side seams of the back and front waistband facings together. Press the seams open. Fold the waistband in half with wrong sides together along the centre of the waistband, then press.

Consider replacing the front edge of the left side facing with interfaced fabric to avoid the waist facing

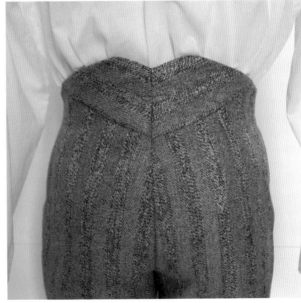

Fig. 8.33 1890s trousers, front view and back with back waist yoke detail.

# Trousers 1890s

1 Square: 2.5cm (1") No seam allowance included

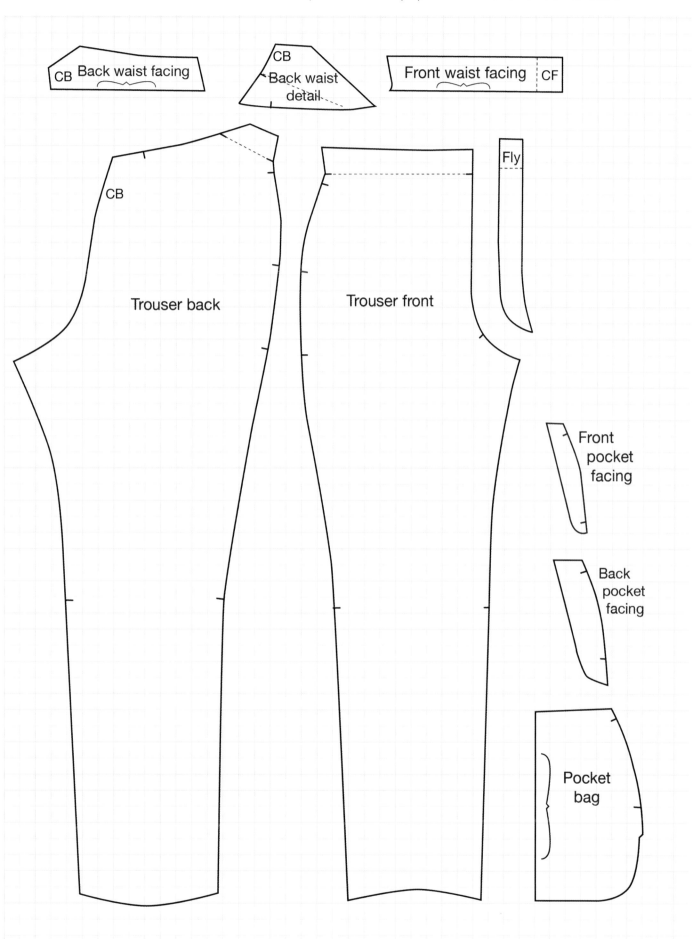

CB Back waist facing

CB Back waist detail

Front waist facing CF

CB

Fly

Trouser back

Trouser front

Front pocket facing

Back pocket facing

Pocket bag

showing at the top of the fly.

Pin the waistband facing pieces to the waist area of the trousers. Sew together along the waist construction line, continuing across the extra seam allowance at the centre back. On the right front, stop before the centre front; the waist facing will be sewn across the top of the button stand after it is attached to the right centre front seam.

Trim the waist seam allowance. Bluff stitch the facing with seam allowances towards the facing. Turn through and press.

Fold the left front waistline with right sides of the front and waistband facing together, then pin together along the centre front.

## Fly

Construct the left front fly lining over the waist facing along the centre front seam; trim off the top of the fly lining above the waistline.

Assemble and fit the fly using the button fly instructions in Chapter 5 for the 1840s trousers, but stop before the 'Fly shape' instruction.

The fly seam allowances on the 1840s trousers are finished with binding. Other methods can be used – a machine zigzag is used for these 1890s trousers.

When the left fly is completed, with buttonhole strip bar tacked to the fly lining and the fly lining and buttonhole strip seam allowances finished off together, trim off the top of the buttonhole stand about 1cm (⅜in) above the waistline. Turn the centre front of the waist and waistband facing through to the right side. Press.

## Fly button stand

Bag out a fly and fly lining piece along the long curved seam, sewing close to the edge of the seam allowance. Turn through to the right side and press. Machine tack the side of the fly closed.

Pin the right side fly piece to the right front. Sew together along the centre front; stop sewing about 2.5cm (1in) before the balance mark for the bottom of the fly. The centre front and fly seam allowances can be finished off after the two legs have been joined.

Sew the right front facing to the top of the fly, from the centre front dropping down at a slight angle by 6mm (¼in) to the edge of the button stand. This will ensure that the top of the button stand is not seen from the outside when the trousers are fastened. Fold the facing seam allowance around the edge of the fly. Sew the facing to the fly at the edge of the fly.

## Fly shape

Topstitch the fly shape, starting at the top edge of the waist, sewing about 3cm (1¼in) parallel with the centre front, following the fly shape, then continuing off the bottom of the fly into the seam allowance below the hook (Fig. 8.36). A hand stabstitch gives a subtle authentic finish.

### Joining the inside leg seams

Sew front and back legs together along the inside leg seams. Press the seams open.

### Joining the two legs together

Pin the two legs together along the crotch line. Sew from the corner of the left front hook (the right-angled shape at the bottom of the fly) and balance mark, then continue along the crotch seam following the construction line to the centre back waist and facing.

Pin the button stand over the bottom of the fly opening. Sew back along the crotch seam starting at the waist facing. Continue sewing over the stitches at the bottom of the hook through to meet the stitches joining the centre front and button stand.

The extra seam allowance at the back waist is for future alteration. Press the centre back seam open.

## Finishing the fly

Close the fly with the wearer's left front slightly overlapping the right centre front seam; pin closed through the button stand.

Bar tack the bottom of the fly opening through all the fly layers.

On the inside of the trousers sew the buttonhole stand to the button stand below the bottom buttonhole.

## Sewing the waist facing to the waistline of the trousers

Pin the waist facing to the inside of the trouser waist area (Fig. 8.37). Check the top of the pocket bags are lying flat and covered by the facing. Fold the facing centre back seam allowances at an angle under the facing.

Topstitch along the tacked waistline through to the facing, sewing from the centre front around the waist to the opposite front.

Fig. 8.34 Back waist detail; on inside, fusible interfacing, construction lines and extra seam allowance at back waist can be seen.

Fig. 8.35 Left front fly layers finished together and bagged out with waist facing; right front button stand partially sewn on; waist facing sewn to front of fly.

**Buttons**

Sew the fly buttons slightly away from what would be the centre of the buttonhole, slightly closer to the centre front.

Braces buttons can be fitted using the guidance in the Glossary.

**Trouser hem**

Angled or shaped hems were used a lot during the Victorian period and continued to be used well into the twentieth century. The hems sit at an angle, longer at the back and shorter at

the front in order to fit neatly over the foot.

Shaped hems curve neatly round the dropped back leg part of the hem. The front of the hem has to be snipped into for the hem to be able to follow the upward shape of the curve. If the hem has been cut at the centre front in order to achieve the dropped hem shape the hem itself cannot be lengthened beyond the cut, thus restricting the usefulness of the hem allowance for future alterations. The method below accomplishes a neat shape hem and retains the flexibility to lengthen the hem for another wearer.

**Shaped hem**

Turn up the hem allowance on the back leg by about 5cm (2in), following the curved shape of the hem. Cut the front hem straight across 5cm (2in) at the side seams.

**Tack the hemline**

Finish off the cut edge of the hem as preferred.

**Fish dart on the front hem**

Fold the front hem with right sides together, folding straight across from the side seam hemlines. The tack line

should appear as a shallow curve above the fold.

Using a large machine stitch, sew along the tacked front leg hemline, starting and finishing close to the side seam; this creates the fish dart. Do not sew onto the side seam as it will increase the bulk of fabric at the hem.

Turn the hem through to the right side; the 'fish'-shaped curve can be lightly pressed towards the hem.

Pin the hem in place following the tack line. The pins should be placed at right angles to the hemline, permitting a small portion of the top of the hem to be folded back in order to sew the hem.

Sew up the hem using a couture hem stitch. To do this, fold back the top of the hem, pass the needle through the fold and catch a thread or two of trouser leg fabric, with the needle through the fabric of both trouser leg and hem. Take hold of the doubled threads at the eye of the needle, draw them back towards the previous stitch and around the point of the needle. Pull the needle through the work and repeat.

A machine blind hem can be effective and strong for holding up hems made in more substantial fabrics.

Fig. 8.36 Fly shape sewn parallel to centre front, with stitching continuing into seam allowance below hook.

Fig. 8.37 Trouser waist facing topstitched from right side along tacked waistline; bar tack sewn through all layers from outside at bottom of opening; inside, fly pieces sewn together on curve.

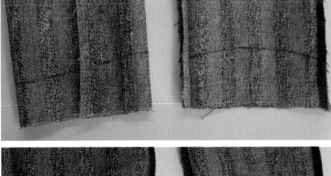

Figs 8.38 and 8.39  Top: Trouser hemline marked; front hem edge is cut straight across. Bottom: Fish dart pinned (right) and sewn (left).

# Chapter 9
# Working Man's Waistcoat and Breeches

*These garments are based on styles from before the beginning of Victoria's reign; they are comparatively unsophisticated garments, suitable for working or poor men. Similar garments would have been worn well into the period, with many variations, eventually being superseded by shorter waistcoats and trousers.*

## Working Man's Waistcoat

The waistcoat front fabric is backed with calico. There are two sets of ties at the back waist, a not uncommon feature, and two large welt pockets placed fairly low on the waist. This waistcoat has a stiffened stand collar.

### PIECES NEEDED

**Main fabric:**

Cut two fronts and welt pockets; cut one collar.

**Calico for backing:**

Cut two fronts and one collar.

**Lining:**

Cut two fronts, four backs, two of each pocket bag piece; cut one collar.

**Woven interfacing:**

Cut two welt pocket shapes and two welt pocket stays. Alternatively, the stays could be linen or cotton tacked to the wrong side of the welt pocket area.

**Collar canvas:**

Cut one collar shape without seam allowance.

**To finish:**

Tape to use as ties for the back.

Fig. 9.2 Waistcoat with welt pockets and a stand collar; back has tape ties to alter waist.

Left: Fig. 9.1 Working man's outfit consisting of shirt, waistcoat and breeches.

**Working mans' waistcoat**     1 Square: 2.5cm (1") No seam allowance included

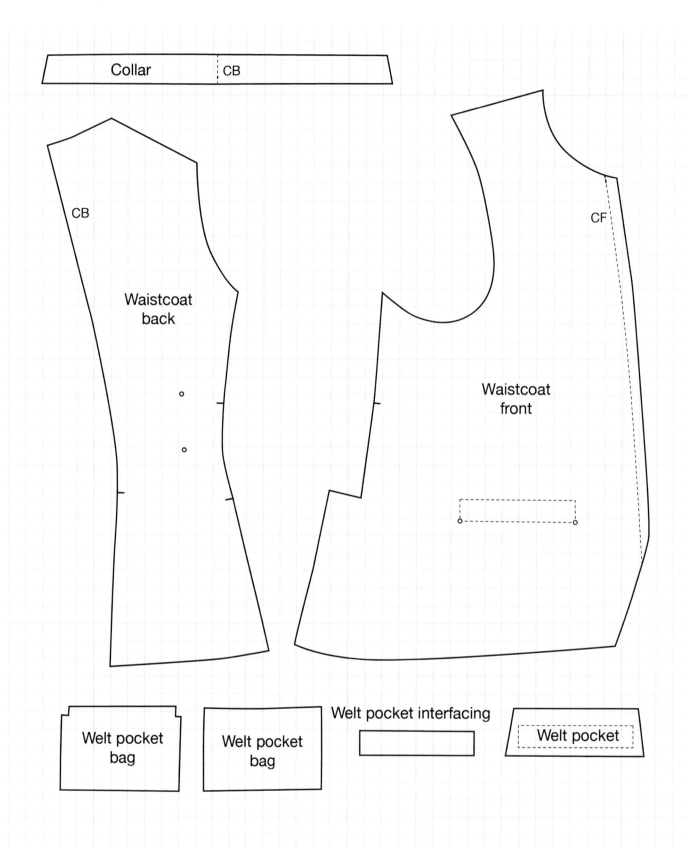

Collar
CB

CB

Waistcoat
back

Waistcoat
front

CF

Welt pocket
bag

Welt pocket
bag

Welt pocket interfacing

Welt pocket

## Marking Up and Preparation

Mark the construction lines and pattern information onto the calico backing. On the front lining, mark the shoulder construction line indicating the conjunction of the armhole and neckline onto the shoulder. Mark all pattern information on the outside back fabric and tailor tack the position of the waist ties. On the pair of inside backs, mark the centre back sewing line including the top and bottom of the line. Also mark the shoulders, indicating the armhole and neckline on the line.

Flat tack the calico fronts to the outer fabric and indicate balance marks by making a stitch on the seam allowance. Tack the pocket position.

## Construction Instructions

### Welt pocket

Always fit pockets at the earliest stage of construction possible. The welt pocket pattern seam allowances are included, 6mm (¼in) along the bottom of the welt. The side seams are offset by 6mm (¼in), the seam being wider at the bottom of the welt and narrower at the bottom of the back of the welt.

The bottom two corners of the welt can be marked from the pattern with a tailor tack; a chalk line or tack line can be used for the bottom line marked through to the right side of the garment. When using a backed fabric tack the welt position. This simple welt is cut and sewn on the grain of the fabric; a clearly marked line for the bottom of the pocket is usually enough.

### Pocket stay

Place the stay behind the welt. Fuse the stay to the pocket area on the inside of the garment; the stay should be a bit bigger than the total size of the welt pocket.

### Interfacing the welt

Fuse the welt interfacing onto the welt 6mm (¼in) up from the bottom of the welt and the same distance from each side at the top of the welt interfacing.

### Pocket bag to welt

Pin the pocket bag with the square cut outs centrally to the top of the welt and sew the two together with a small seam allowance. Press the seam allowances towards the pocket bag.

Press the seam allowance at the bottom of the welt towards the inside along the edge of the interfacing, fold back the fabric along the top of the welt

Figs 9.2, 9.3 and 9.4 Top: Stay and tacked pocket and pocket bag sewn to welt. Centre: Welt sewn to pocket bag with seam allowance pressed toward pocket bag; small seam allowance has been pressed over welt interfacing. Bottom: Top of pocket bag pressed over welt interfacing.

interfacing, then press lightly with the right side out.

### Welt pocket sides

Fold the welt along the top fold with right sides together. Keep the cut edges of the side seams together and sew from the top at the interfacing, stitching parallel with the cut edges of the side seams. Do not sew the pressed seam allowance at the bottom of the welt into the side seams. Turn the corners through carefully and press lightly, following the straight grain and the side of the interfacing. The side seams of the welt have been offset, ensuring the side seams will pull towards the back or inside of the welt.

### Joining the welt to the garment

Pin the fold at the bottom of the welt to the marked line for the bottom of the welt, matching up the bottom corners of the interfacing with the thread-

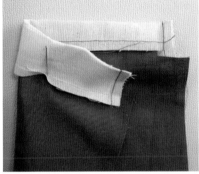

Figs 9.5 and 9.6 Top: Closing welt pocket sides, sewing from folded top of interfacing parallel with edge of pocket. Bottom: Pocket turned through and pressed lightly, seam is not visible from front.

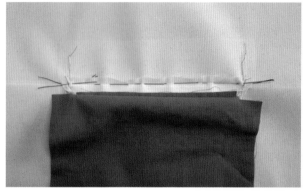

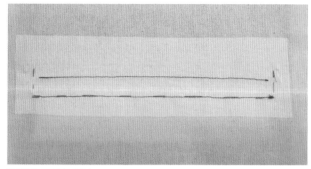

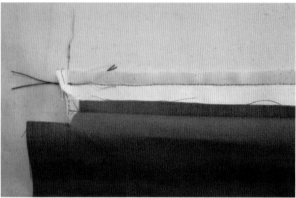

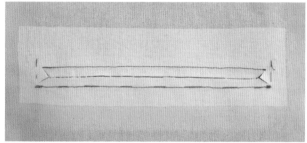

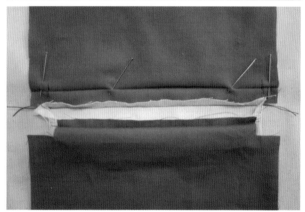

Figs 9.10 and 9.11 Welt pocket and pocket bag sewn to garment (viewed from inside). Top: Welt is sewn to edge of pocket marking; pocket bag sewing stops slightly short of pocket opening. Bottom: Pocket is cut open between sewing lines and snipped to within a thread of last machine stitch, creating triangles.

Figs 9.7, 9.8 and 9.9 Top: Fold of welt is pinned to pocket line on garment. Centre: Welt is sewn to garment. Bottom: Remaining pocket bag is pinned to garment above welt.

marked bottom corners of the welt. Sew close to the edge of the interfacing, securing both ends; it is important to make a precise and secure finish so walk the machine back and forward one stitch at a time. Do not sew beyond the interfacing or welt marked on the garment.

### Joining the pocket bag to the garment
Press back a seam allowance of 1cm (⅜in) on the remaining pocket bag, place the folded edge centrally on the pocket area with its cut edge just under the small seam allowance of the welt. Sew along the groove of the fold parallel to the first line of sewing, stopping and starting the sewing 3mm (⅛in) inside the sides of the welt and first line of sewing.

### Cutting the pocket open
Cut between the two lines of sewing on the garment. At 6mm (¼in) from each end make a triangle by snipping from the central cut up to the last thread before the last stitch on the parallel lines of sewing.

Press open the seam between the welt and the garment, ironing gently with the point of the iron. Carefully manipulate the seam allowance at the sides of the welt so that the pressed seam continues towards the sides of the pocket. The pocket bag joined to the welt can be passed through the cut opening.

With the welt-to-garment seam open, using either a machine or hand ditch stitch, sew along the welt-to-garment seam, stopping and starting about 1.3cm (½in) from each end. This will hold the lining in place and reduce the chance of the welt sagging or changing shape. The other pocket bag can be passed through the welt opening to the inside of the garment.

### Making the pocket bag
With the face side of the garment down, smooth the two pocket bag pieces and pin the sides together with one or two pins on each side. With the right side up, fold back the main body of the garment exposing the side of the

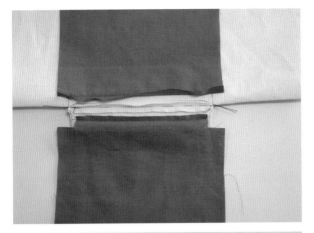

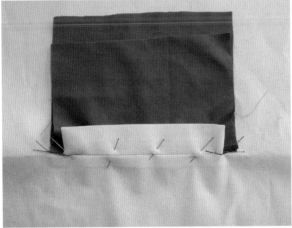

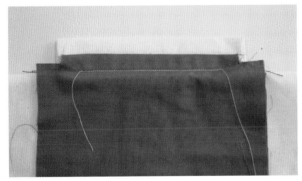

Figs 9.12, 9.13 and 9.14 Top: Seam between welt and garment is pressed open. Centre: Pocket bag pinned over seam. Bottom: Ditch stitching between welt and garment through to pocket bag.

pocket bag and sew along the side of the pocket. Near the bottom of the pocket bag, with the needle in the fabric, pivot the bag and fold back the bottom of the garment parallel to the bottom of the pocket bag. Continue along the bottom and repeat for the other side. This is to keep the pocket bags very flat while sewing them together.

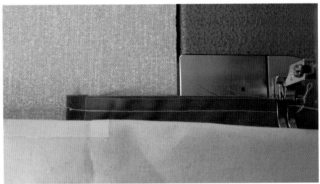

Fig. 9.15 *Pocket bag from inside:* Sewing round pocket bag, face of garment is uppermost; it has been folded back, exposing pocket bag to be sewn closed.

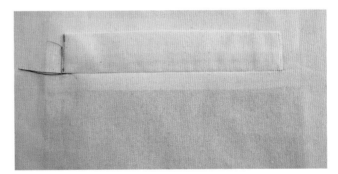

Figs 9.16 and 9.17 Top: Sides of pocket topstitched to garment. Bottom: Welt can be secured invisibly from inside by hand sewing through to welt seam allowance.

### Sewing the sides of the welt pocket to the garment

There are two possibilities here: (a) topstitch along the sides of the welt, sewing through the garment and pocket bag, or (b) from the inside, hand sew through to the welt seam allowance along the sides of the welt. The latter has the advantage of being quite strong and not having visible stitches; it could be finished off on the outside with decorative hand sewing or stabstitching (Figs 9.16 and 9.17).

### Constructing the main body

Sew together the centre back seam on the outside back and lining. Press the seam open.

Sew the backs and fronts together at the shoulders. Press the outside shoulder seam towards the back; press the shoulder seams on the lining open.

### Joining the centre front

Join and offset the lining to the front along the centre front line. With the shoulder seams together, smooth the fronts; matching the centre front of the fabric and lining, pin the front edge and machine the fronts together about 3mm (⅛in) outside the construction line. Trim off the excess seam allowance. Press the seam allowances towards the lining, turn through to the right side and press along the construction line to ensure that the lining will not be seen from the outside.

### Preparing the front and back hem and the armhole

After pressing with wrong sides together, match the shoulder seams and smooth the lining and top fabric together; pin to hold and stop movement.

The seams of the waistcoat and lining need to be level. Trim level the seam allowances of the front hem and side vent, trim the two layers of the back hem and trim around the armholes. All these seams will be offset slightly but precisely, which is easier if they start off equal.

At the front hem, with right sides together, fold back along the centre

Fig. 9.18 Waistcoat and lining offset and joined at centre front; after pressing, thin line of front fabric can be seen on inside.

Fig. 9.19 Hem has been offset, sewn, trimmed and pressed. Side vent is sewn at an angle from side seam; other side of waistcoat has been turned through and pressed to show result.

front line. Pin the front fold, pin along the hem with the lining showing by 6mm (¼in) from underneath the top fabric. Sew starting at the front construction and hemline; over two or three stitches move out 3mm (⅛in) to continue along the bottom of the front parallel to the construction line. Trim off any excess seam allowance. Press the seam allowance towards the lining and fold and press along the construction line.

### Side vent stand

At the side front, fold the hem towards the lining. Pin and sew up from the hem, making a right angle at the top of the vent. Sew to the side seam; at the point where the side seam joins the vent, pivot and continue sewing at an angle through to the edge of the seam allowance to create a reinforced area of sewing. The side vent stand is going to be under the lining so the seam does not need offsetting.

Trim off the excess seam allowance and snip close to the stitch at the bottom of the side seam and top of the vent stand. Turn through and press.

### Back hem

With the two backs right sides together, the inside lining hem should be visible from the outer fabric hem by about 6mm (¼in). Sew together just outside the construction line. Press the seam allowance towards the lining; turn through to the right side and press along the hemline.

Pin the lining to the armhole, offsetting the seams. Trim, turn to the right side and press (see the 1840s waistcoat in Chapter 5).

The waistcoat fronts and back should all lie flat at this point, with the right side of the fabric just visible from the lining side.

### Front side seams

Tack the side seams of the outer front to the front lining; the front side seam can now be treated as one piece of fabric and will be sandwiched between the waistcoat back and back lining.

### Closing the sides

With right sides together, pin the front to the outside back side seam. Sew from the armhole to the top of the side vent stand on the side seam construction lines.

Wrap the back lining over the waistcoat front so that the front side seam of the waistcoat is sandwiched between the inside and outside back. Pin in place and sew on top of the first line of sewing to the back hem. Turn the waistcoat through the neck. Press the side seams and lining at the lower back opening. Leave the side seams on the back and lining as long as possible for future alteration.

### Finishing off the side vent and stand

From the outside, with the lining on top of the vent stand, pin the lining over the stand by an even amount along the length of the stand. Sew through the lining and across the top of the vent stand.

### Centre front neck

Start with the front folded back along the centre front construction line and the front seam allowance toward the lining. Sew from the front fold along the neckline to the centre front balance

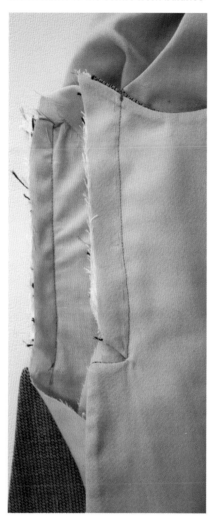

Fig. 9.20 Front and outside back seamed together to side opening extension.

mark. At the mark, pivot and continue sewing at a right angle towards the edge of the seam allowance. Trim away the seam allowance parallel with the stitch lines and snip to within a thread of the right angle at the balance mark. The picture here shows the blue stitches on both sides of the front neckline with the seam allowance trimmed down on the right. Turn through to the right side and press.

With the front and back panels lying flat, tack the neck seams together along the outside construction line.

### Collar

Stiffen the collar by fusing and machine pad stitching the collar canvas to a backing fabric (Fig. 9.22).

The machine pad stitch worked across the collar; this consists of a large zigzag made with a straight stitch across the body of the collar.

The backing is flat tacked onto the outer fabric close to the edge of the canvas.

### Lining the collar

Start by offsetting the collar lining. Lay the collar onto the lining with right sides together, pin them together at the centre back, at the centre front move the top fabric in to expose 6mm (¼in) of the lining along the front seam. At the neckline fold up the lining seam allowance in line with the neck edge of the canvas. Sew both front edges about 3mm (⅛in) outside the sewing line. Trim off the excess seam allowance.

Fig. 9.21 Sewn centre front, trimmed on one side; notch allows collar to finish edge to edge.

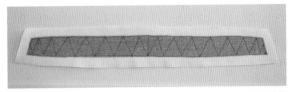

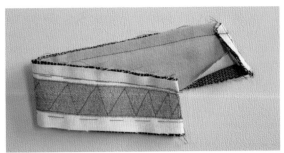

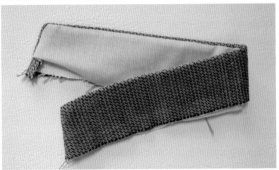

Fig. 9.22 Collar canvas machine pad stitched to backing fabric; centre front offset and lining turned up; top of collar sewn; collar turned through to right side and pressed (lining must not be visible from outside).

Press the seam allowances towards the lining. Turn through and press along the front construction line.

With right sides together, pin along the top of the collar; the lining will be a little tight so distribute the fullness along the top of the collar. Machine from the edge of the canvas at the centre front, sewing away from the canvas in about three stitches and continuing parallel to the canvas. At the other side sew three stitches to finish back at the edge of the canvas on the centre front. Turn the collar through, ensuring both the corners are the same shape with neat well-defined points. Trim off excess seam allowance. Press the seam allowance towards the lining and fold and press the collar along the top edge of the canvas.

### Joining the collar to the waistcoat

With right sides together, pin the collar to the neck edge, matching the construction lines. Place the pins in line with the construction line, ensuring the construction lines match. As the seam is sewn, remove pins as the machine needle approaches them.

Trim off any excess seam allowance from the neck edge and collar, then press the seam allowance towards the collar. Sew the collar lining to the neckline covering the seam allowance.

### Back waist ties

With the back lying flat, pin or tack around the thread marks indicating the position of the waist ties. Place the ties over the marks with the tie lying towards the side seam; sew the tie through the back layers a small seam allowance. Fold the tie over the seam allowance and sew in place covering the seam allowance. The ends of the ties are then rolled over and sewn down by hand.

### Button and buttonholes

Mark the top and bottom button positons, measure the distance between the marks and divide the measurement by number of spaces between the buttons – there is one less space than there are buttons.

Make a sample buttonhole to check how the buttonhole looks and make sure the button will fit through it. Make the buttonholes and sew on the buttons.

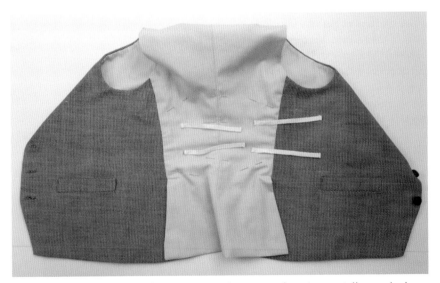

Fig. 9.23 Waistcoat back with pins securing layers together, ties partially attached on right side and fully on left; sewing at top of side opening, welt pockets and buttonholes can be seen.

## Working Man's Breeches

Breeches have been around in one form or another for hundreds of years, persisting into Victoria's reign, and continuing to be used for some formal dress liveries and sports to this day.

The liveries of certain Victorian household servants retained breeches as part of the uniform. Footmen in particular wore the old styles of dress; they were more visible than other servants as they answered the door to visitors as well as serving at the table during meals. Footmen would also be seen away from the house with 'the family' in or on their vehicle.

The fall front type of opening was also used for some fashionable styles of trousers and military uniform trousers well into the period and on riding breeches into the following century.

Breeches were already outmoded at the beginning of the Victorian period although still worn every day and as part of evening dress for the elderly and unfashionable until the middle of the century (Byrde, 1992).

This breeches pattern is intended to be a fairly timeless style, based on an original pattern from *The Complete Guide to Practical Cutting*, plate 26 (Minster, 1993).

### PIECES NEEDED

**Main fabric:**

Cut two fronts with the fall front cut open; cut two backs, bearers, posts, waistbands, knee bands.

**Cotton lining:**

Cut two waistbands, bearers, knee bands, fall front waist facings, fall area.

**Woven fusible interfacing:**

Cut one waistband without seam allowance.

**Fusible interfacing:**

Cut (with seam allowances) two waistbands, knee bands, posts. Cut pieces to cover the extensions for the knee openings on the front and back legs, from the outside edge to cover the dotted line that marks the side seam in each case. Cut two small pieces for reinforcing.

**To finish:**

Buttons, two buckles, six eyelets, cotton tape.

These instructions include a back waistband opening that can be used to alter the waist. The opening above the knee band has no fastening but could have buttons; the knee band is fastened with a buckle but could also be buttoned. In this case the fabric has been cut with a 1.3cm (½in) seam allowance. The exceptions are the posts and knee bands, where a much smaller seam allowance has been cut.

### Marking Up and Preparation

Fuse the interfacing onto the wrong side of the fabric.

Fuse a second layer of fine interfacing over the top of the main interfacing, continuing into the seam allowance on the waistbands, knee bands and posts.

Fine fusible interfacing could be bonded to the wrong side of the fall front openings

A small piece of lightweight fusible could be applied over the bottom of the seam allowance at the top of the button stand on the back leg pieces; this area will be snipped into so that the side seam and button stand will lie flat.

On the posts, press back the seam allowance around the edge of the main

Fig. 9.24 Breeches, front and back views, showing fall front fastening and eyeleted fastening at back waist to adjust waist size.

**Breeches**    1 Square: 2.5cm (1") No seam allowance included

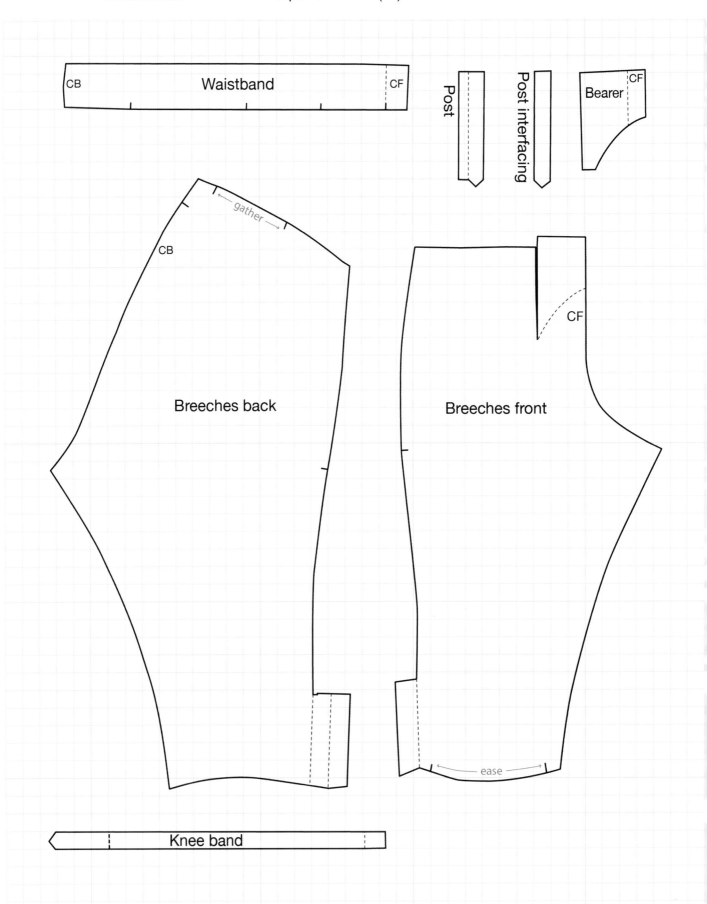

shape along both sides and the point.

Mark the pattern information on the wrong side of the fabric or cut with a consistent seam allowance and indicate the balance marks with a snip or mark as desired.

## Construction Instructions

### Finish off the seam allowances
Trim the crotch seam to 1.3 cm (½in) and finish.

### Ease stitches
Put in ease or gather stitches between the balance marks at the back waist and at the front knee.

### Press the knee opening extensions
Press towards the inside along the fold lines on the fronts and backs. The opening on the front is in line with the side seam; the back leg has an extension that goes under the front leg opening.

### Outside leg seam
Sew the fronts and backs together along the side seams, stopping at the top of the knee opening.

Press the seam open to the top of the opening and snip the back seam allowance 3mm (⅛in) above the last stitch of the side seam above the opening. The snip will allow the seam and opening to lie flat.

### Finishing off the knee opening
The folded edges of the knee opening can be sewn down, either by hand or machine. Make buttonholes for the opening now, if required.

With the knee opening neatly closed, secure the top by sewing through all the layers at right angles to the end of the side seam stitch line. This can be done by hand stabstitching or machine sewing.

### Inside leg
Sew the back and front legs together on the inside leg seam. Press the seam open.

### Knee band
Sew the fabric to the lining along the bottom edge of the knee band about 3mm (¹/₈in) away from the construction line.

Trim the lining level with the top fabric between the pointed end of the knee band and the first balance mark on the band top.

Press seam allowances towards the lining and press the band along the edge construction line to complete the bottom edge of the band.

Take the area between the first balance mark and the point. With right sides together, offset the lining from under the fabric and pin with about 3mm (⅛in) showing.

Sew from the balance mark to beyond the point, stitching 3mm (⅛in) away from the construction line. Snip in towards the sewing line at the balance mark on the fabric.

With the seam allowances folded towards the lining, sew round the point, making one blunt stitch at the point. Trim, turn the point the right way out and press.

Fig. 9.25 Breeches knee area with fusible interfacing and opening folded back.

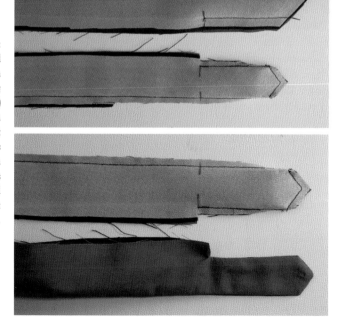

Fig. 9.26 From top: Knee band and lining are sewn together along bottom (long) seam; short seam to point is offset and sewn; point is sewn with seam allowance towards lining and turned through to right side.

Bag out the other end of the band, turn to the right side and press.

### Joining the knee band to the bottom of the leg

With right sides together pin the band to the leg; the pointed end of the band is on the front of the breeches. Pull up the ease stitches to fit onto the band. Sew the band to the bottom of the leg, distributing the ease evenly. Wrap the lining over the seam allowances, sew the fold of the lining covering the stitch line area.

### Joining the two legs

Sew the two sides of the breeches together, from the centre front to the balance mark just below the back waist. Sew the seam again close to the first line of sewing; after the first line of sewing has been completed the second can be a fairly small zigzag stitch sewn over the top of the straight stitch. Press the seam open.

### Finishing off the back waist opening

Roll the seam allowance along the back opening and sew the rolled seam down. Make a small bar tack straddling the seam at the bottom of the opening to reinforce the opening.

### Fall front

Sew the fall front waist facings together along the centre front line and press open.

Finish off or press under the seam allowance along the bottom of the fall front waist facing.

Sew the fall front waist facing to the breeches front along the waistline. Press the seam allowance towards the fall front waist facing and bluff stitch

the facing through the seam allowances. Press so that no facing is visible from the outside. Match up the centre front seams and machine tack the main fabric to the fall front waist facing close to the cut edge of the opening for the fall front. Continue the machine tack round the opening to act as a stay stitch.

Sew the centre front of the facing to the breeches centre front seam allowance with a few stitches. Trim off excess lining close to the machine-tacked front edge.

### Bearer

Press back the long side seam allowance of the bearer lining. With right sides together, sew the bearer and lining together along the bottom (curved) edge and short side seam. Turn through and press.

### Attaching the posts to the openings

Place the right side of the post extension to the lining side of the lined fall front opening and sew together with a 6mm (¼in) seam allowance (Figs 9.28 and 9.29). Press the seam allowance towards the opening.

Bag out the top of the post level with the finished front waistline. Sew the post front and extension together slightly above the level of the finished front edge. Turn through and press.

### Joining the bearer to the outside of the opening

Pin the bearer along the side of the opening; sew with a small seam allowance on the breeches and 1.3cm (½in) allowed on the bearer (Figs 9.30 and 9.31). The bearer and sewing should finish parallel to the end of the

opening; secure it. Snip the breeches seam allowance close to the last stitch on the bearer. Press the seam allowances towards the bearer. Sew the lining over the seam allowances.

### Finishing off the post

Pin the open side of the post onto the front of the breeches. Sew from the top of the post along the fold of the pressed-under seam allowance, continuing around the point at the bottom and up the other side by about 2cm (¾in). With the post and bearer closed and lying flat, sew across the post at right angles towards the first line of sewing, then finish securely.

### Waistband

Press under a seam allowance on one long side of each waistband lining.

At the centre front, offset the join between the waistband and lining, sewing 6mm (¼in) away from the construction line. Press the seam allowances towards the lining and press the front edge fold along the construction line to ensure the lining is not seen along the front fastening of the waistband.

To offset the seam allowances along the top of the waistband and lining, sew the top of the waistband and lining together starting at the front fold and construction line. Sew away from the construction line after a few stitches and continue to sew parallel to it. Press the seam allowances on the top edge towards the lining, fold and press along the construction line.

Bag out the centre back of the waistband, then press.

### Joining the waistband on

With right sides together, pin the waistband to the breeches, pulling up the ease stitches to fit the waistband. Sew the waistband to the breeches. Press the seam allowance towards the waistband. Sew the folded seam of the lining over the seam allowances to close the waistband.

### Finishing touches

On this pair of breeches there are two buttons fastening the waistband and

Fig. 9.27 Back waist opening finished off with seam allowances rolled under; bar tacks and ease stitches are visible.

three on the bearer; the posts have one button (Fig. 9.32). The knee bands are fastened with buckles. There are three eyelets on each side of the back waistband with a cotton tape threaded through to alter the waist size.

Figs 9.30 and 9.31 Top: Post sewn onto fall front and bearers sewn to side of opening. Bottom: Top of post bagged out.

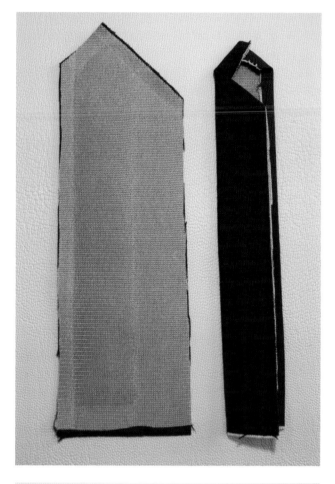

Figs 9.28 and 9.29 Top: Interfaced post with seam allowances pressed under along construction line. Bottom: posts sewn to lined fall front.

Fig. 9.32 Fall front opening; centre front waist is fastened with two buttons, posts with one each.

Lacour & Cie dessᵗᵈ                    October 1872.                    Imp. Lemercier & Cⁱᵉ Paris.

# GAZETTE OF FASHION.

## EDWARD MINISTER AND SON

*8, Argyll Place Regent Street*

London, w.

# Chapter 10
# Sport and Leisure

*The Victorians did not necessarily originate the concept of sports and leisure activities but conditions during this period meant that a growing population, particularly a much larger middle class, had enough leisure and resources to have access to such pursuits. Employment legislation changed, leading to better pay and more free time for the workforce. There were new, faster transport systems, many technological inventions and there were developments in all areas, including fabrics and waterproofing. These all had repercussions for leisure clothing.*

The countryside pursuits of hunting, shooting and fishing had always been accessible to the upper classes, but now the numbers of people with the time and disposable income available to indulge in sport and leisure activities grew. Wages increased considerably from around the 1850s, with all classes exhibiting a noticeable interest in outdoor activities.

## Football

Football had been played in the streets from the fourteenth century; by the seventeenth century it had become dangerous and extremely violent. Public schools developed the initial rules for the game and these were formalized and amalgamated in the 1860s in order for different school teams to compete against each other.

Football's rise in popularity outside the public schools was due to a general improvement in living standards, communication and transport; this meant that there was free time to watch and play; many more people could afford to travel to matches and pay for entry, and there was a rise in sports

journalism.

The design of football shirts was based on woollen undershirts; striped, long-sleeved jerseys were also worn for many other sporting activities.

Other popular outdoor ball games included lawn tennis (introduced in the 1870s), croquet, golf, rugby union and cricket, which all attracted huge crowds by the end of the century.

Fig. 10.2 Lord George Robert Canning Harris, 1889 (from *The Strand Magazine*, volume 1, 1895). By the 1890s, white flannels, white shirt, dark cap and V-necked pullover constituted accepted cricketing costume.

Left: Fig. 10.1 Football outfit of 1872 consisting of breeches with belt, striped socks, jaunty cloth hat and a very tight knitted shirt. The footballer is accompanied by a man in a hat wearing a double-breasted jacket with contrasting collar and striped trousers. (National Museums Liverpool)

## Bicycling

What we would recognise as bicycles started to appear in the 1840s after pedals and brakes were added to hobby horses. Early cycling outfits were close-fitting garments allowing free movement.

The advent of the safety bicycle in 1885 changed the machine from just a sporting apparatus to a convenient form of transport. Modified everyday informal dress was worn instead of specific cycling outfits.

Fig. 10.3 Racing cyclist J. Green in specialized cycle clothing (from *The Strand Magazine*, volume 1, 1895).

## The Norfolk Jacket and Other Outfits

The Norfolk jacket is a tough, weatherproof and multipurpose outfit that became very popular by the end of the century. The jacket was less stiffly structured than other coats and jackets and incorporated pleating for movement. It was usually made from green and brown wool tweed to blend with the countryside. It could be teamed with breeches, knickerbockers or trousers and was used for many outdoor activities, including hunting, walking, riding and bicycling. The Norfolk jacket was adapted for golfing with extra pleating to permit the range of movement needed at the shoulders.

The accepted male sports outfit for summer consisted of an open-necked shirt with attached collar and a blazer, generally worn with trousers.

The country house weekend was a popular middle-class activity and involved holding or attending house parties and related sporting events, thus requiring several specific outfits.

Once again the number and variety of possible outfits worn for sport or free time was huge, depending on the activity, social status and available budget, from visiting the local park with the family to equestrian sports with all the paraphernalia and expenditure entailed.

It is impossible to do the full range of Victorian leisure-time clothing justice. This chapter can only show a glimpse of the sports and leisure activities from sixty-plus years, illustrated with a few images that I found appealing to inspire the reader into looking further into the possibilities of Victorian sport and leisure wear.

"I THOUGHT THAT YOU ADMIRED KITTY MORISON."

Fig. 10.4 Illustration by H. R. Millar (from *The Strand Magazine*, volume 1, 1895). A story character wearing a Norfolk jacket, possibly at a country house.

# Chapter 11
# Completing the Look

*The last part of garment construction is usually making buttonholes and sewing on fastenings. Another final essential stage is giving the item a finishing press and removing tacking threads; this is a valuable opportunity for quality control, to ensure everything is as you wish. For many costumes there are two additional areas to be considered to prepare for its ultimate use: accessories and breaking down.*

## Accessories

### Braces

Braces literally held together the outfit; trousers were held up and the shirt stayed tucked in, while the waistcoat covered any gaps. Braces could be made in the home and increasingly used the improved elasticated fabrics.

### Collars, Cuffs, Bib Fronts and Fastenings

There were many relatively small changes to collars and the associated items over Queen Victoria's reign of sixty-three years. Men wore collars appropriate to their income, profession and status; for period-accurate styles some research will be needed. Simple universal styles of Victorian collar are available to buy and possible to make.

For evening wear and later in the period, detachable stiffened collars, cuffs and bib fronts were attached to the shirt with studs and cufflinks. For the wealthy, studs for evening wear shirt fronts might be made in gold, diamond or other splendid materials.

Fig. 11.2 Illustration by W. Thomas Smith from *The Strand Magazine*, 1895. A character from a story is tying his tie; his braces are attached to his trousers but hanging down, ready to be put into use.

Left: Fig. 11.1 Studio photograph of a man from the 1880s; the trousers and waistcoat are creased from sitting down.

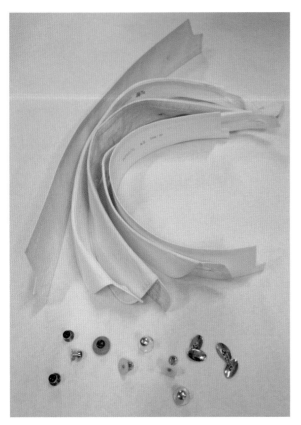

Fig. 11.3 Detachable collars, studs, collar studs and cufflinks.

Fig. 11.4 Illustration from the *West End Gazette*, November 1873 (National Museums Liverpool). Man wearing a morning coat, with a top hat, umbrella, gloves, wing collar and cravat with pin; note the hair and beard.

## Neckwear

Although there were countless necktie styles, cravats are an enduring type; a large square of starched fine or lightweight fabric was folded diagonally and wrapped around the neck over the collar, with some of the collar showing above it. The amount of collar seen changed with fashion; at some times the collar folded out over the top of the cravat. Cravats progressed from plain to decorative or imaginative and had a selection of quirky names and tying instructions.

## Hats, Shoes, Gloves, Hairstyles and Accessories

Fortunately, there is a wealth of Victorian reference material that can be used to see the range and variety of costume accessories and hair styles available to men. We are lucky that some Victorian-style items are still available; for example, Oxford shoes and (for evening wear) evening pumps or opera slippers. Gloves can be quite similar to Victorian originals, as can some sticks and umbrellas.

All but the very poorest men would wear a hat out of doors, with wealthier men having particular hats for use with specific outfits. If your costume appears to be worn out of doors a hat is essential.

Victorian men's hats can be broken down into a few basic types: straw boater-style hats for summer, top hats with straight sides, flat top hats with a brim, bowlers or derby rounded-top hats with a smaller brim, softer felt hats and soft fabric caps, with many variations within each broad type.

## Breaking Down and Why It Is Necessary

'Breaking down' is an umbrella term used to describe many different processes and end results. It is a procedure applied to a costume to give it a narrative or history; it is evidence of the story you want the costume to tell, whether it is to provide signs of authenticity or offer evidence about the character or lifestyle of the wearer.

The possible stories a costume can convey are numerous:

- Who is wearing the clothes?
- What is their character?
- What is their profession?
- Are they rich, poor?
- Where do they live?
- Where have they been?
- What have they been doing?

At the very least, to look real many costumes need to appear as if they have been worn regularly; new garments can look rather flat and lifeless. Breaking down can be any method of making a smart costume look as if it has been lived in or perhaps as if it had belonged to someone for a long time who has cared for it with washing, ironing patching and repairs. At the extreme you might want to convey that it has been worn for years and is very dirty and ragged.

Breaking down has to be carefully considered. Where does a garment get dirty and worn? If the garments belong someone with a particular occupation, what effect will that have on their garments? Which areas will show marks, dirt or wear? Do these effects need to be removable?

Find some references, either photographs or garments showing the type of wear patterns required.

## Some Suggestions on Breaking Down Costumes

The most obvious process for washable items is to wash them thoroughly.

Creasing in areas of wear, like those displayed by the man from the chapter opening photograph, is ideal for some characters.

Crumpled elbows, crotch and bulging knees can be very effective and reasonably easy to remove.

Jackets or coats can have their pockets stuffed; cord can be passed through the arms and drawn up to the neck; the arms can be creased at the elbow and steamed lightly.

### Shirts and linens

White shirts can look very bright and modern, particularly under stage lighting. A classic technique to make whites less bright or appear grubby is washing in black tea. Commercially available dyes can be used to give a permanent shade.

### Coats and thicker garments

Dirty Down is a company which provides a range of products that give a variety of finishes, many of which are removable.

Wear away areas of the fabric with a cheese grater for a more heavily worn look.

Saddle soap gives a greasy look to suggest grime on cuffs or a greasy collar and can be easily removed.

Dry brush painting can be used to reproduce grime and shading. Dab the very edge of the brush in a small amount of paint and brush it over paper to remove the excess paint. When the brush is almost dry, brush the costume with it.

## Lastly

*Making Victorian Costumes for Men* has provided me with an unparalleled opportunity to accompany you through the process of creating key outfits of Victorian men's clothing, using a variety of efficient tailoring and costume-making techniques, essential skills and inspiration. You are now equipped to create your own men's Victorian costume or to make costume using elements of Victorian styles while broadening your range of technical abilities.

I do hope you have found this overview of how to make Victorian costume for men both practical and enjoyable.

# Suggested Reading and Information Sources

Audin, Heather, *Making Victorian Costumes for Women* (The Crowood Press, 2015)

Byrde, Penelope, *Nineteenth Century Fashion* (Batsford, 1992)

Cabrera, R. and Flaherty Mayers, P., *Classic Tailoring Techniques: A Construction Guide for Men's Wear* (Fairchild Publications, 1983)

Croonborg, F.T., *Grand Edition of Supreme System for Producing Men's Garments*, Primary Source Edition 1867 (Reprint from Croonborg Sartorial Co., 1867)

Davis, R.I., *Men's Garments 1830–1900: A Guide to Pattern Cutting and Tailoring* (Players Press, 1994). Many of the basic patterns were drafted from the instructions in this book, an essential and easy-to-follow guide.

Doyle, R., *The Art of the Tailor: With a Needle, a Thimble and 10,000 Stitches* (Sartorial Press Publications, 2005)

Ettinger, R., *Men's Clothing and Fabrics in the 1890s* (Schiffer Publishing, 1998)

Gernsheim, Alison, *Victorian and Edwardian Fashion: A Photographic Survey* (Dover Publications, 1981)

Hopkins, A. and V., *Waistcoats: From The Hopkins Collection c.1720–1950* (The School of Historical Dress, 2017)

Johnston, L., *Nineteenth-Century Fashion in Detail* (V&A Publications, 2005)

Leoni, C., *Sewing Machines* (BE-MA Editrice, 1988)

Levitt, S., *Victorians Unbuttoned* (George Allen & Unwin, 1986)

Maclochlainn, J., *Victorian Tailor: Techniques and Patterns for Making Historically Accurate Period Clothes for Gentlemen* (Batsford, 2011)

Minister, E. & Son, *The Complete Guide to Practical Cutting* (1853) (R.L. Shep, 1993)

Osborne, Roger, *Iron, Steam and Money: The Making of the Industrial Revolution* (The Bodley Head, 2013)

Peacock, J., *Men's Fashion: The Complete Sourcebook* (Thames & Hudson, 1996)

Rowland, Suzanne, *Making Edwardian Costumes for Women* (The Crowood Press, 2016)

Sadako Takeda, S., Durland Spilker, K. and Esguerra, Clarissa M., *Reigning Men: Fashion in Menswear 1715–2015* (Prestel, 2016)

Shep, R.L. and Cariou, G., *Shirts and Men's Haberdashery 1840s to 1920s* (R.L. Shep, 1999)

Von Nordheim, T., *Vintage Couture Tailoring* (The Crowood Press, 2013)

Walker, G., *Early Victorian Men. The Tailors Masterpiece: All Kinds of Coats* (R.L. Shep Publications, 2001)

Waugh, N., *The Cut of Men's Clothes 1600–1900* (Faber & Faber, 1994)

Weightman, Gavin, *What the Industrial Revolution Did for Us* (BBC Worldwide, 2003)

Willett, C. and Cunnington, P., *The History of Underclothes* (Dover Publications, 1992)

Wilson, A.N., *The Victorians* (Hutchinson, 2002)

Wingfield, M.A., *Sport and the Artist, vol. 1: Ball Games* (Antique Collectors' Club, 1988)

## Stockists and Suppliers

The fabrics and trimmings used throughout this book were sourced from many different places. Listed below are the principal suppliers used.

**Fabworks Mill Shop,**
Providence Mills,
Bradford Street,
Dewsbury
WF13 1EN
A shop with varied and random stock, well worth visiting if possible.
www.fabworks.co.uk
Tel: 01924 466031

**Dugdale Bros & Co. Ltd,**
5 Northumberland Street,
Huddersfield,
West Yorkshire,
HD1 1RL
Suppliers of a huge range of tailoring supplies and trimmings; they also sell beautiful tailoring fabrics.
www.dugdalebros.com
Email:
web_enquiries@dugdalebros.com
Tel: 01484 421772

**Whaleys (Bradford) Ltd,**
Harris Court,
Great Horton,
Bradford,
BD7 4EQ
Suppliers of a vast range of fabrics and backings and interfacings.
www.whaleys.co.uk
Email: info@whaleysltd.co.uk
Tel: 01274 576718

**Sew-Rite,**
Units 4–6,
Moor Market,
77 The Moor,
Sheffield,
S1 4PF
I am fortunate to have access to this haberdashery store local to me, which is run by Mrs Nahida Fearn.
Tel: 0114 2758365

# Glossary of Terms and Sewing Techniques

**Back tacking:** a few stitches over the top of each other to secure the end of the sewing thread.

**Bagging out:** sewing two pieces of material with right sides together; when turned through to the right side the raw edges are encased within the piece. Offset the seams to make the lining smaller.

**Balance marks or notches:** marks made on the pattern to match pattern pieces together and to ensure that seams join at precise points. Balance marks can be indicated with a small snip, chalk mark or as seems appropriate.

**Bar tack:** a series of several short parallel stitches sewn closely together to make a bar that reinforces and strengthens a particular area on a garment. Bar tacks can be sewn by hand or machine.

**Bias:** a line that is at a 45-degree angle to the grain line; fabric cut on the bias has more flexibility.

**Blind:** fabric seen through a pocket opening which hides the pocket bag.

**Bluff stitch or under stitch:** a line of stitching close to the edge of a facing, sewn through the seam allowances; it stops facings becoming visible from the outside.

**Blunt stitch:** when machine sewing around corners at the conjunction of the construction lines make one stitch at an angle to both lines; this blunt stitch helps the corner turn through neatly and sharply.

**Braces buttons:** whether on the inside or the outside of the waist area, these buttons are strongly sewn with at least one stitch going through all the waistband layers. At the front of the garment, two are sewn 6cm (2$^1$/2in) apart above the centre front line of each leg. At the back, they are sewn one at each side of the centre back seam about 7.5cm (3in) apart or on the tips of the peak.

**Breaking down:** a finish or process

applied to a costume to make it look more 'authentic', thus giving it a narrative or a history (see Chapter 12).

**Break line:** the fold line of the lapel.

**Bridle:** a tape running next to the break line to support the lapel fold. The break line does not follow the grain line and is liable to stretch: the tape counters this.

**Buttonhole stand:** the part the buttonholes are applied to, as compared with the button stand to which the buttons are sewn.

**Buttonhole stitch:** used to create a knot with each stitch, making the finished edge strong and decorative. With the needle partly through the cloth, take hold of the threads at the eye of the needle and draw them back towards the previous stitch and

around the point of the needle. Pull the needle through the work and repeat.

**Canvas:** traditionally various types of linen were used to support and shape the garment. For the examples in this book the coat fronts have been 'canvassed' with hair canvas used across the chest. Canvas comes in various weights, usually stiffer across the weft. Collar canvas is mainly used on the coat collars.

**Corner/point turning method:** put the index finger inside into the corner, carefully fold the seam allowances over the corner onto the fingertip, place the thumb onto the fingertip holding the seam allowances in a pinch, then pull the fabric from the finger over the thumb.

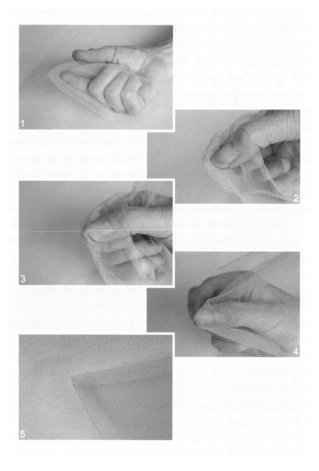

For corner turning, put index finger into corner, fold seam allowances over corner onto index finger, hold them with thumb and fingertip together, and pull fabric over to thumb.

**Couture hem stitch:** a widely spaced buttonhole stitch. The advantage of this method is that each stitch has its own knot; thus if the hem thread is caught the knots stop the whole hem from puckering, or if the thread is broken the knots slow the rate at which the hem can fall down.

**Ditch stitching or stitching in the ditch:** sewing along the join between two pieces of fabric and securing another layer underneath. Ditch stitch by hand or machine. With precision sewing along the 'ditch' between the panels the sewing line can disappear into the join, thus becoming almost invisible.

**Ease:** the process of bringing two disparate lengths of fabric together where a longer construction line is made to fit to a shorter one; also the amount by which the two differ. Ease is commonly found on the back shoulder seam, which is usually 1.3cm (½in) larger than the front shoulder seam. Sleeve heads have around 5cm (2in) ease; that is, the measurement around the armhole of the sleeve should be about 5cm (2in) bigger than around the armhole of the jacket. On Victorian men's coats the skirt waist area is bigger than the body waist.

For a small amount of ease, push some of the excess fabric evenly along the seam length and pin until the ease fits the required area. For a longer area of ease, quarter the length to be eased, pin it at an angle to the construction line, then the pin the construction lines together to flatten the ease down, then sew along the matched construction lines; while sewing it may be helpful to use a pointed tool or pin to push the ease down as the machine moves along the line. The eased area must not have any pleats or tucks in it. Fabrics can be eased by different amounts; felted wool is very malleable and will distribute much more ease than closely woven cottons or linens.

**Edge tape:** commonly used to join canvas to the front edge of coats or jackets. The tape can be fusible or

Top: Edge tape has herringbone stitch straddling canvas and fabric. Centre: Edge tape is sewn to canvas and tacked onto fabric seam allowance. Bottom: Fusible edge tape straddles canvas and fabric; tacked construction line is marked through onto edge tape.

hand-sewn with a herringbone stitch straddling the canvas and fabric or sewn to the canvas front edge and tacked to the fabric. It can be useful to mark the construction line onto the tape.

**Finishing methods:** these include overlocking, trimming with pinking shears, zigzag stitching, binding the edge or using a hand whip stitch. Even when specified in the instructions, finishing off has to be considered and completed at an appropriate time in the construction process using a method suitable for the fraying capacity of the fabric being used.

**Finishing seam allowances:** this process is essential for unlined garments made from fabrics that fray. The seam allowances can be finished either prior to construction or as each seam is sewn. Neaten the cut edge using the most expedient finishing method (see Finishing methods), taking into account whether the inside of the garment is going to be seen.

**Fish darts:** these came into use during the Victorian period, primarily to

shape the waist area of evening wear and tailcoats, giving a close fit. They are also used on slanted trousers hems or military hems, helping to give the slanted shape without having to cut into the hem allowance.

**Flat-fell seam:** sew a seam with one seam allowance up to double the width of the other. Press with the long seam allowance covering the short one. Wrap the longer round the shorter and sew the folded edge to the garment. The flat-fell seam can be formed on the inside or the outside of the garment by starting with either right or wrong sides together. (This seam method is used on the early Victorian shirt in Chapter 4.)

**Flat tacking:** used to join two (or more) pieces of fabric together, after which they are to be treated as one piece of cloth. Flat tacking can be performed by hand or machine, keeping the fabrics flat while being sewn. Hand-sewn flat tacking is a large running stitch sewn on or close to the construction line marked onto the backing. Knots must not be used at the end of the thread as fabric can be damaged as the tacking thread is removed; instead secure the ends with a double backstitch. Tack balance marks in the seam allowance. A fairly weak cotton thread is ideal; strong thread could damage the fabric or seams when it is removed.

**French seam:** a double seaming process where the second seam encloses the raw edges of the first (see drawers instructions in Chapter 4).

**Gather stitch:** a double row of large machine stitches or zigzag over a cord.

**Gimp:** cord wrapped in a filament, traditionally silk, now viscose. It is used to reinforce and raise buttonholes; the buttonhole stitch is sewn over the gimp.

**Gorge:** the meeting of the top of the lapel and the collar.

**Grading:** the process of trimming various seam allowances to different lengths to reduce bulk.

**Grain:** the direction of the warp and weft threads. Straight grain is in line with the warp threads, parallel to the

Top: Fabric is gathered by two rows of large machine stitches. Lower: Zigzag stitch is applied over strong bold thread and then pulled up.

selvedge (sides of the fabric); the bias is cut is at a 45-degree angle.

**Hem or hemming:** the process of finishing the lower end of the garment. See also Couture hem stitch. Herringbone stitch is suitable where the hem will not be seen; for example, behind a lining. Paper-backed hemming tape can be fused and can not be accidentally caught along the hem between the seam allowances but this tape must not be fused along or close to the hemline as it will make a very sharp and flat hem. It is really only suitable for behind a lining, and the seam allowances of the hem should also be sewn together.

**Hind arm seam:** the back seams of top and under sleeves.

**Hook or back hook:** a right-angled step or notch at the bottom of the centre back seam on or below the natural waistline. It enables one side of the skirt to overlap the other down to the hem. It is often seen on Victorian coats and is still used on some modern tail coats and morning coats.

**Inlay:** in tailoring this term means a large seam allowance to allow for adjustments between fittings and for future alterations.

**Jiggers:** in this book these are the waist adjustment tabs on the back of waistcoats that are joined with a lace or cord to alter the waist fit.

**Ladder stitch or drawing stitch:** used to join the turned-under seam allowance of the collar to the lapel much like a running stitch. It is made by taking one stitch at a time on each side, ensuring the stitches are opposite each other, thus creating a ladder effect. When the thread is tightened the two folds pull together and the stitch disappears.

**Machine tacking:** a large machine stitch used for temporary sewing.

**Melton:** a thick twill-weave wool fabric with a nap that has been closely sheared to give a smooth surface.

**Nap:** the finish found on pile fabrics like velvet or corduroy. When the pile is stroked it feels smooth in one direction and slightly rough in the other. Cut pattern pieces with the nap running one way only, to avoid panels looking faded or unmatched.

**Offset or offsetting:** this term is used to mean making the lining or facing a little smaller than the top fabric. To offset a lined panel, cut the two pieces to be offset the same size, but when pinning the seams together expose around 6mm (¼in) right sides of the lining or facing, making it visible from under the edge of the main fabric, then sew together just outside the construction line. This makes the inside smaller than the top fabric and the finished edge is on the construction line, therefore less likely to be seen from the outside

**Pad stitch:** formed by making a stitch at a right angle to the direction of sewing. This is used to join canvas to the fabric, as pad stitches add stiffness, improve the body and encourage shape into the area. With the canvas uppermost take a very small stitch through the canvas, just catching a thread of the fabric below.

Pad stitch the lapel in order to encourage it to roll back over the front of the jacket. Arrange the work over your non-dominant hand, the index finger and ring finger and little

Ladder stitch is made by single stitches taken opposite each other; when thread is tightened, fabrics join neatly.

finger supporting the cloth, with your middle finger directly under the part being sewn. Make a very small stitch perpendicular to the direction of sewing, not visible on the underside, the needle just touching the middle finger when coming through the canvas and cloth. The underside will be covered in tiny dimples.

Start at the break line, sewing parallel to it and pulling each stitch slightly tight to join the fabrics firmly. As you work back and forwards away from the break line with the work rolled over the fingers the lapel will gradually take shape. Make each stitch mid-way between stitches from the previous row. (See the picture at the start of Chapter 3.)

After the pad stitching press the lapel area flat; this can seem brutal but it is necessary and the lapel area retains the memory of the shape.

**Pad stitch tacking:** used to hold the jacket front to the canvas. Working from the outside, large stitches are made at a right angle to the direction of sewing to reduce the flow of the thread; if a pad-stitched tacking thread is accidentally pulled it will only pull up to the next stitch and not create a gather as a running stitch would.

**Press and iron:** these terms are used to describe applying heat and/or steam and sometimes pressure as a stage in the construction process.

**Quartering:** a process to evenly distribute a larger length of fabric onto a smaller area. Distribute the ease along a seam by hand or fit different shapes together evenly. With the larger area uppermost, pin the outside edges or balance marks of both pieces together; find the centre of both parts and pin together, then continue to divide the areas in half and pin until there are pins at regular intervals holding the same amount of excess fabric between them.

**Reinforcing triangle:** a V shape of stitching which reinforces a potentially weak area and helps control fraying where a snip has to made into a seam to allow an area to lie flat. For extra stability prior to sewing, fuse lightweight interfacing over the area.

**Secure/securing:** this ensures that stitching does not unravel during construction or wearing. Hand sewing must be started with a knot and/or a back stitch and finished with at least two back stitches. Machine sewing is secured with a few stitches back and forward or a back tack, usually at the edge of the fabric.

**Stabstitch:** a hand stitch where the needle is put into the fabric very close to the thread emerging from the fabric, creating a barely visible stitch.

**Stays:** these are used on the wrong side of the fabric to add stability and strength. Traditionally strips of linen would be tacked in place, but fusible interfacing can be used if suitable. Stays are commonly used for pocket openings.

**Staystitch:** sewing used to strengthen and stabilize areas on a garment.

**Tacking:** any unseen sewing that is to be removed or will not be seen on the finished garment.

**Tailor tack:** a stitch or loop of thread

Reinforcing triangle sewn in seam allowance touching construction and fold lines.

used to mark information from the pattern onto the fabric.

**Toile:** a version of the garment made from an inexpensive fabric (often calico) to test out the pattern and check the fit, shape, proportions and details of the garment. It is assumed a toile of the garment has been fitted before the altered pattern has been cut from the 'real' fabric.

**Topstitching:** hand or machine sewing visible on the outside of the garment.

**Yoke:** The neck and shoulder area; on shirts it is a separate pattern piece, while the coats and jacket have a yoke backing fabric to strengthen the shoulder area.

## General Points

### Construction lines
Usually these are at the edges of the pattern piece without seam allowance, either where it joins to other pattern pieces or the cuff or hem lines. Often the construction line is the sewing line.

### Cutting
Most of the pattern pieces in this book need to be cut as an opposing an identical pair, left and right, there are a few exceptions so do check you have all the pattern pieces you need and you know how many pieces to cut out of each fabric; main fabric, contrast fabric, backing fabric, linings, pocketing, canvas and interfacing.

It is very important to lay the pattern pieces out onto the fabric on the straight grain ensuring the desired amount of seam and hem allowance is available before cutting.

If the fabric has a pattern, check or stripe consider how to use it when laying the pattern on the fabric. If practical fold the fabric double in order to cut both sides at once.

Double check grain direction, number of pattern pieces needed, seam and hem allowances, fabric right or wrong side and any pile or nap direction before cutting into your fabric.

### Pinning
This must be practised so that construction lines are joined accurately

and balance marks meet. Place a pin at a right angle through the balance marks and construction lines; then, with another, pin down and up through the layers of fabric without the first pin moving; check the pin has gone through both construction lines. Continue pinning the lines together. Machine sew the layers together on the construction line, pulling the pins out when the machine needle approaches. Check that the sewing has passed through both construction lines with the balance marks still together. Keep practising.

### Process
When constructing, assume right sides go together unless otherwise directed. Always match balance marks and, where possible, match centre fronts or centre backs, hemlines, etc.

Always carry out a single step on both sides of the garment at the same time; right and left sides are often identical (although they may vary sometimes). One example might be sewing the front sleeve seam together on both sleeves, then taking them to the pressing table together and pressing both seams at the same time before moving on to the next process. It is particularly important with pockets; if you totally complete one pocket and then start on the pocket on the other side, it is very difficult to get the second one to look like the first. It does not take any longer to go step by step and ultimately it is more efficient and gives better results.

### Sewing
Sew to the edge of the fabric unless otherwise directed.

'Sew' as an instruction can mean sewing by hand or machine.

Hand sewing must be started and finished securely. Start with a knot and or a back stitch, and finish with two back stitches. Start or finish lines of machine sewing with a few stitches back and forward or back tack, usually at the edge of the fabric; sometimes you will need to do this precisely at a balance mark or at the end of a construction line.

# Acknowledgements

I am very grateful to the many people who have provided help and encouragement at all stages of writing *Making Victorian Costume for Men*, first and foremost Pauline Chambers, the course leader from the Northern College of Costume, who made the original suggestion that I might be interested in writing this book.

Huge thanks also go to Martyn 'Tol' Tolson, without whose support this book would not have been possible. I also would like to thank my family and friends for their constant backing, support and advice.

I must certainly also mention those professional colleagues who provided help during the writing of the book: Huddersfield University and the Costume with Textiles course team; at the Crucible Theatre, Debbie Gamble (wardrobe supervisor) and the whole wardrobe team; and the Northern College of Costume.

Jane Taylor kindly donated some fabrics, without which I might never have begun making the costume examples for this book.

Thanks also go to the people who agreed to read the book as it was being written: Kate Harrison, Merle Richards, Elaine Hallet, Becky Graham, Liz Garland and Siatta Kpakra. Additional thanks to Kate Harrison and Merle Richards-Wright for helping with finishing the costumes for the photo shoot..

I was greatly helped along the way by Siatta Kpakra, who provided early editing, and by technical editor Jema Hewitt. Zi Young Kang was a source of great patience and of clear and meticulous instructions while I was trying to produce my own pattern illustrations.

Laura Newill, pattern illustrator, took on the mammoth task of turning the garment pattern photos into beautiful diagrams. Mandy Lock photographed the finished garments and took all the extra photos. With Rob Broadhurst, she also undertook the photo editing.

I must also thank Liz Garland for encouragement and for finding the Victorian photo album; Laura Green, course leader for the Creative Pattern Cutting Masters who gave me the skills and confidence to undertake writing a book; Yorkshire Artspace for my studio and backing; the Crowood team for their patience and guiding me through the writing process to the finished book.

## Museums Visited

Integral to the research for the creation of the patterns in this book was the opportunity to look at original garments. I am very grateful to the following museums and curators for generosity with their time and making available the museums' collections of Victorian men's clothes so that they could be looked at and photographed.

At the National Museums Liverpool, Pauline Rushton, Curator of Costume and Textiles, allowed me to look at the Victorian tailoring books in the museum's collection, kindly gave me permission to use images from them, and introduced me to *Victorians Unbuttoned* by Sarah Levitt.

At Museums Sheffield, Clara Morgan, Curator of Social History, and Olivia Froment, Curatorial Assistant for social history, were most helpful in giving permission to photograph the sewing machine archive.

At Leeds Museums and Galleries, Rachael Cooksey, Curator of Costume and Textiles, provided expertise and advice.

# Image Credits

The main photographs for this book were taken by Mandy Lock and edited by Mandy Lock and Rob Broadbent. The garment-making photographs were taken by Sil Devilly. Laura Newill created the pattern illustrations.

National Museums Liverpool kindly gave permission to use the following images from their collection of tailoring books:

**Fig. 0.1**, from Joseph Couts, *A Practical Guide for the Tailor's Cutting Room, Being a Treaties on the Measuring and Cutting Clothing*, in all styles for every period of life from childhood to old age (Blackie & Son, 1848), accession no. 1962.70.1.

**Fig. 3.2**, from C. Compaing and L. Devere, *The Tailors' Guide; A Complete System of Cutting every Kind of Garment to Measure*. Second Volume Plates (Simpkin, Marshall & Co., 1855–56), accession no. 1962.70.3, Plate 21, pattern diagram for a pair of trousers from the 1850s.

**Fig. 10.1**, from Edward Minster & Son, *The Gazette of Fashion – The Cutting Room Companion, vol. XXVI*, October (Kent & Co., 1872).

**Fig. 11.4**, from *Edited by a Committee of Metropolitan Foremen Tailors' Society, West-end Gazette of Gentleman's Fashions, vol. XI*, November (Kent & Co., 1873), Plate 1, 'English Costumes'.

Museums Sheffield kindly gave permission to photograph sewing machines from their collection:

**Fig. 1.2** (with accession numbers): Jones hand sewing machine, c. 1900, 1976.653; Jones 'D' sewing machine, c. 1880s, Z50; Weir sewing machine, c. 1860s, 1963.126; S. Davis & Co. 'Beaumont' sewing machine, c. 1900, manufactured in Germany, 1972.195.

Images from *The Strand Magazine*, edited by George Newnes (George Newnes Ltd, London):

**Fig. 1.1**, vol. VIII, 1894, July to December, p. 63, from '*The Quinton Jewel Affair*' by Arthur Morrison, illustration by S. Paget, 'Martin Hewitt, Investigator'.

**Fig. 10.2**, vol. VIII, 1894, July to December, p. 481, from '*Portraits of Celebrities at Different Times of their Lives*', 'Lord George Robert Canning Harris born 1851, photo taken age 38 in 1889'. From a photo by E. Hawkins, Brighton.

**Fig. 10.3**, vol. VIII, 1894, July to December, p. 726, from '*Athletes of the Year*', '*J. Green, racing cyclist*'. From a photo by Barrass, Newcastle-upon-Tyne.

**Fig. 10.4**, vol. IX, 1895, January to June, p. 235, from '*A Tramp's Romance*' by Denzil Vane, illustration by H. R. Millar.

**Fig. 12.2**, vol. IX, 1895, January to June, p. 685, from '*Lenster's End*', by Mrs E. Newman, illustration by W. Thomas Smith.

Photographs from the author's personal collection: **Figs 1.3** and **12.1** from Victorian photograph album from the Huddersfield area.

# Index